STONES OF REMEMBRANCE

Foreword by Don McClure

PAM ROZELL

LAMP POST publishers

This is a book you can't put down. Pam is open and honest about her struggles with her marriage, how God divinely intervened, and their journey serving Jesus together. Her life's story is about God's redemption and the restoration of a ruined and broken life due to poor choices. A must read!

Gail Mays, Retreat & Conference Speaker, Author, Pastor's Wife
for over forty years with her late husband, Pastor Steve Mays.

The Rozell's story is a compelling "God story" of honesty and hope that will inspire everyone. An awesome story about a unique and creative ministry that's touching thousands of lives around the world. This book will give you hope on your faith journey.

Jay Edgerton, Television Producer / Director

In a time when so many are searching for a quick fix, Pam Rozell has written a road map for spiritual success that touches the deep pain we all have to face in this life. As she unfolds the Potter's Field story, she makes it clear there are no short cuts to surrender. I am convinced that God is crazy about people when they yield to Him and His ways. You don't need to be famous or rich or beautiful — in fact sometimes those things make it more difficult. You just have to learn to yield, and this book will help you learn that.

I have had the privilege of watching what God has done with Michael and Pam for fifteen years now. Our mutual desire to rescue children around the world led us to Cambodia together, and what God is doing through them in that country alone is amazing! I am certain that what He has done with them He can do for you; but it takes faith and courage to fight the battles and pass the tests life hands us. Reading their story will build your faith and give you the courage to step out on the water and allow God to give you a story like theirs which seems beyond impossible.

Pastor Dan Carroll Water of Life Community Church

With her Southern Belle charm, Pam shares the "riches to rags" story of how she went from worldly success, to the depths of despair, to the joy of the Lord. Like Joseph, who went from the pit, to the palace, to the prison, and then to second in command over an entire kingdom, Pam candidly shares of her personal pits, prisons, and palace experiences. With each turn of the page you will be drawn into her life's story, and be encouraged as you come out with her on the other side! This is a must read for anyone who is in an unequally-yoked marriage, who's ready to throw in the towel, who battles with abuse, or who believes that they or their spouse cannot be changed. You will be encouraged as you read how Mike and Pam were able to take what the enemy intended for evil in their lives and use it to bring God the glory!

Michelle Randall, Senior Pastor's Wife,
Bible Teacher, Author, Speaker

Fifteen years ago I was saved through Potter's Field Ministries. I am so grateful to God for Mike and Pam answering the call God had for their lives.

Pam's book is an amazing testimony as to what God can do with a person's life when they surrender their will and step onto the potter's wheel for molding and shaping. Pam's story is inspiring and will encourage all those who read it. I am blessed by the friendship we have today.

Denise Toth, Biblical Science Institute

STONES OF REMEMBRANCE
by Pam Rozell

Cover and Portrait Photography: Marianne Wiest Photography

Published by:

LAMP POST
publishers
SPRING VALLEY · CALIFORNIA
www.lamppostpublishers.com

Trade Paperback: ISBN-13 # 978-1-60039-238-2
ebook: ISBN-13 # 978-1-60039-743-1

www.pottersfield.org

Therefore, I tell you, her many sins have been forgiven—for she loved much. But he who has been forgiven little loves little.

— Luke 7:47

Dedication

For Jim and Michael,
The two most important men in my life.
My daddy, the first man I ever loved

My husband, the love of my life, partner & best friend…
I would say "I do" all over again…
it has been the biggest adventure in my lifetime…

FOREWORD

My wife Jean and I have known Michael and Pam Rozell for over twenty years. We were first blessed with their presentation of Potter's Field as Michael worked the potter's wheel and the clay while Pam sang, and their witness for Jesus Christ unfolded before a mesmerized audience. The response from the congregation was always tremendous as so many in the world are hurting just as they were. The Lord anointed them then, as He has continued to anoint them thousands of times all over the world.

As we got to know Michael and Pam personally, we found them to have a truly deep passion for the lost, and particularly hurting children. Some years ago we took them to Central America where they had the opportunity to see personally the plight of many orphaned and street children. That trip seemed to add a new dimension to Potter's Field as they first began supporting children in Central America, and now in a number of places around the world. With the added vision came the need to train and disciple young people to get involved and help oversee the work as it grew. Soon they added a school for training, followed up with six months on the mission field. And it seems that the Lord just keeps adding and adding and adding to the vision, adding leaders, adding students, adding interns, and adding missionaries. As you read about the lives of Michael and Pam in this wonderful book, you will see before your eyes and heart how the Lord took two people so deeply entrenched in this fallen world and lifted them out into being incredibly used by the Lord.

King David reflected on the Lord's work in his own life in Psalm 40. And it seems that every verse was also written for Michael and Pam.

> *I waited patiently for the Lord;*
>> *and he inclined unto me, and heard my cry.*
> *He brought me up also out of an horrible pit,*
>> *out of the miry clay, and set my feet upon a rock,*
>> *and established my goings.*
> *And he hath put a new song in my mouth, even praise unto our*
>> *God: many shall see it, and fear, and shall trust in the Lord.*
>
> *Blessed is that man that maketh the Lord his trust,*
>> *and respecteth not the proud, nor such as turn aside to lies.*
>
> *Many, O Lord my God, are thy wonderful works*
>> *which thou hast done, and thy thoughts which are to us-ward:*
>> *they cannot be reckoned up in order unto thee:*
> *if I would declare and speak of them,*
>> *they are more than can be numbered.*

Michael and Pam have become very dear friends of ours. I believe as you read their story they will also be endeared to you as well.

Don and Jean McClure

STONES
OF REMEMBRANCE

Chapter 1

BEFORE CHRIST

I wanted to be a beauty queen and Broadway performer. These were the dreams that filled my girlhood imagination – and that of most little girls who were growing up in Thomasville, Georgia, during the 1960s and seventies – and I would grow up to fulfill them. The hope of beauty, of a career on the stage, of adoration and fame, seemed to be a one-way ticket to a better world, far away from the doldrums of small town living.

I grew up watching such TV shows as *Lawrence Welk*, *The Ed Sullivan Show*, and *The Carol Burnett Show* – variety programs – endless singing, dancing, and acting, with glamorous movie stars trussed up in those Bob Mackie designer costumes that nowadays you find only on late-night infomercials or *Nick at Night*. Waltzing around in priceless gowns under sparkly stage chandeliers, singing glass-shattering operatic arias, performing to the swell and crash of full symphonic orchestras: such was the stuff my dreams were made of.

Little did I know how truly important it is to "be careful what you dream for." Dreams really do have a way of coming true, but maybe not in the happily-ever-after way such dreams dance around in childish heads.

My mother, Nita, was a homemaker, and my dad, Jim, was a former Master Sergeant in the Marine Corps. Together with my brother, Greg, we moved to Thomasville after having lived in Battle Creek, Michigan, where I was born, and Fairfax, Virginia. Dad had worked in the Pentagon before being transferred to work for Civil Defense in disaster preparedness (FEMA).

In Thomasville, we lived in a tidy, tree-lined neighborhood, not unlike those portrayed in shows like *The Andy Griffith Show*, on a street called Wimbleton Drive. Three years later we moved to another neighborhood on Tuxedo Drive that was closer to town and we could ride our bikes to school. We had friendly neighbors, and everyone always helped each other out and looked out for each other's children. We also had wonderful maids that helped raise us kids. If you've seen the movie *The Help*, this is an accurate description of what it was actually like for us in the early sixties.

Our maid was Leona Griffin, and I loved her a lot. She was a kind, helpful, selfless woman and I knew that she truly cared for me. Leona would watch her "stories," the soap operas, everyday while she ironed my dad's shirts and handkerchiefs.

The political and social climate during this time was tumultuous. There was racial prejudice and violence, and civil unrest was rampant. I remember the day that John F. Kennedy was shot. We had just moved into a nicer neighborhood on Tuxedo Drive close to the elementary school my brother attended. I was five years old and had just returned from kindergarten, and my next-door neighbor, Mike Taylor, came over for lunch. Leona gave us soup and a sandwich; she stood before the television crying. My parents didn't particularly like Kennedy, and I think that Leona's emotional display for the President that day started something brewing in my mom, and she wanted her gone.

I remember the day my mom fired her for a reason that I knew wasn't true about her, even at such a young age. When my mom died three years ago, Leona's granddaughter worked at the Assisted Living facility where she lived in Georgia, right before she passed. She took care of my mom, and I know it was a gift from the Lord when I visited the home after her death when her granddaughter came up to me and said, "I got to take care of 'Miss Nita' at the end. I want you to know that my grandmother, Leona, loved you a lot. She had pictures of you up in her house even up until she died a few years back." So it had come full circle that Leona took care of us and her granddaughter took care of my mom at the end.

I had previously gone to see Leona in 1999 when I had gone back to my hometown to choreograph a local Music and Drama Troupe show. She hadn't changed a bit, and the love and respect that we had for one another hadn't faded since childhood.

As far back as I can remember, I loved to sing and dance around the house.

My next-door neighbor's maid, Mabel, would make us lunch on occasion of tomato sandwiches, slathered in mayonnaise on Wonder Bread, along with a glass of skim milk. We didn't drink skim milk at our house, and when I would drink it I thought it tasted like thick water. My best friend, Deborah Balfour, lived down the street (she is still my bestie today). Her maid, Bertha, would teach us southern etiquette and manners, and as all the maids would do, she would show us love by feeding us good southern food. Our moms would play bridge together on a weekly basis, and they would go to the Garden Club and the Country Club for their friendship and "community."

For us kids, it was a carefree time. Lots of playing with the neighborhood kids, building forts in the woods, swimming, jumping on the trampoline until dark, "kick the can," and catching fireflies in a jar until we all would fall into bed afterwards with the exhaustion that only accompanies childhood, unknowingly establishing lifelong friendships, some of which are still in my life today.

As far back as I can remember, I loved to sing and dance around the house. I had a knack for memorizing songs immediately after hearing them and would pretend to tap-dance along with them. By the time I was four, I already had a repertoire of Glen Miller tunes and 40s music swirling around in my head from listening to Mom and Dad's record collections, or from listening to them sing their favorite songs as they went about their daily routines.

At the First Baptist Kindergarten, I would fight for the pink tulle ballerina costume everyday during "dress-up." The teachers recognized, even then, that I could sing pretty well and chose me to perform a solo of "Oh Dear, What Can the Matter Be?" at the Kindergarten Graduation. This song would resonate throughout the rest of my childhood and through my twenties. I wore little red shoes that flared against my white graduation gown, and had to walk around in the middle of a big circle of all the graduates, belting out, "Oh Dear...," and I loved the fact that others paid attention to me and kept commenting on what a good voice I had for being so young.

My next-door neighbor and good friend, Cayla Miller, began to take dancing lessons at five years old with a local dance instructor, Ruth Salter. From her recitals, Cayla had the best dance costumes. The glittery sequins, the flirty skirts, and gloves with smart shiny cuffs activated my imagination to days in the future where I would dance on the stage in a world that I knew was bigger than where I was presently. The rhinestones and bugle beads with blinding "bling" seduced my mind daily where I would be transported to the Miss America stage, pretending to be one of those girls I would watch each year with my family in front of our TV. I would go over to her house and try on those costumes every day, and I discovered two new things – the clickety-clack wonder of black shiny tap shoes, and the ever-graceful, pink silk and ribbons of toe shoes! Oh, how my world expanded! I would put those tap shoes on and tap around Mrs. Miller's kitchen linoleum until she shooed me out because I was putting black streaks on her newly cleaned floor. I knew even at seven years old that I wanted to be a tap dancer and a singer! I begged my mom endlessly for months to let me take dancing lessons. Finally, after much begging and whining, I secretly persuaded my daddy to let me take lessons, and Mom finally relented. I know now that she knew that she would be my taxi service for the thousands of lessons to come until I could drive myself.

> I learned at a really young age how to wear the public "mask," and it started in the organization called "church."

I loved the discipline of learning to dance, the structure of the steps and movement, and the sheer delight of learning how to maneuver my body into a graceful Giselle or to tap out rhythms like a drum with my feet while remembering a full dance routine. I took ballet, tap, and jazz, and couldn't wait to go to classes two or three times a week. I loved listening to Ruth tell her stories of how she dreamed that one of her students would one day end up on Broadway and how she would expound with delight as she spoke of her sister, Nancy, who was a Radio City Rockette Dancer in New York City.

My dreams and ideas of a world much larger than my small town in South Georgia grew along with my repertoire of dance routines. I am so grateful that both of my parents sacrificed their lives, along with their time and money, to help mold and shape their kids' gifts and talents to help them become what God had intended them to be in this world. Little did I know that I would have the privilege of gracing the Miss America stage as Miss Georgia, and that five years after that, the dream of Broadway would become a reality in this small town girl's life!

I grew up in a Christian home. Mom and Dad had introduced us to the "church life" ever since I can remember. However, where we lived in the South – which I've learned is truly a subculture in America – everyone goes to church. It is the politically correct thing to do: Put on your "Sunday best," show up at church, and act as though you have it together in front of your friends and peers. I learned at a really young age how to wear the public "mask," and it started in the organization called "church." It is such a shame, because church is the place where Jesus invited sinners to come and drink His living water, to come and be healed, and in actuality, to bear all of our scars and warts and all. But NOT in the South! I knew even as a young girl that there was something wrong with this picture. It was more of a social circle and a place to be seen. And over the next two decades of my life it would be a journey to find the "real Jesus," and to establish a relationship with this God who wants to call me His "friend."

While I was still in kindergarten, my family attended the First Baptist Church for a while, since this is where I was in preschool. They had just moved to Thomasville and didn't have a lot of friends yet, and this seemed a logical choice to attend since it was the largest church in town, but they didn't really care for the formality of the services, or the "social ladder" status they felt was accompanied with attending there.

I sang in the children's church choir after Mrs. Stegall, my kindergarten teacher, had informed the choir director, Billy Ray Hearn, that I had a "gift from God" to sing. He gave me a lot of good direction as a child, so my foundation in singing was being laid. Billy Ray later went on to establish and run the famous Christian record label, Sparrow Records, after leaving Thomasville. He was there only a short while, providentially during my formative years.

After kindergarten, my parents decided to attend the Christian Church on Broad Street because someone at work had invited my dad to come and visit the church. Since they weren't "sold" on First Baptist, they decided to give it a try. The congregation was warm and inviting, and was filled with salt-of-the-earth-type people that appealed to my parents. My dad had been previously married, and the Baptist church was extremely judgmental of divorced people in the early sixties. He wasn't allowed to become an elder in some churches because of his divorce, or even to be an usher or distribute communion. This new church embraced my parents wholeheartedly and opened their arms without condemnation. They not only allowed him to usher, but to serve communion as well. Needless to say, this is where we stayed until I graduated high school, although we moved into a new building along the way on the other side of town a few years later.

I remember the first time I felt the movement of the Holy Spirit. I was eleven years old. On various occasions before this, I had experienced a "feeling" that I was "special," and had a special "call" on my life. I know now that the Holy Spirit was prompting me deep inside my heart, although I didn't know what it was at the time – I just trusted it.

One morning at our church, we had a guest-touring artist, a man who was a singer with a beautiful operatic voice. We were going to have a Revival that week and he, with his wife and children, were there to share special music for the morning service. It was announced that for the evening service, he would be giving a concert. When he was introduced that morning, I sat in awe as a man under four feet tall – a dwarf – got up to share his music. He opened his mouth, and the sound that came out of that little body was nothing short of miraculous, splendid, resounding, and spellbinding. How could a sound that loud and glorious come out of someone so small? I remember thinking that God uses all shapes and sizes of people, kind of like the potter's vessels, to use to His pleasure. God didn't just need to use the beautiful people of the world; He could choose to use anyone, the foolish things of the world to confound the wise.

I knew that something special and unworldly was happening, but I wasn't quite sure how to articulate it.

At the conclusion of the sermon I started crying as I watched my brother Greg go forward at the altar to give his life to the Lord Jesus Christ. I knew that something special and unworldly was happening, but I wasn't quite sure how to articulate it. All I knew was I couldn't wait to get back to the church that evening to hear that little man sing again and talk about a Jesus that was personal and real to him, like He was his friend and had transformed his life; a God that used him to spread the Good News of the Gospel no matter how limited or unusual or different he may be in this world. At the end of the concert, when the invitation came to accept Jesus as my Lord and Savior, even though I didn't entirely understand what was going on, I felt a presence and a power that I had never felt before. I remember that I needed to go forward to accept this Jesus. My heart was practically beating out of my chest and into my throat, and I felt as if there were hands carrying me to the front of the church, floating me forward to become a child of God. I couldn't have stopped going forward even if I had tried. Something beyond myself was in control. Before I knew it, I was at the altar, dissolved in tears and feeling as though I had been cleansed of something that I didn't understand.

I wasn't entirely sure of what I needed to be cleansed from, considering I felt that I was a "good kid" and didn't get into too much trouble (yet)…and I was young. All I knew is that I wanted this gentle and kind, loving and wonderful Jesus that I heard about from the traveling singer. I came to find out that I was cleansed of sin – something that we as humans are all born into. I felt new!

I learned that what I had done was called getting "saved," or being "born again." The Great Awakening in the 1740s called it the "new birth." It would be a journey throughout my life and well into my marriage to learn that we all sin and fall short of the glory of God. It would be a life lesson practiced over and over again that we truly need to learn how to forgive one another seventy times seven from the heart, never withholding that grace from one another, that there are no degrees of sin, and only through grace by faith can we truly be saved.

The Christian Church denomination believed that you needed to get baptized as soon as possible. I was immersed – "dunked" as opposed to being "sprinkled." I had always wanted to get in that large bathtub in a white robe and get baptized ever since I had seen the first one performed in church, because everyone would applaud and be really happy after someone went down into the water and then came back out; but I didn't understand the reason to have it done to me. I was told this was symbolic of going down in a watery grave, leaving your sins there, and coming out cleansed, starting new and fresh and clean.

Unfortunately, over the next few years, I never really grew in the knowledge of the Lord past this evangelical plea of getting saved, and I soon grew tired of not learning more about Jesus. I knew there had to be more to what I had done. I knew I wanted to surrender to Him and serve Him with my life. I knew in the core of my being that He had a plan for me, and I wanted to see it come to fruition.

The religious climate during this time was that church was a very politically correct place to be on every Sunday morning and evening. Wednesday's weren't ever as well attended as the weekends. The civil affairs in the late sixties and early seventies were still extremely racist, and the south had not accepted the "free love" and "make love not war" and "integration" that was beginning to progress in other parts of the country.

Unfortunately, in the southern states, referred to as the "Bible Belt," many churches are filled with vocational pastors that are only taught in seminary to give topical teachings each week, not really delving into the entire Bible from start to finish, verse-by-verse, chapter-by-chapter. So each sermon is stuffed full of "what to do and what not to do," basically trying to get a congregation "saved" each week. However, the majority of the congregants sitting in the pews have already made a profession of faith and become "members" of their particular church. It's not like the larger churches in big cities where at any given time you will have plenty of heathens and "backslidden souls" to go fishing for in their pond. So needless to say, I became bored very quickly of not knowing how to apply the Scriptures to my life, or to grow beyond the basic evangelical plea each week. I knew that the Lord, as He had spoken to me in the depths of my soul, had a special plan for my life (Jeremiah 29:11), but I wouldn't know what that was until my late twenties, after walking away from my faith altogether, and returning as a "prodigal daughter" after meeting my husband, Michael.

I hadn't really seen any success stories of Christians, either. I would see people raise holy hell during the week, and then go and play church, wearing a mask on the weekends, and that would seem to be okay with them. I knew there was something wrong with this, and the phoniness bothered me even as a young person. Interestingly enough, this would be one of the major themes that would be a driving force in our ministry to come in the future.

Unknown to me at the time, there was a major "Jesus Awakening" taking hold across our country. Even our little town of Thomasville was experiencing pockets of the movement of the Holy Spirit. My brother, Greg, was getting so on fire for the Lord that it kind of scared my parents. There was a family down the street, the Malones, who had a weekly Bible Study at their home which they called "The Way," and they used *The Way Bible*. I remember that my parents tried to discourage such a radical view of Christianity. We had just come out of the sixties, where civil unrest was prevalent and cults were forming, and the Manson murders had just taken place. So fear was pervasive during this time, and it was not uncommon for parents to be overprotective of their children. I attended a few Bible studies with

> I would see people raise holy hell during the week, and then go and play church, wearing a mask on the weekends, and that would seem to be okay with them.

my brother and remember loving the worship and experiencing what I know now as the presence of the Holy Spirit in that home.

On the other side of the country in Southern California, there was a movement going on called "The Jesus Movement" – the "Jesus Freaks" were born out of this – and a pastor named Chuck Smith, who was tired of denominational church bureaucracy, decided to start a church called Calvary Chapel. I wouldn't know of this man who was to become my pastor until the late eighties. I have learned in the past few years that the Holy Spirit was moving mightily across this nation during this time in all denominations, and anyone who was open to His mighty power was getting caught in its wake. Hippies were coming to know the Lord in droves, and when Pastor Chuck had his first church building – his first church started in a tent – one of the elders of the church didn't want barefooted "hippies" coming in and walking on the new carpet. Pastor Chuck told them to tear the carpet out. He ended up on *Life Magazine* baptizing hundreds of this generation. And the rest is history. Some of the most influential churches and Pastor's of the Twentieth and Twenty-First Centuries have been birthed out of the Calvary Chapel movement. And how perfect that we have ministered in thousands of Calvary Chapels and other denominations for the past twenty-five years!

Chapter 2

MY SOUTHERN UPBRINGING

When I was in third grade, around eight years old, a new girl moved to town. This was exciting for the neighborhood kids because we could learn new things about new people – and this girl was an Army brat! She had already lived in many different places; yet another promise the world was bigger than we knew. Her name was Cindy Watt, and she was destined to become a bosom friend, or a "lifer," as I call it today. She came bounding into class, vivacious and loud, and immediately the two of us were connected at the hip. She was my kind of people! We would spend afternoons together, laughing from the bottom of our toes until tears rolled down our cheeks. I always marveled at how big Cindy's laugh was, that it bubbled out of her, and I loved watching her mouth get wide and the laugh bellow from her bowels. To this day I have never laughed so much or as hard as we did in those years.

We explored many new things over the next few years and were the best of friends. We would pass "dirty notes" around class, which today are considered so innocent, exploring what sex was and where babies came from, or writing things about our teacher, Mrs. Clifton, on the walls in the bathroom with soap, and then we

15

would get caught and have to write a hundred times while staying after school: "I will not write bad things about Mrs. Clifton," or we would talk so much in class we would write: "I will not talk in Mrs. Clifton's class."

We would make horrible drinks at her house, strange concoctions of any liquids we could find, mixing in chili powder, garlic, salt and pepper, and anything else in the cupboard that we considered gross. When my dad would come to pick me up, or when her dad would come into the kitchen, we would convince them it was the best drink ever and watch them take a gulp with mischievous anticipation as they would wince in disgust nauseated at the taste of our nasty mixtures.

Cindy taught me how to put on make up. I wasn't allowed to wear it in public, but we would sneak different clothes to school and put make up on while there. Of course, we would invariably get caught and would always have to pay the consequences with our moms: not being able to have a sleep over on the weekend – which seemed at the time like the worst punishment ever! She taught me how to kiss a boy, talking me through it, and she was there to share the nightmare stories of our first kisses, how slobbery and slippery and awkward they felt.

It was with Cindy that I had my first "taffy pull." Her grandmother taught us that is what they used to do for fun when they were kids. We would laugh and laugh as we pulled the gooey mess of taffy and see how far we could stretch that sweet candy across the kitchen, then we would eat it until we would almost get sick. Those were the days of precious innocence, a friendship that was divinely appointed before time began.

Cindy had to move away when her father was deployed to Italy. I learned for the first time how it felt to have one's heart ripped in two, and the agony of having to say good-bye to my best friend since the third grade. (She's still in my life today, by the way.)

My best friend, Deborah Balfour (also still in my life today), lived down the street on Plantation Drive. Having known her since kindergarten, she and I have shared many things throughout our lives together, but between ages nine to around fourteen, the most impactful was our love of horses! She and I would ride all day long during the summer months and on the weekends during the school year at a place right out of town called Butler's Pony Farm. We would carpool for these adventures, spending from morning until the sun went down in this magical place! It would cost about fifty cents for the day. Mr. Butler had so many horses, from small ponies to every breed, size, and color. As young girls we would always compete and run the horses from the back of his property, which we called the terrace, all the way to the barn

> As I sang, a hush came over the place, and everyone joined in to sing with me.

to see who was the best and fastest equestrian. Mr. Butler had some eighty acres of unspoiled land, with a pond and a large barn with numerous stalls.

I started off on a pony named "Spring," and she was a sassy little thing. Some friends down the street owned her, and I used to ride her in the neighborhood until they transferred her out to Butler's. One day she bit me, and I turned around and bit her back in the hind end. I didn't realize at the time that's what horses do to each other, and she never bit me again!

I graduated up to a faster, normal sized horse about fifteen hands, a mare named "Cricket," and Deborah always rode "Buddy Boy." We had a make shift wedding for the two of them one day!

On weekends we would spend the night in the stalls with our horses on occasion when our parents gave us permission, and we would swim with our horses in the pond. It was a time of innocence, establishing "best friends for life" and instilling a love of horses in my life that has never left me. These majestic creatures got me through my tumultuous adolescence. They have a sensitivity that is God-given, and they live in the moment. I've told my secrets to more horses than I can count, sharing my heart with these wonderful, healing animals, and telling them that Jesus says He will be coming back on a white one. It was a stone that God was erecting as He was weaving the tapestry of my life.

The summer of my twelfth birthday rolled around, and it was as typical as usual until I received a call from my next-door neighbor, Cayla. She was going to attend a summer camp up in Montreat, North Carolina, with First Presbyterian, the church she and her family attended. It was a camp that Billy Graham owned and operated that invited young people to attend each summer to learn more in depth about the love of Jesus Christ. It ran for one week, and she asked if I wanted to go with her. I was so excited, though a little apprehensive, because it would not only be a week away from my family, but also, in my young mind, far away in a brand new state where I'd never been.

It was decided that I would go. This week was an eye opener for me because it opened a new world into this "Jesus thing" that I had done. It was filled with beautiful music, and this new type of "worship music," complete with cool rock bands for the Lord, was expanding my view of Christianity in a way I had not seen in Georgia. There were wonderful speakers and hundreds of preteens and teenagers that were "on fire" for the Lord. There was a band called The Archers there, and I loved their music and had my first crush on the lead singer, Steve Archer. He had a thick head of beautiful, wavy, dark hair and could knock the socks off any girl and make her swoon, even if it was for Jesus. I found myself drawn to this young man, and would try to get as close to the front row as I could every time they sang on the program that week.

The last night of the camp, they announced that there would be a talent show, and anyone interested in being in the show could sign up. Cayla encouraged me to sign up and sing. Someone had a guitar and showed me a few chords, and I learned a song called "Kum By Yah – Come By Here My Lord." It came my time to sing, and although I was nervous, I felt a warmth surround me as the spotlight hit me, and I began to strum and sing the words, "Kum By Yah my Lord… come by here…someone's praying Lord, Kum by Yah, someone's singing Lord…" As I sang, a hush came over the place, and everyone joined in to sing with me. As I recollect on this time, it was truly the first time that I had led worship for the Lord.

You might as well have told me that I was the most desirable girl on earth, and in reality, God really did feel that way about me.

After the show was completely over, I was giggling and doing what any twelve-year-old girl would do with her friends, and I looked over and Steve, the tall, dark, handsome lead singer of The Archers, was heading right for me. My heart was beating hard and my palms were sweating. You must know how important this was, especially because this was the time that I was going through my "ugly duckling" adolescent stage of life. I had a relatively low self-esteem about the way that I looked at this time in my life, especially since I felt that I was being held back in becoming a young woman, not allowed to wear makeup or even shave my legs yet. I was very self-conscious and aware that I wanted to feel attractive, but in this stage of life I was definitely in my awkward years. The Lord knew that I needed some encouragement.

Steve Archer walked right up to me and proceeded to tell me that he thought I had a beautiful voice, and that the Lord could use my talents one day if I would let Him. You might as well have told me that I was the most desirable girl on earth, and in reality, God really did feel that way about me. These years in a young girl's life are one of the most tumultuous times she will experience because her body is changing and hormones are bouncing off the walls, and the need to know that she is accepted and loved by God and her family is imperative to healthy development. I left this event in my life uplifted, and a little giddy, by what had happened to me there in Montreat. It was another stone upon which the Lord was building to lead me to what He had planned for me in serving Him. God was wooing me even when I was twelve years old. He is so patient with us, and is tireless and relentless in His pursuit of His precious children. He will leave the flock to go after even one lost sheep…

It was sometime around my fourteenth year that the Lord also planted a seed of desire to work with children from the third world. I was viewing some literature one evening for an organization called World Vision. My heart was broken over the state of the children I saw in those images, children who lived in a third world country, dwelling in destitute conditions my young eyes hadn't ever seen before. There were children with no food or water, they were dirty and had flies landing upon their little faces. I was crying uncontrollably from a place deep within my soul. It touched me at such a primal level, I knew I wouldn't be able to ignore this calling I felt deep within. I wanted to help these young ones. I uttered a prayer,

"Lord, let me work with these children one day and do whatever I can for them when I become an adult."

This prayer that was lifted up from deep within my heart as a teenager was not forgotten by our Lord. I pray even today that the things that break our Lord's heart will always break mine. That I will never take for granted what we have, and if it's within our power to act and help others that we always will.

> *Do not withhold good from those to whom it is due, when it is in the power of your hand to do so.*
> — Proverbs 3:27 NKJV

> *...But he who has mercy on the poor, happy is he.*
> — Proverbs 14:21 NKJV

This is yet another stone upon which the Lord was etching upon my heart for my future.

Chapter 3

HIS SOUTHERN CALIFORNIA UPBRINGING

M ichael came from a broken home. His mother, Roberta Hanks, got pregnant at a very young age while still in high school. In those days, parents decided that, for the sake of the unborn, you would get married. In the south, we called it a "shotgun marriage." His dad, Jim Rozell, still had a lot of wild oats to sow — he was a "player." He and Roberta both were a strikingly handsome couple, but the marriage was pretty much doomed from the start. Michael's brother, Steven, was born in 1955, and four years later, Michael came along. Unknown to Roberta, Jim had been seeing another woman on the side and had gotten her pregnant too, and the child was going to be named "Michael." That baby didn't make it to full term, but Jim ended up marrying that woman, and one more after that.

Jim and Roberta divorced when Michael was only two months old. They moved in with Roberta's mom, Louise Hanks ("Gram"), and Michael's granddad, Harry. He died of a massive heart attack at fifty years old; Michael was just five years old.

Michael was raised by two women and learned early on that they had no control over him. He was a hyperactive youth and would throw fits in stores, writhing on the floor and yelling and making a scene when he wouldn't get what he wanted from Gram. Roberta would just resign and say, "give him what he wants." He played practical jokes on these ladies for years (he still does on his mom), and eventually would intimidate his mom so much that she would acquiesce to him, a role reversal of sorts. She would be so tired and weary from working long hours at Rockwell International that she didn't have the energy to discipline him the way she should've as his mom. So she would give into him on most anything he wanted just to keep peace.

Michael would go through his youth being promised by his dad that he would be picked up for a weekend visit, and he and Steven would pack their bags and sit on the stoop waiting for their dad to show up, but he never would.

The rejection, abandonment, neglect, lack of discipline, permissiveness, and disappointments that Michael experienced as a young boy would scar him and cause hurt, pain, and anger to start churning within him at a very tender age. The issues that resulted developed over time, came into full bloom, and followed him into his adulthood. Subsequently, he would carry them into his marriage.

He had a problem with authority, or even understanding the structure of it, and because Michael didn't grow up with a father as a role model, and his biological father wasn't the picture of the ideal, he had a problem trusting others, especially men. Later, when he came to know Christ, this presented a problem for him in learning to let God alone be his "Abba", his "Daddy." The family ordained by the Lord as an authority structure, with the man being the head of the home, treating his wife with honor as Christ loved the Church. Michael had none of this modeled for him. Throughout his life, he would have to learn not to substitute other men in the place that God should alone hold, not to seek their affirmation as a substitute for finding his significance in Christ, and find that delicate balance of not giving too much of a voice to others instead of listening to Jesus. He always jokes that he has "Daddy issues."

Christmas was a dreaded time for Michael. He would have to spend one holiday with his Mom and Gram, and the other one with his dad and whatever "stepmom du jour" he would have to endure. When it came time to open the presents, it was always particularly awkward and painful. He and Steven would sit for what seemed like forever while the stepchildren and his dad and stepmom would open numerous presents and "ooh and ahhh" while he and Steven only had one present each to open. He describes it as being like that Norman Rockwell painting of the guy looking from the outside in while the family was having a great time. He felt like an outcast, and not part of his dad's family. Even to this

> Michael left that encounter thinking to himself that he wasn't worth very much...

day, Michael gets weird about opening presents at Christmas, so I've made a concerted effort to make Christmastime a happy family time for us each year. We also invite people that have no place to go or can't be with their families to come over, and I lavish presents on all who are in attendance.

During his teens, Michael's dad would drive over to his house sometimes to take him to lunch. Driving up in a convertible Mercedes, Michael was worldly enough to know how much one of these luxury cars cost. He looked at his dad and asked, "How much child support do you pay mom for Steven and me?" His dad said, "fifty dollars each." Michael's pain seared deeply into his heart, and it must have been evident on his face when he asked his dad, "Can you raise Robbie (his stepbrother) on fifty dollars a month?" "Of course not," he answered. He knew that his dad didn't even think about things such as this. Michael left that encounter thinking to himself that he wasn't worth very much, and that material things were definitely more important to his dad than he would ever be.

The two women raising Michael had a hard time keeping tabs on him in the neighborhood and the places he would run off to by himself, which resulted in a hideous incident that could've been disastrous. Michael was seven years old, and he was lured one day into a tunnel by a pedophile – a pervert. Just as this man was about to do something hideous while playing "show and don't tell," to Michael, by divine appointment a stranger called out shouting, "Hey, what are you doing down there?" Thankfully, the guy was startled and ran away, leaving Michael unharmed, but emotionally damaged by the encounter.

He had no outlets to talk about anything growing up. It's no doubt that Michael started using recreational drugs and alcohol at the very tender age of twelve because of the pain he had already experienced in his young life. Trying to numb himself so he wouldn't have to feel anything, Michael had become a full-blown alcoholic by the end of his freshman year of high school. When he took his very first drink he had a "black out," meaning he didn't remember anything he did after ingesting his first alcoholic beverage. He knows now that he has what we call "blood alcohol poisoning." There were alcoholics on both sides of his family, so he was genetically predisposed to become one as well.

His mother and grandmother worked full-time just to keep food on the table. No one would show up for his ballgames. He would look over his shoulder, hoping that his dad would show up to watch him play and be proud of him. He was a good athlete, but no one was there to spur him on to greatness or to give him the pat on the back that all children need for proper development. He would have to ride to McDonald's in the rain at times to feed himself from the money his mom would leave him on the counter as she left for work in the mornings, knowing she wouldn't get back in time to feed her boys. On occasion, Gram would fix his favorite meals and give him the love that he so desperately needed. Michael loved his Gram tremendously. She doted over the boys when she could, and in all reality, acted as the mother figure in their lives. I'm so glad that Gram got to see me in my wedding gown for our renewal ceremony before she passed away.

In Junior High School, a counselor that his school appointed would pick him up in a yellow van once a week so Michael could talk and have a male figure in his life to help guide him. He still talks about this man today, and he was a good influence in his life. Through it all, the Lord saw all of this happening and knew that Michael would be one like David who had a heart after God, and that He would choose Michael to preach the gospel to a dying world many years later. Michael would understand the hurts and pains of this generation. He would understand what it was like coming from a divorced home and the pain that accompanies growing up without two parents in the home. He would be able to understand and empathize with those that experienced the pain that accompanies neglect. He could relate with feeling like you aren't worth the time or the effort to feel cared for and safe. How would he know that in the late fifties that only six million homes would have divorced parents, as opposed to today where there are over forty six million. The Lord does choose the foolish things of the world to confound the wise.

The saving grace in Michael's young life at fourteen was when he went to the Pomona County Fairgrounds in Pomona, California, with a couple of his childhood buddies. His friends from the neighborhood, David Holder and Don Scheck, were running around the fairgrounds, and they couldn't wait to go on the rides. As they were going through all of the exhibits to get to the rides and start having fun, Michael's feet stopped and his eyes became transfixed on an old man making a pot on a potter's wheel. It was an old school "kick" wheel that the potter would have to kick on the bottom to keep it turning. Michael asked his friends, "Isn't this the coolest thing you've ever seen?" They were like, "No, let's go and ride the rides." Michael's friends left to go have fun and Michael stayed watching this man make something artistically beautiful from a seemingly worthless lump of clay for the rest of the evening. That night, he knew that no matter what it took, he was going to find a place to do this thing called pottery.

His dad told him he'd be a bum if he tried to make a living doing pottery, that he needed a "real" job.

The next year, his brother, Steven, started taking a pottery class at school. Michael was chomping at the bit to take pottery classes. He found out that he had to be fifteen years old to start. Unwilling to wait another year, he found a place that was teaching classes near his home called Hudson Adult School. He went in and said that he would do anything to start taking classes early. The teacher said that if he would clean the studio and make clay from the scraps on the pug mill then he could use the wheels. Michael thought that was a reasonable request and he couldn't wait to touch the clay for the first time. The very first time that he tried to make – or "throw" – a pot, he had a God-given talent to start making large vases immediately! He was hooked! He couldn't wait to get to the studio everyday and have an outlet for creativity and a way to expend his energies in a more productive way. Little did he know how this would all play out later in his life, even though it had been years since he touched clay when he met me.

Michael was asked if he would do an exhibition to help promote Hudson Adult School. He was going to throw pottery for as long as he could to try to make it into the Guinness Book of World Records. They hoped that this would bring attention to the school and raise enrollment. He did this event hoping that his family would come and support him. No one from either side came to see him, but Michael, being who he is with his competitive nature and fortitude, ended up throwing pottery for twenty-eight hours! This garnered him the nickname "Marathon Mike." He definitely would've been put into the World Record books if the school had submitted the statistics. Michael told me that neither his mom nor his dad were ever that interested in his pottery gifts. His dad told him he'd be a bum if he tried to make a living doing pottery, that he needed a "real" job. His mom, after getting saved in her fifties (she's eighty now), is now totally supportive of his artistic talents. She has many pieces in her home here in Whitefish and wants more anytime he will make her one. But until that time, he told me that neither one of them had owned a piece of art created by him.

His two pottery teachers have come out to see our ministry in the past years. They both loved it, and marveled at how Michael's life had turned around.

Michael has two pictures on his desk today. One is a picture of me, who he still calls his bride after thirty years of marriage, and the other is a picture of him at fourteen throwing a tall, large vase during his twenty-eight hour exhibition. This was a stone in Michael's young life that he wouldn't revisit for thirteen more years.

Chapter 4

THE SHOW BUSINESS YEARS

Throughout my entire adolescence, I couldn't wait to leave this small town life behind. My dreams and goals were much larger than what my provincial surroundings could offer. My home life was becoming more volatile with the typical mother-daughter tensions and fights that seemed to escalate with every passing year. However, now at fifteen, many pivotal things were taking place.

A year before, a man had moved to Thomasville from New Jersey with his wife and young daughter. His name was Fred Allen, and he had been a former talent scout, an A & R director for RCA records. He had a master's degree in Sacred Music and a PhD in Psychology. He had also studied voice at Julliard as a tenor. My world was about to split wide open. The Lord had led him to Thomasville.

He shared with me once that he had just stopped to gas up his car en route to another location when he had a visitation of sorts: a man told him that he was going to change many young lives in this small town. He and his family decided to stay, and many people were so glad they did, because over the last forty-plus years he has helped mold and change the course of many young lives – including my own.

was a divine appointment for many teenagers seventh
gh twelfth grades, when Fred founded the Thomasville Music
and Drama Troupe. It was a stellar group of young people who
Fred, along with his wife, Winnie, as a team, taught us all to appreciate musical theatre and dance, and would put on spectacular
shows each spring. We would take enrich-

"That's going to be me one day, all the way to the Miss America Pageant."

ment trips each year to New York where
we would see Broadway plays and meet the
actors afterwards for a Q&A. It was there
that Fred came up to me and said, "You want
to do this don't you?" Of course I said, "Yes."
And he declared, "So you will."

We went to London and and saw the
crown jewels and a Broadway show, and we
also visited Oxford and Wales. I was actually
seeing things I only read about in books. He
was one of my first mentors that helped me believe in myself, and
he told me that my potential was unlimited. He taught me to sing,
and working with him set the foundation for my theatrical and
musical career. I've yet to this day met anyone quite as talented
as Fred Allen, who not only was a choral maestro, but a musical
genius who played the piano beautifully – and I've worked with
some of the Industry's best through the years.

When I was seven, I started taking dance lessons three times a
week from Ruth Salter at her School of Dance. I took ballet, tap,
and jazz. In addition to these, in junior high I added gymnastics,
unicycle – where we would ride in parades and do halftime shows
at basketball games on them while doing tricks, and piano twice
a week. Then I added voice lessons as I got older, and Troupe
twice a week. I was a cheerleader my freshman year, in the marching and concert band as first chair flutist my sophomore year, a

baton-twirling majorette in my junior year, and in my senior year, I was Co-Drum Majorette, where I led the band. Ironically enough, the director of the Troupe today, Raymond Hughes, was Drum Major at the same high school six years before I was. He has gone on to be a renowned choral director for the Metropolitan Opera in New York and other Opera houses around the world. I guess I was what some would call a "super achiever." But for me, it was just what I loved to do.

There was another man in our town named Tom Faircloth who worked alongside Fred at times. He and his wife, Janice, would assist in any way they could, and Tom started mentoring young women for the Miss Thomasville Pageant that was affiliated with the Miss America Scholarship Program. I was always up for a challenge, and I could use the funds for college, so my interest was peaked. I had also attended a pageant with my mom one year, and had been enamored with the sparkling crown and glittery gowns since childhood. I wanted a crown! One of our neighbors down the street won that year, and I turned to my mom and said, "That's going to be me one day, all the way to the Miss America Pageant." She giggled and then realized it could look like she was laughing at my dreams. I told her, "You will see one day." I must've only been twelve at the time.

In 1973, my across-the-street neighbor, Gail Bullock, won the Miss Georgia title. I was amazed while we watched it on television. Pageants are still a really big deal in the south to this day. The whole town was thrilled that a hometown girl won the title. Gail used to babysit my brother and me. Her sister and I got braces and carpooled to the orthodontist together! This dream could really be within my reach. The next year when I auditioned and made the Troupe, there was a girl named Seva Day that could sing beautifully, and I looked up to her. Tom knew that this girl could win, and he started grooming her to become the next Miss Georgia – and in 1975 she won the title! After winning the crown, when I went to her homecoming she took me aside and said, "You're next!" I was thrilled. (Seva and I just attended the 2017 Miss Georgia Pageant together. It was my fortieth anniversary since I had won the title at eighteen years old. It was a great reunion, and we talked about that night when she told me that I was next...such fun memories!)

Tom took me under his wing and started grooming me to become the next pageant winner from Thomasville. I won the title in 1977, and my homecoming was amazing, nothing short of the whole town coming out to celebrate another win. I had sung an aria from the opera *La Traviata* called "Sempre Libera," which had vocal acrobats that no eighteen year old should be able to do, and it literally brought the house down complete with a standing ovation, not only at the Miss Georgia Pageant, but at Miss America as well.

This was the eye for talent and development skills that Fred Allen was known for. Tom had taught me to walk the runway, talk and carry on conversations, and how to sit and be a lady in every sense of the word. He knew how to pick out wardrobes and make a winner. Tom subsequently chose two more girls from our hometown through the end of the eighties that won the Miss Georgia title before retiring from pageantry altogether. I had a dream one year prior to winning that I was chosen as queen, and even saw the dress in which I won, even though I hadn't even bought my gown yet. So when my mom and I went to Lillie Rubin and I saw the dress hanging there, I knew it was my gown. The Lord gave me a dream to prepare me for what was coming!

When I won the Miss Georgia title, my life changed overnight. I was presented a new car for winning, and a large monetary scholarship for winning talent, was well as for the title itself. I won diamonds, jewelry, furs, wardrobes, and a trip to New York to buy couture gowns and clothes for Miss America. My appearances – which I got paid for all year – started up right away (I had to take a year off from college to represent the state), and my schedule was intense. Tom's wife, Janice, was one of my many chaperones who traveled with me all year, and she said that I gave her gray hair because it was all she could do to get me to my appearances on time. I moved into the home of one of the directors of the pageant for two-and-a-half months to prepare for nationals. The stress of my life changing so fast and being uprooted and away from my family, preparing with mock interview panels everyday, numerous television appearances, being in parades, singing the National Anthem at the Atlanta Braves and Flames games, singing at the White House for President Jimmy Carter (since he was from Georgia), singing at the Mets game at Shea Stadium, and having appearances with Burt Reynolds and Sally Field at the Omni in Atlanta – just to name a few highlights – was almost too much too soon for this sheltered eighteen year old from Thomasville to bear. I moved back home before I competed for the national title. Everyone used to ask me, "How did you do in Miss America?" I always told them, "Top fifty!" I put that line in my show later on when I headlined around the world. I'm forever grateful to be a part of an elite sorority that only a few women can say that they were a part.

I went back to college the following year, after relinquishing my title, to finish my degree at the University of South Carolina. Fred wanted me to study with Evelyn McGarrity, a voice teacher there that he knew was wonderful. I had completed my freshman year at Wesleyan College in Macon, Georgia, when I won the pageant. I had gotten a full scholarship to USC in voice, and that, along with the Miss Georgia and Miss America money and the funds my dad had set aside for me for years, paid my way through college and enabled me to live off campus in a nice apartment for my last three years of school.

I ended up graduating with honors in 1981 with a Bachelor of Arts in Journalism and a minor in music. Throughout my college years, I was a member of the Ballet Company, the Opera Company where we did many performances. I also auditioned and got a job at Opryland in Nashville, Tennessee. Adjacent to the Grand Ole Opry, it was a place where you would do shows during the summer months and during the fall, if you signed up for it, and it was a training ground – an apprenticeship of sorts to prepare you for Broadway. Every summer I would go and do a different show each season, and one year even drove every weekend during the fall show schedule from Columbia, South Carolina to Nashville, Tennessee, which was a nine- to ten-hour drive each way, depending on weather conditions. I'd drive there on Friday after classes and do shows all day Saturday and Sunday, then get back in my car and drive home Sunday evening, only to get up for classes again on Monday. Needless to say, I was vigilant and determined to make it and prepare anyway I could to be on Broadway.

> I was at a crossroads. Would I make the decision to give in to my flesh, or let the Lord use me like He had told me He wanted to?

I met a lifetime friend at Opryland named Teresa Lee. She was a Christian, and she and I hit it off. One year we ended up doing a show together called *For Me And My Gal* where I had the lead as "Mama Cohan." It's a role that Mary Elizabeth Mastrantonio did before me, and I set my sights on the role. She is a star today, playing in movies such as *Scarface, Robin Hood: Prince of Thieves, The Abyss,* and *The Perfect Storm,* and the lead on *Law and Order,* just to name a few.

One summer while performing at Opryland, I knew that I was in the battle for my soul. I met a guy that I loathed at first, but then started to have feelings for him. I knew he wasn't a good guy; he had a girlfriend, and he had his sights set on me as a conquest. I was extremely attracted to him. I felt as if all my hormones were on full tilt. I truly felt as if I was in the middle of a spiritual battle for my life. It was a critical, determining time. I had started writing songs for the first time at twenty-one years old. I never knew that I even had that gift. I knew that the devil was sifting me like wheat. I literally felt as if I had a devil on one shoulder, telling me to give in to my desires, and an angel on the other, telling me to be strong. My sexuality was in full bloom. I was at a crossroads. Would I make the decision to give in to my flesh, or let the Lord use me like He had told me He wanted to?

This man pursued me with a vengeance, and I found myself in a car with him and every fiber of my being was being enticed by the evil one. My conscience was screaming to get out of the car, but my flesh was so enticed and so weak that he eventually wore me down to where I went to his apartment and ended up giving in and compromising my whole belief system, knowing that it was a wrong decision.

My walk with the Lord was derailed and thrown off course because I couldn't say "no" to my flesh.

> *For all that is in the world – the lust of the flesh, the lust of the eyes, and the pride of life – is not of the Father but is of the world.*
>
> — 1 John 2:16

I fell with him, and gave my heart to the wrong man. This relationship ended up hurting me like I'd never been hurt before, and that's but one reason why God wants us chaste and pure. He wants to protect us by not bringing baggage into the right relationship. He doesn't want our hearts damaged.

> *Keep your heart with all diligence, For out of it spring the issues of life.*
>
> — Proverbs 4:23 NKJV

This started a process of backsliding that would last a total of seven years…until I met my future husband, Michael.

The Lord took my gift of songwriting away right then and there, and didn't give it back to me until twelve years later. He couldn't trust me with the gift. However, the Bible tells us in Joel 2:25, *"And I will restore to you the years that the locust hath eaten…"* (KJV), and today I mentor young women why the Bible teaches us not to have sex before marriage. I was never told why not to biblically, I was just told not to, and that doesn't give a strong-willed person like myself a reason to make the right decision.

> *Flee sexual immorality. Every sin that a man does is outside the body, but he who commits sexual immorality sins against his own body. Or do you not know that your body is the temple of the Holy Spirit who is in you, whom you have from God, and you are not your own? For you were bought at a price; therefore glorify God in your body and in your spirit, which are God's.*
>
> — 1 Corinthians 6:18-20 NKJV

I was being led by Satan down a path of destruction, slowly and methodically, that would eventually lead me back to the true and living God. It would just take seven long years.

After graduating college in 1981, I headed straight to New York City. I didn't know anyone there, but I had a connection with some people at Opryland who hooked me up to room with some girls in Queens. I boarded a train in Eustis, Florida, where my parents lived at the time, and I will never forget the look on my mom's face when I left. She thought I'd never make it back to them. I arrived in New York full of hope and promise, with the determination and drive to make it into a Broadway show.

I quickly got an agent for auditions, and a commercial agent with the William Morris Agency, where I started going out on "go-sees" for commercials. I landed a regional commercial rather quickly and started receiving paychecks regularly. I immediately got my SAG and AFTRA union cards.

I made enough money to move into Manhattan. I lived in three different apartments during the two years I lived there. I started out in Hell's Kitchen on 43rd Street with a friend that I worked with at Opryland. Then I moved on up to the Upper East Side, on 72nd and Third Street in a doorman building where I lived with two former Miss Americas, and then ended up in Chelsea on 16th Street between Fifth and Sixth Avenue.

I acquired a vocal coach named Joyce Bryant, a singing star in the fifties that was known for her sultry belt voice. Since I was only operatically trained at the time, I needed to learn to "belt" to get jobs. I was a quick study and learned to belt like any Broadway singer could. I also hired Phyllis Grandy, a vocal coach who helped me with repertoire for Broadway audition songs and how to present myself professionally. She was known as a coach that could get you on Broadway quickly. I also studied with vocal coaches at

Julliard to maintain my operatic voice as well, so I wouldn't lose those chops, and I regularly took dance classes to be ready when the auditions would arise.

In order to make money, I became an in-house wedding gown model for Bergdorf Goodman's. I would wear the most glamorous, expensive wedding gowns and sachet around in dresses costing thousands of dollars on each floor of the store, showing off the gowns while people shopped. I loved this job! I also became a model/mannequin for the Seventh Avenue Fashion houses. I felt just like an inanimate object that could fit the sample size of two or four, and they didn't care about who I was or what my name was. I was also a model for the New York Health and Racquet Club, and I taught exercise for a living for a while at Body by Gilda, in order to pay the bills. I figured I might as well get paid to stay in shape for when that audition would come along to change my life. I became a pretty popular exercise instructor, and would have stars in my classes like Kevin Bacon and his then-girlfriend, Tracy Pollan, who is now married to Michael J. Fox.

I was searching for significance at every level of my being instead of looking to the right source – Jesus Christ. I was partying and hanging out with friends that I shouldn't. *"Do not be deceived: Evil company corrupts good habits"* (1 Corinthians 15:33 NKJV). Or I like the version, *"Bad company corrupts good character."* I was definitely testing my wings and boundaries, and I became a promiscuous young woman. My conscience was becoming seared with each man I would pursue. It became my sport of choice to trifle with them. What God had made to be a beautiful act between a husband and wife, Satan had distorted in my young life.

Looking back, I can personally relate to the woman at the well in John chapter 4, when Jesus spoke to her saying, *"Whoever drinks of this water will thirst again, but whoever drinks of the water that*

I shall give him will never thirst. But water that I shall give him will become in him a fountain of water springing up into everlasting life" (NKJV). The woman said to Him, *"Sir, give me this water, that I may not thirst..."* Jesus told her to go call her husband, and she said she didn't have one. *"You have had five husbands, and the man you now have is not your husband. What you have said is quite true."* She couldn't believe He "knew" her so well, and she knew that she had encountered a prophet. And then Jesus went on to reveal that He was indeed the Christ that had come. I can imagine that she went to tell everyone in her town about this man, becoming an outspoken evangelist. My life was heading down the same path as this woman. How might my life have been different if I had lived it knowing that God knew what I was doing? Even so, in His grace and loving pursuit of me, Jesus would come and reveal Himself to me, and one day I would also be His outspoken evangelist!

> "I'm so lonely. I thought all of this would make me happy. I bought the lie that this was glamorous. What am I doing?"

I found myself experimenting with the occult by going to mediums and psychics to find out what my future held instead of relying upon the true and living God. I couldn't believe the height from which I'd fallen. One psychic in particular, on the upper West Side, was especially memorable. I walked up the stairs into a dark space that felt eerie, filled with newspapers all the way to the ceiling in every nook and cranny of her apartment. She was a hoarder, with a bunch of Siamese cats running around. I sat down, and she proceeded to tell me that at age thirty-three I would still be doing what I'm doing (singing), but it would look differently, though she didn't know what it would be. When I think about this, I was thirty-three years old, my "coming of age," when Potter's Field Ministries actually began. It just goes to show you that even powers of darkness "know" things – but God is over all! I had unknowingly invited demonic activity into my life. I would walk around Greenwich Village after being in a club with friends until 3 a.m. and pray up to the sky, "I'm so lonely. I thought all of this would make me happy. I bought the lie that this was glamorous. What am I doing?" I was living a life that was the antithesis of how I was raised.

One day, I heard through the grapevine that the Broadway show *42nd Street*, by David Merrick, was holding replacement auditions at the Majestic Theatre. It was a "Catch-22" to get into these auditions because you needed your Actors Equity union card to even get in to be seen. I decided right then and there that I was going to be seen, despite the fact that I didn't have my Equity card. I found out when the auditions were and marched myself down to the stage door at the Majestic Theatre. I knocked on the door and introduced myself to the Stage Manager with all the fearlessness, tenacity and moxie that accompanies youth. I proceeded to tell him, "I'm a great tap dancer and singer and I want to be seen for the replacement audition!" He asked me if I was "Equity" and I said no but I should be! I'm sure that this sort of thing doesn't happen too much in today's world. This guy was so impressed with me that he took my phone number and said he'd get in touch with me if he could work it out. In two days, I got a call for an audition and found myself in front of Karen Baker and Randy Skinner, auditioning for a spot in *42nd Street*!

Three callbacks later, Karen Baker said, "Where have you been? You got the job!! " I couldn't believe it! I landed my first Broadway show after two years of beating the pavement. I immediately got my Equity card. They asked if I wanted to take the place of the gal I was going to replace on Broadway in a few months, or I could choose to be a part of the brand new company they were opening in Los Angeles which was starting rehearsals in a couple of weeks time, and I could compete for my own spots in the show. I chose to move to Los Angeles because I wanted to get out of New York, and I wanted to compete for my spots in the show. And living in California would fulfill yet another dream.

We did the show for one year at the Shubert Theatre in Los Angeles to a resounding success. We performed eight shows a week, and I soon discovered that it was monotonous, and didn't fill the hole in my heart that I thought it would. I thought that reaching the pinnacle of where I'd put all my energies these past years to achieve my goal would magically turn off that emptiness buried deep within my heart, but this wasn't it either, and I turned down the next contract for the San Francisco Company. I would end up doing two more companies of this show in the Los Angeles area in the years to come, working my way to the lead role, "Dorothy Brock."

I also had a cabaret act in Los Angeles, playing in popular venues like The Rose Tattoo, and I developed quite a following. The Executive Producer/Director/Writer at ABC Television, Don Colhour, hired me to become the in-house choreographer for ABC. I choreographed shows for them such as *ABC Night of Stars,* and *A Tribute to Aaron Spelling,* and also the UCLA Men's Chorus. I also choreographed a show for Michael Feinstein at the Hollywood Bowl called *A Gershwin Tribute,* where I tap danced solo in a Bob Mackie costume to, "I've Got Rhythm," while the stage rose from underneath on hydraulics with me on it. Through contacts, I ended up having a job as Ginny Mancini's personal assistant for a short time. Ginny is the wife of now-deceased, renowned conductor and composer, Henry Mancini, known for such songs as "Moon River" from *Breakfast at Tiffany's* and "The Pink Panther Theme." She herself had an illustrious career as a singer before marrying. I got Ginny the gig of hosting *The Bach Festival* for ABC, and I got to sing solo during this event. Ginny was a very helpful woman, and she kind of took me under her wing. I must've reminded her of herself when she was starting out in her career. She asked me to sing at Henry's birthday party at their palatial home in Bel Aire. I couldn't believe it. Stars came out in droves for the party. People that I'd grown up watching on television, and singers I had admired, and celebrities from my parent's era were in attendance. I was in the Mancini's living room with such greats as Carol Burnett, Andy Williams, and Dionne Warwick. The renowned composer, arranger, lyricist, and conductor, Stan Freeman, beautifully played the piano for me that evening while I sang. It was a surreal experience.

Using money I made during my jobs and shows, I put together a one-woman solo act with full orchestrations for each song. I became a headline entertainer on seven major cruise lines and traveled the world. It was a great gig at first. They paid large, and I was treated as though I was a passenger. I got great outside cabins with balconies, and could take anyone with me for free. But just like anything else, it got old fast. I only did one show per week so I had way too much down time. All this time, I was having liaisons off and on, with two actual relationships thrown in between. My heart was getting harder with each passing tryst. Proverbs 28:14 – *"Blessed is the man who always fears the Lord, but he who hardens his heart falls into trouble."*

I also was a headline entertainer in shows in Florida, New York, and Monte Carlo, France. Although it seemed I had the world by its tail, I was actually progressing down the abyss of a sinful lifestyle that didn't show any signs of stopping. I had bitten the apple and bought the lies of Satan that all that glitters is gold and silver. It's definitely not; silver, in time, tarnishes.

Sin is only pleasurable for a season.

> *By faith Moses, when he became of age, refused to be called the son of Pharaoh's daughter, choosing rather to suffer affliction with the people of God than to enjoy the passing pleasures of sin, esteeming the reproach of Christ greater riches than the treasures in Egypt; for he looked to the reward.*
>
> — Hebrews 11:24-25 NKJV

Chapter 5

HIS COLORFUL PAST

Michael is one of the most unique people I have ever met. As a matter of fact, I've *never* met anyone like him. I adore him in so many ways. I love that he tells the raw truth no matter what. I've grown so much as a person and a Christian since I've been married to him for the past thirty years, but it hasn't come without deep pain and wounds. The truth can truly cut deep sometimes, though I'd much rather know the truth so I can change, or at least improve myself – and it works the other way around as well. We both have grown deeper in love through the years. We trust each other, and each other's opinions. We have each other's best interests at heart. He still makes me laugh after all this time. I couldn't imagine a more suitable spouse, and knowing that God had a plan all along that we would be together before time began is mind-boggling.

Trust in God – even when things look bleak. He can make beauty from ashes. Michael has an inordinate amount of energy. He has been diagnosed with ADHD and dyslexia. Personally, those are just letters to me. I feel the Lord made him with this much energy to accomplish the things He has for his life. One thing I've discovered about the learning disability of dyslexia is that many people who are affected by it have high intelligence, and show true brilliance in certain areas of their lives. They just have different learning styles.

Michael hears the voice of the Lord and then obeys. I used to try to keep up with him when I was younger, but now that I'm older I don't even try. I just let him run with the horses the way God intended him to, and I sit back and marvel. I believe he is truly a "man after God's own heart" as David was (Acts 13:22). When he started out, however, I'm sure it didn't look that way. So be encouraged.

Michael has always been a daredevil. He never really displayed fear, nor did he think of the consequences of his actions until much later in his life. He was pretty much a terror, or a whirling dervish, in his neighborhood. Michael was born in Downey, then grew up in Hacienda Heights, and then moved to various places throughout Southern California before settling into a condo on the water on St. Moritz Drive in Huntington Harbor. He would wake up at the crack of dawn and run over to his neighbor's house, the Holders, at 6 a.m., where he would start knocking on the door asking Eileen if his friends could come out and play. Michael jokes today that she'd see him coming and close the blinds, hoping he'd go away.

Michael was good at everything he attempted to do, and if his brother did something, he would pick it up and end up doing it better. He started snow skiing at a very young age. He and his friends would drive to Mammoth Mountain, skiing quite often throughout his youth. He became an expert skier, able to ski double black diamond runs and do jumps and flip on skis. He's still an excellent skier to this day. A neighbor down the street who he didn't know well had a trampoline. He "hired" three underclassmen to help him steal it, and for helping he would get them a case of beer. He wanted it so he and his buddies could practice flipping on their skis in his backyard. When his mom came home, she asked where the trampoline came from, and Michael made up a story that he bought it. His mom, being trusting and a bit gullible, believed him.

His antics didn't stop there. Michael started experimenting with drugs and alcohol. He and his friends decided one evening to go and steal some marijuana growing in a field not too far from his home. They had to be really careful, because they knew if they got caught taking it that the consequences would be dire. They ended up successfully stealing a great deal of fresh weed, and Michael took it back to his mom's home and decided that he would string it up to dry in one of his mother's closets. She wasn't happy about this, but he basically told her to be quiet

Looking much older than his age, his dad started taking him to Las Vegas to gamble and play blackjack.

about it, and that he was going to do it anyway. Michael ruled the roost over the two women raising him. This also became the beginning of his amateur drug dealing before graduating to a more sophisticated operation after high school.

By the age of sixteen, Michael had a full mustache, and long luxurious hair that would make the girls swoon. Looking much older than his age, his dad started taking him to Las Vegas to gamble and play blackjack. This began an addiction to gambling that lasted until he got saved. His dad would make him take dark mascara and fill in his mustache so he would look old enough to sit in the casino. This is also where he learned that some men were unfaithful to their wives on these trips – thankfully, this was never one of Michael's vices. Michael loved the thrill and the adrenaline rush of losing just as much as winning.

Gambling in his adult years, after having lost the all money he had brought with him, Michael would borrow thousands of dollars from his friends, always saying that he'd be good for it and pay it back. He has told me stories of coming home after gambling all night, taking an early flight home the next morning, hung over after losing so much of his and his friends' money that he would hate himself. But still the lure was there, drawing and beckoning him back to do it again.

One of Michael's first jobs was a government job where he drove a forklift. He was living in Seal Beach at the time, and one day, while he and his buddies were so busy partying and skiing, he hurt himself badly flipping on his skis. He told his work, however, that he had hurt himself on the job. He was able to go on workman's compensation, and they settled a lawsuit with him for thousands of dollars. He was heavily into a cocaine addiction by this time – as well as alcohol – and he bought so much coke that he ran through the entire settlement in no time.

Michael was broke. He had to sell his car to live. He got a job as a busboy in Sir Winston Churchill's Restaurant at the Queen Mary. This was a five-star establishment. Since he sold his car, he had no way to get to work, but he remembered that he had a pair of roller skates. So until he could afford another vehicle, Michael roller-skated to work from Seal Beach to Sir Winston's in Long Beach every day. He didn't realize it, but since he got hired at the restaurant he automatically became a member of the waiters union – which meant they couldn't fire him. One of the waiters took Michael under his wing and taught him everything he knew about fine wines and tableside dining. He eventually got promoted to the position of waiter and, like everything else he did, he became an excellent one. He later rose to the rank of "Captain." This is when he learned to cook fancy desserts tableside, such as flaming the sauce for bananas Foster.

Michael's waiter friend told him about Regent Air, a new airline that was holding auditions to for flight attendants with specialty positions such as chefs and hairdressers. It was going to be an exclusive airline that flew celebrities and wealthy clients from New York to Los Angeles and back. At twenty-one, Michael decided to go to the "cattle call" and audition – there were only twenty-nine job positions. Twelve of these would be in-house chefs. Over ten thousand people showed up across America over a one-year period! After many months of interviews and callbacks, Michael was one of the twelve that got the job! He was elated. Limos would pick up the clients and drive them to the airplane where they would be greeted by the staff, the male attendants wearing Halston tuxedos. The airplanes were

His girlfriend genuinely cared about him... Her dad wanted to give Michael money to go away.

exquisite, with suites, a hair salon, and a galley where Michael was chosen to be the in-house chef cooking gourmet meals. Wolfgang Puck created the official menu, so Michael was trained by his staff on how to make all of Wolfgang's gourmet meals. He especially loved making caviar omelets in the mornings for such people as Lucille Ball and Barbara Walters, to name but a few. Even though this was a glamorous job, make no mistake – they were flight attendants and could evacuate a plane if it went down. After a while, the job got really old for Michael; the money wasn't all that great for the weird hours they were required to keep. He wanted a new job…and adventure.

His dad called him one day and asked if he wanted to come and work with him in the financial industry. He knew that Michael had the "gift of gab" and could probably sell ice to Eskimos, so he asked him to learn the business from the bottom up, starting in the mailroom. He told him that if Michael could stick it out, he would eventually have the potential to make a lot of money. His father always said, "Give me a waiter with the "gift of gab" that can sell, rather than someone with a business degree that can't." Michael certainly fit the bill. I'm sure it doesn't happen often in today's world, but back then it did. Michael learned the business very quickly, and he rose up into the ranks, cold calling all day long and securing investments under his dad's license pretty much from the start.

All the while this was going on, Michael's cocaine addiction was becoming out of control. He sold it on the side, and he was hanging out with big-time drug dealers and partying with a friend who was in the thick of that lifestyle. His friend didn't even have a social security number; he bought and did everything with cash. Michael had fast cars and fast women – amongst some who were mud wrestlers – and he lived with a handful of them. They would party hard with plenty of alcohol, cocaine, and anything else their hearts desired. The debauchery of his lifestyle was so far and above anything I'd ever experienced. He would struggle with rage issues in each relationship, and would eventually end up kicking the girl out of his house while in a rage, throwing her clothes over the balcony railing into the water in the harbor below.

He started dating an accomplished young woman who was a college graduate, choosing to because she was vastly different from the girls he had been with until this point – his father would kick him out of parties at his house when he would show up with some of the women he chose to hang out with. This girl was in love with Michael and they decided to get engaged.

Problems began early on in their relationship, both because of Michael's addictions, as well as her own deep-rooted problems. Michael had bought his dream car, a 911 red Targa Porsche, and they had put the car in his girlfriend's name. She had a great driving record and it was easier this way. Michael had two DUI's and a reckless driving violation – driving with an open container and in excess of 130 mph. Problems escalated in their relationship due to Michael's increased cocaine use – he started smoking it – compounded with her issues, and tensions continued to mount. His girlfriend genuinely cared about him and was worried about him. Her dad wanted to give Michael money to go away. She decided to take the drug paraphernalia she found to Michael's dad to reveal the extent of his drug use. Michael came clean to his dad about it. She was actually committed to see him through rehab, but as weeks passed, she saw that Michael wasn't committed in getting the help he needed. I think she saw the writing on the wall that this wasn't going to end in a marriage, like she'd hoped. They broke up.

Two months later, her dad called Michael's father. She had found another car and wanted to exchange the Honda she was currently driving, and she needed the Porsche back because it was in her name. Plus she was liable if Michael had any accidents or tickets while driving it. His dad called Michael into his office and asked one question: "Is the Porsche in her name?" He answered, "Yes." Then his dad said, "Give her the keys! You're about to make a big commission and you can buy a new one." He left that meeting in the car that she had been driving, while his now ex-girlfriend drove off in his prized Porsche.

A couple of months later, Michael received a call from his ex-girlfriend asking him to buy the car back because she had found a car to purchase and needed a substantial down payment for it, but she wanted to offer it to him first. He gave her a hard time, but he bought it back and went to the bank to have it transferred into his name. When they went in, the lady behind the counter politely asked for the thousands of dollars in taxes that he would owe on it. He hit the roof! He told her that he'd already paid those taxes once when he bought it and put it in his girlfriend's name, and he wasn't going to pay it twice. He then asked, "Is there any way around me not paying taxes on this car again?" She told him, "Yes, there is one way. You could marry this girl and that would take care of it." He looked at her and they both decided that they would go down to the justice of the peace that afternoon, get married in name only, then go back and have the title transferred. They went down to the justice of the peace, got married, and went back and did the transfer. They told each other goodbye and didn't see each other again! Michael and I met only a few weeks after that transaction. We fell in love, and got married three weeks after meeting each other.

I didn't learn about this story until a few months into our marriage. And when I did, a panic came over me, wondering if he'd ever gotten a divorce or dissolution of marriage! When I asked him he wasn't sure, and that led me to a mad research of records to find out if he was really married to me. I was so relieved when I found the actual dissolution of marriage certificate on file at the courthouse. That could've been a close one – living with a man I wasn't legally married to!

A few years later, the girlfriend was getting married herself. She was joining the Catholic Church, and a monsignor of the Orange County archdiocese tracked Michael down to interview him to see if the stories lined up about what she said had happened, as she was seeking an official annulment by the Church. They granted the annulment. Before he hung up, the priest asked Michael if he wanted absolution from the Catholic Church. Michael began sharing with the priest, telling him that he was now a "born again

Christian," and that the Lord had forgiven him. "So thanks, but no thanks!" he said. The priest promptly ended the call.

Oddly enough, this girl married a man that has family ties to Whitefish, Montana, where we live today. They ended up buying a nice condominium in Whitefish as a vacation home! Though the connection was unknown to us, we bought one of these condos in 2005 for my mom when she moved here after my dad passed away in 2003. We found this out from friends of theirs that now live in Whitefish who knew both Michael and her when they were dating back in the eighties. This couple bought a unit for themselves – right across the street from the one we bought! And the name of the street it is on – St. Moritz Drive! Needless to say, they sold it a few years ago.

Chapter 6

PAY ATTENTION TO ME

"**P**AY ATTENTION TO ME!!*" The voice resounded in my head and through the core of my body. It shook me awake from a deep sleep during an afternoon nap before my show that evening. It was 1985, and I was the headline singer in the show *Pizazz*, a Miller-Reich Production at the Sheraton Bal Harbour in Miami, Florida. We performed eight shows a week to a sold-out crowd for a full year, and received great reviews. These words jarred me at such a level within my soul that there was no doubt it was the voice of the Lord trying to get my attention! It was electric and audible.

I was encountering something supernatural. It was frightening in a way, yet familiar at the same time. I knew God was trying to get my attention because I had been ignoring all of the "cues." I had been living for myself for so many years, walking away from the convictions of my youth when I had received the Lord Jesus as my Savior. My singing and dancing talents had taken me all over the world, and I was trying to fill that vacuous hole in my heart with all the accomplishments, glamor, and debauchery I could, and it left me wanting – it still wasn't filled. The message of *"pay attention to Me"* was an accurate depiction using the acronym of my name: PAM. In God's economy, there are no accidents.

My life had become the things dreams were made of – hob-knobbing with the likes of Donald O'Conner of *Singing In the Rain,* and Eddie Fisher, who at different times was married to Debbie Reynolds and Elizabeth Taylor. They were headlining down the street from us at The Fontainebleau. We would go to their hotel, just down the street from ours, and dance until the wee hours of the morning with the now-senior citizen stars from classic movies that my mom had me watch while I was growing up – movies that instilled the love of singing and dancing into my life. My mom, Nita Souders, with my great Aunt Lois, was visiting to see our show, and she was giddy and thrilled that she could dance with these icons of the cinema. These were the men she would see on the silver screen during her youth and escape into another world, far away from her upbringing in Bartow, Florida. I was really glad that I could bring a little excitement into mom's life, knowing her daughter was "living the dream" she had played in her mind. Little did she know that Eddie Fisher, who was at least thirty-plus years older than me, was hitting on me. And I'm thinking, "Not even on your birthday!!"

Although incidents such as these seemed to follow me my whole life, I looked at them as a novelty, comical in a way. I had my pick of any "eligible man" I wanted – Cindy Adams from *Page*

> I was living a life that I thought would bring me success, but I was walking away from the convictions of my youth and rewriting my "normal" as I went.

Six once reported in *The New York Post* that Mike Tyson was seen with me and it wasn't even true. I had my pick of princes, racecar drivers, and any of the younger available men on the smörgåsbord.

I was on another journey, however. Looking for something deeper, more meaningful. I didn't know what that something was, but I was going to find out. Except I was vacillating between living a life that my mother would love and wish for me – which invariably had its foundations rooted in sin – and the deep pull of a spirituality that had taken a deeper root in my soul years before in Thomasville, Georgia, back in that little country church.

I was having regular anxiety attacks where my asthma would escalate and I would almost hyperventilate. I would have to call someone that I knew and loved, just to hear their voice to ground me emotionally so I wouldn't feel as though I was losing my mind. These are the things that panic attacks are made of. I really didn't know what was happening to me during these episodes, but I knew if I could hear my grandmother's voice, it would bring me back to some semblance of reality. I was living a life that I thought would bring me success, but I was walking away from the convictions of my youth and rewriting my "normal" as I went. I never realized that this would cause volcanic eruptions in my soul, evidenced by the occurrence of panic attacks so severe that I thought I was dying. I *was* dying – spiritually – with every willful sin I would walk into, and with all the debaucheries this "prodigal daughter" would rebelliously encounter.

My grandmother, Ida Pearl Bennett, was a stabilizing force in my young life. She was always there for me, to listen when I needed to talk about life, or to help me navigate through teenage issues, or problems between my mom and me. She seemed to understand me better than my mom, with no judgments or expectations. She allowed me to be fallible me. She accepted me as I was along with my faults, attitudes, and teenage angst. I remember as a child I would fall asleep in her lap while she would stroke my hair, singing with her sweet voice, "Go to sleepy little baby, go to sleepy little baby...when you wake you can have some cake...ride the pretty little ponies, ride the pretty little ponies." To this day, I still love having my hair stroked; I love cake and adore horses!! I miss my grandmother's unconditional love, tenderness, warm lap, and the sense of being valued by another woman.

I was young and hadn't really experienced much death in my life yet.

On this day, when I heard the audible resounding voice that startled me awake, I called my grandmother. She had been sick for a few weeks and was in the hospital. She had been diagnosed with cancer of the mouth, and I had been to visit her a few weeks prior in Bartow. Life was swirling so much around me, I never stopped to think about life without my grandma. All I knew was that I needed to hear her voice.

"Hi Grandma!!" I breathlessly uttered. "Hi Pam," she responded in that calm tone that was so familiar and comforting. When I heard her voice on the other end of the line I immediately relaxed, and the anxiety level that had been a ten went down to about a five. I could feel my heartbeat start to slow down. My breathing became less labored and my mind was averted from "nervous breakdown" mode to "I'm okay again." Grandmother is here, and I'm okay. I am safe.

She and I talked that evening for about an hour. I asked her questions about life, what to expect in my future. "Do you think I will ever get married Grandma?" "You will if you want to, sweetie," she calmly reassured me. "You can do anything you want." (That was something my dad had told me all my life.) All the while, she was lying in a hospital bed, slowly dying from mouth cancer. I really couldn't wrap my mind around the fact that she was actually in the last days of her life! I couldn't envision a world without her in it. I was young and hadn't really experienced much death in my life yet, and because of my naïveté and immaturity, the reality that she wouldn't be around hadn't resonated into my consciousness.

We had always spent family vacations at Grandmother and Granddaddy Bennett's house. Even when Daddy would have to go out of town, Mom, my brother Greg, and I would load up in the car and make the five-hour jaunt from Thomasville to Bartow to have wonderful adventures at their modest house. Greg and I would climb the cumquat tree in her backyard, watch *Friday Night Fright Night* horror flicks in front of her little TV and build forts under the beds in the guest bedroom.

Their humble, brick stucco home was full of love, fellowship, and great food. Many wonderful childhood memories were formed there. I learned how to make "sun tea." Grandma would steep the teabags in a large pitcher and put it out in the sun for hours. She would fill it with large amounts of real sugar, and to this day it is the best tea I've ever drunk. My Grandmother was one of the very best cooks I've ever known, and she would take hours to make out-of-this-world homemade cornbread in a small black iron skillet. She would sleep late into the mornings and start to cook around ten or eleven, slaving over the stove all day. Then she'd do laundry – which she would hang on a clothes line – and to this day I can still remember the fresh smell of the sheets that had been basking in the sun for hours, and when I would pull them up over me at night I would drink in the awesome, aromatic mixture of sunshine and Downey. I try to mimic that smell with my laundry to this day, and there is no substitute for fresh laundry and sunshine drying on a clothesline. She would end up going to bed around two in the morning, and then the next day it would start up all over again. She was a wonderful example in serving my sweet granddaddy, "Slim" Bennett, with no complaints all the days of their married life. Those were precious, sweet days and simple joys that I often return to in my memories.

After our conversation, I remember being so thankful for having spoken with her, for her calming me down once again with her soothing voice and calm demeanor. Everything was copasetic once again in my world. Little did I know that a few days later, my precious Grandmother would be ushered into Heaven, having succumbed to the cancer that had invaded her body.

When I spoke with my mom after her passing, I shared the conversation that I had with her just one week before. My mom was in complete shock when I told her how long we had spoken. She proceeded to inform me that Grandmother had been in a deep coma for the last week!! To this day, I believe that it was a gift from my Lord for me to have a last sweet time with her – for some last parting words of guidance, love, and promise to prepare me for what was to come in my future. My mother and I, until the day she herself died in May 2014, still marveled at the Lord for giving me that opportunity to say "goodbye for now," and to know how intricately He loves us and knows what we need. And He is able to provide all we need, even in the face of death. I look forward to our reunion on that day we see each other in Heaven.

After the show closed in Florida, I was offered another headlining position with Miller-Reich in New York City at a supper club called Café Versailles. Since I didn't have another job, I accepted, and loaded everything up and moved back to New York. I was doing twelve shows a week – two shows a night. It was more work than I had ever done, and it started to take a toll on my body. The pay wasn't enough for the workload, and where I lived in Chelsea – back in 1986 – a studio apartment was $1,500 a month. Although the club was nice, the working conditions weren't great, and dealing with the head of the production company was less than ideal. I ended up getting mononucleosis again (I also had it in high school, resulting from too much activity and exhaustion) and my mom and dad came to New York to take care of me for a while. Somehow, I needed to get out of this job.

One evening, I attended a Christmas party with my cast after a show. On that fateful night I struck up a conversation with a producer who was in the process of casting a show in Monte Carlo, France, and he asked if I would be interested in headlining in Monaco. The very thought of this was exhilarating, and the possibilities were promising. Would this be another stone by which the Lord could get my attention?

Chapter 7

MONACO BOUND

It was the dream jobs of all dream jobs – and I had landed it! So many girls would've given anything for this opportunity, but by some twist of fate, I was scheduled to headline in Monte Carlo! I had just met a producer named Larry Vickers at a party in New York. He had just seen me sing in my show at Café Versailles that evening and was asking about my career, and if I'd ever thought of singing in Europe. He had a great opportunity to put together a show in Monte Carlo, and hoped I'd be interested in being one of two headline singer-entertainers at the Casino du Monaco and The Sporting Club – two of the hottest places on earth to headline. I was trying to play it cool and gave him my number in case this truly panned out. I had been in show business long enough at this point to know that you don't have a job until you put your name on the dotted line.

On March 14, 1987, I got the call – the job in Monte Carlo was mine! Along with five other girls, we would have our lives transformed performing eight shows a week. At the Casino du Monaco, in their Le Cabaret, they would call us "The Girlfriends." This was indeed the premier show in Europe! I had to start rehearsals in New York the very next week; we were scheduled to arrive in Monaco on April 6th.

I couldn't sleep the next evening because I was so excited. I was going to perform in the French Riviera! I would visit Paris, Cannes, St. Tropez, numerous places in Italy, and have experiences that most girls would only read about in novels. In reality, this would be a life-altering, eye-opening, spiritual journey, instrumental in leading me back to the Lord.

On our way to Monaco, we all stopped off in Paris to tour a bit. We went to the Louvre Museum, the Eiffel Tower, and ate some wonderful French food. When we arrived in Monte Carlo we got checked into the Hotel Villa Boeri, which we would call home for the next three-and-a-half months. A bubbly, friendly French woman named Natalie and her husband Maurice would welcome us girls as if we were celebrities from America. I was checked into Suite 7, a really nice, clean European room with a hand-stuffed mattress that was extremely comfortable, complete with a Juliet balcony overlooking the Mediterranean Sea. This is where I would sit every morning, sipping my café au lait or herb tea that Natalie would make me. The smell of the sea would waft into my nostrils and the sunlight would warm my face as I would sit and contemplate life, wondering what exciting adventures lay ahead of me.

> Could I be bought? Would I become a mistress and sell out for worldly goods?

Monte Carlo is a small, lavish town where everyone knows everything about each other, and wants to be in each other's business. There are video cameras on every street corner where the police and palace monitor what goes on. As a result, there is very little crime there. But it is a bit unnerving knowing you are being watched.

Le Cabaret at the Casino du Monaco was beautiful, awesome, and beyond my wildest expectations. The stage was white lacquer that moved into the audience and back, with a beautiful orchestra stand in the back of the stage. The sound system was the finest money could buy. They spared no expense in this theatre. This would be the best venue I had played yet, including at the Schubert Theatre in Los Angeles. I was one of two headline singers, with four backup dancers and a full orchestra from London called The London Express.

Larry didn't waste anytime introducing us around town, and he took us to a discotheque named Jimmy Z's where we met the hosts, Bernard and Frank. Everyone was buying us drinks on the house, and we were throwing tulips at the singer. We danced until the wee hours under the stars – the disco's roof would open up completely and we were under the night sky, and we would just let go of ourselves, feeling free and being alive. That first week, in between rehearsals at Le Cabaret, we met some Swedes that took us in their Porsche to San Remo and Ventimiglia, Italy, to go shopping and have delicious food at Ristorante Cuneo. The food was delectable and the gelato was to die for. This was just a typical day off.

A couple of weeks into our show, I met Amad, the Prince of Iran. He had a crush on me, but he was married. He showed off his Ferrari, Rolls Royce, and his yacht – complete with a helicopter on top – to try to impress me. Before our opening night, he sent me a magnum of Cristal champagne backstage for us girls to enjoy with hopes to woo me. He was nice looking and smart, and this was the first of many temptations that I would be faced with, trying to decide who I was, and who I wanted to be. Could I be bought? Would I become a mistress and sell out for worldly goods? This was just the first of many questions I would be confronted with during this time in my life. I know now the Lord was taking me to the most decadent, richest, opulent place on this planet to show me that nothing could fill the void in my heart or satisfy my thirsty soul except Him. I would be asked to make life decisions during this turning point – not only about who I would become, but whether I truly believed in the God of the universe.

I had never had such an array of male suitors in such a concentrated time and place. I had caught the eye of Frank, the owner of Jimmy Z's, and The Girlfriends always got in for free and got preferential treatment every time we went. It wasn't uncommon that I'd have a dentist on one side of me and lawyer on the other, vying for my attention as they would buy the whole entourage magnums of champagne as we all danced until night turned into morning. I would just toy with these dalliances on a nightly basis, with no intention of it going any further.

Amad would take us to eat at the Fois Gras in the Lowes and would spend so much money – the wealth of the people we were meeting in France was unparalleled to that of anyone I'd ever met in the States. He was trying to wine and dine me at least four times a week. Most of the time, I would only go out with him when my friend, a dancer named Melinda Phelps, came along. (Melinda would later introduce me to my husband back in Southern California.) Amad would take us in his helicopter to shop in Nice, take us to phenomenal restaurants, and we would go gambling with him where he would lose $8,000 in minutes – and it didn't phase him. He was pulling out all stops with me. His relentless pursuit even made me a bit frightened. I was playing in a league that at twenty-eight years old I hadn't yet played. But I played it so cool with him, not giving in one bit, that I knew that he would soon tire of the game.

He decided to take the entire cast of The Girlfriends to the Monte Carlo Open Tennis Tournament, where he bought us all box seats at $500 a pop. We sat by tennis great Iliad Nastasi, and we all made the front page of the Nice newspaper for our show with a picture of us with the tennis player that won the tournament that day. Amad would just show up to see me unannounced at my hotel at times, and I would send him away. When he left for a ten-day business meeting one week, I knew that I probably wouldn't hear from him again. When he did return, he started hitting on the singer in the band, a girl named Jilly, so our relationship was severed. Our director, Larry, said this was good practice for me, because it was going to force me into deciding who I was and what I really wanted out of life. I knew I was experiencing a pivotal moment in my life that would define the course of it. Would I compromise?

The suitors continued to mount as time ticked on. A French clothing designer pursued me, sitting in the audience night after night, making artistic renderings of me in clothes he designed that he thought would look good on me. He would send these drawings backstage with love notes, complete with flowers, champagne, and Coco Chanel parfum. I wasn't interested, but I thought it was sweet.

Being a part of this wonderful show, we met everyone who was "someone" in this town – plus, Larry had connections. After a show, a typical night on the town might look something like this: "The Countess" of Menton would invite us all to a party at Le Pirot (The Pirate). Back in 1987, this cost five hundred dollars per person, and there were at least ten of us in attendance. But we were her guests, and we would stay overnight in her palatial mansion overlooking the Mediterranean. We would all arrive at the restaurant, and the wine and sangria would be flowing with the mariachi band in full swing. We would then be seated for the beginning of a multiple course meal, starting with crevettes (shrimp, with heads on them, still looking up at you) and beluga caviar. Then the pirates would come out shirtless, toss the spaghetti in large bowls and then serve us. We would conclude with dessert, and were then instructed to get up and start smashing our plates – and a stack of clean plates – into the fireplace. The energy escalated as we would throw our glasses into it as well, signifying that we liked the music. The after-dinner drinks continued to pour, and we'd all start playing "air drums," or drumming on the pots and pans or whatever was in front of us, and throwing streamers all over each other, dancing to the music. To top it all off, at the end of the night they'd bring in a donkey to eat watermelon off the tables. It was decadence like I'd never experienced up to this point in my life. Then The Countess would have the disco across the street opened for us, and we'd dance until 5 a.m.

> I had a knot in my gut that the Holy Spirit was nudging me to pay attention to.

While I was experiencing all these new adventures, I had a knot in my gut that the Holy Spirit was nudging me to pay attention to. Although sin is pleasurable for a season, I knew deep down I had a calling on my life. I was in the middle of the battle for my soul. It continued when I decided to have a liaison with the drummer in our band, Matthew, who was only twenty. He would be my "go to" after all the other men I continued to see would wax and wane. Looking back, I think his innocence and family values attracted me, grounding me somewhat to help keep my feet on planet earth during this spiritual crisis in my life. However, there were consequences to dragging in someone that pure into my debaucheries at that time. Hearts can get broken unintentionally. I've prayed many times for him throughout the last thirty years.

My next liaison would be with a blond, Swedish, drop-dead-gorgeous Grand Prix racecar driver named Stephan. The Girlfriends would hang out together most nights after our show at a charming little bistro called Cristal's and have champagne cocktails, and people would flock to come and see us there. I was sitting by Matthew one evening, and Stephan was making eyes at me from across the room. When he came over and put his arm around me, Matthew was furious. I whispered into Stephan's ear to call me at my hotel the next day, and he did. This started a month-long tryst with this handsome adrenaline junkie, until he had to leave to go to Belgium to pick up his car to race in the Grand Prix.

A friend from Los Angeles who starred with me in *42nd Street* called to fix me up with a friend of hers named Jacob. He would fly me to Paris for my day off to show me more of that romantic city. I figured I would do it since I trusted Cathy and she knew him. I flew to Paris, and he had a limo meet me at the airport to escort me to my five-star Hotel. When I met him I was very shocked, because he was a very unattractive, short, little man. I decided to make the best of things for twenty-four hours and allowed him to take me to such high-end stores as Lavin and Nina Ricci, and he bought me two beautiful, long cashmere coats, purses and belts, chocolates, Cristal champagne, and roses. He had reservations at a wonderful restaurant, and then he took me to The Lido to see the can-can girls. I figured I would make the best of things and avoid being alone with him like the plague. Boy was I going to have a conversation with Cathy after this! After the Lido show when we went back to the hotel, of course he tried to make the moves on me and I rebuffed his advances at every turn. "You can't buy me!" I was screaming in my head. I managed to get through the night without any major incidents, and we slept in separate hotel rooms.

The next day, I couldn't wait to get back on the plane to Monaco! Jacob had bought me a business class ticket, so when I got on the plane, I was seated next to a really nice, jovial man named George. We struck up a conversation and started laughing hysterically, and we were having a great time together. About four rows in front of us, a man sitting with an attractive woman kept looking back at us like he wanted to be with us. I finally said something to George, and he told me that the man looking at us was Prince Albert of Monaco, and he was sitting with the Princess of Spain. George was sure he would rather be back sitting with us and laughing – after all, George was Albert's bodyguard! The planets were aligning for me on every level during this time in France. As we exited the plane, Prince Albert was waiting for me on the jet bridge, and as I approached him, he introduced himself, adding, "You guys were having such a fun time back there..." We exchanged pleasantries, and he asked what brought me to Monaco and wondered where he knew me from. I told him I was in the show at Le Cabaret and The Sporting Club, and he told me he had attended the Le Cabaret show one week before. He and his family were coming to the show in a few weeks at The Sporting Club after the Grand Prix. He asked, "Can I show you Monte Carlo?" Of course I told him "Yes" and proceeded to give him the name of the Hotel where I was staying, and wondered if he ever would really call me.

Albert called within two days, and for that first week we talked for hours on the phone. He then made a date for us on my next

The night came for Prince Albert to pick me up for our date, and everyone at the hotel was buzzing.

day off. I was ecstatic, and I called my parents and other people back home who would be thrilled to hear about it. During the following week, Melinda and I went shopping for a dress and I found a beautiful white couture suit at Lilas Spak that looked like it was made for me. I got my hair and nails done, and we went to the Spa at the Casino du Monaco. Since we worked there, we could go there anytime, a perk we girls got to enjoy that was well worth it.

Stephan, the Swedish racecar driver, had returned from Belgium where he placed second in his race, and old feelings resurfaced. We scheduled a date at La Cremailler. I told Stephan that I liked him more than I had realized, more than anyone in a long time, and I was scared. He asked me out, but I told him I already had a date planned with the Prince of Monaco. I could tell he was really jealous. I told him that I'd rather be with him and he said, "The choice is yours." We planned a rendezvous after my date with Prince Albert, and I hoped he would follow through, since I wouldn't see him until after The Grand Prix race.

The night came for Prince Albert to pick me up for our date, and everyone at the hotel was buzzing. They all wanted to meet the prince in person; none of the employees at this particular hotel had met him. When he pulled up in his silver Porsche at 8:30 p.m. sharp, everyone was hanging out of the windows to catch a glimpse of him, calling his name and waving. I was in my room, nearly hyperventilating with excitement that Prince Albert was arriving. I came down the stairs in my white dress, and Natalie and Maurice were there, with Melinda by my side, and everyone in the cast. He said, "Good evening, Pamela," kissed me on both cheeks, and asked if I was ready to go.

We headed off to a dinner party with heads of state and other important people in attendance. I felt a little out of place at the dinner because everyone was speaking different languages, I counted at least three different ones. As a result, I couldn't engage in many conversations, and Albert felt how uncomfortable I was, reassuring me under the table by placing his hand on my knee, holding my hand, and looking at me with a smile. After dinner, we hung out with a guy who showed us his battery powered sports car – that was super boring for me. He finally said to me, "I've had enough of this, let's get out of here and have some fun!" I was all for that! He took me to the Lowe's for a drink, which was a hot spot in town, and everyone was pointing at us and talking, wondering who I was.

We talked for hours, and I asked him about his mother, Grace Kelly. We actually had some really deep conversation, and we had a connection, however, I wasn't really attracted to him like I was with the racecar driver. It is surreal thinking that the two most eligible bachelors in Monte Carlo were pursuing me!

Albert's security team was following us the whole night. He took me to his apartment – he had many different dwellings in Monaco. This is where he took his potential conquests. He tried to get me to go to bed with him and I told him I wouldn't, that I wanted to take it slowly and become friends first. He couldn't keep his hands off of me, and would whisper in my ear, "Pamela, I want you so badly." I'm sure this worked for him every time in the past. It was not going to happen – on this night or any night. When he knew I meant business, he took me back to the Villa Boeri, and Melinda and Natalie were waiting up to see how everything went. I told them it was a nice enough evening with the exception of fighting off his octopus hands the later part of the night, and that he promised to call within the next few days.

He indeed delivered on his promise, and we talked for a long time on the phone. We were never at a loss for words that's for sure. I kept hearing a clicking noise in my phone on these conversations, and Nancy, my "den mom" who looked after us, and our director, said that they were probably tapping my phone and listening to our conversations now that I'd had a date with the prince. I also noticed in the subsequent weeks after our date that I would find people following me. It was a little unsettling. When he called to ask me out again, I informed him that I already had a date that evening, and he asked, "With another man?" I told him that I did – I had a date with Stephan – and I could tell he was a little jealous. We made plans to meet at the California Terrace the next day, but he called and canceled. I wasn't surprised. I knew that our relationship would be a fleeting one, especially since I wasn't going to deliver what he wanted.

My date that evening with Stephan at Café de Riz was less than stellar, he was preoccupied, getting ready to race the Grand Prix the very next day. Melinda and I were invited to attend the Grand Prix Formula One Race by an Italian man who owned Polpetta's, and to join him for brunch on the terrace at the Hotel de Paris. After brunch, which consisted of Rose Tattinger, lobster, and Beluga caviar by the scoops, we joined him and his friends on a fourth floor suite to have a ringside seat with a view of the race which ran on the streets of Monaco below. It was thrilling, energizing, and we could watch it live outside on the balcony and on television at the same time. We were located at the best spot there is, looking down past the Bistroquet and the turn at the hotel. It was incredible! Early on into the race, Stephan wrecked his racecar. He was not injured, but he was out of the race. Melinda and I were asked by the Italian man to accompany him to the Salon de Jeux – only for high rollers at the special Baccarat tables – at the Casino du Monaco. We watched him lose over sixty thousand dollars in less than thirty minutes – it was nothing to him. He just ordered up magnums of champagne and we sat in disbelief that he wasn't fazed by his loss. I guess she and I weren't that much of a good of luck charm to him!

We did the Gala show after the Grand Prix event at The Sporting Club, opening for Lionel Hampton. I was excited about it because this was the night that the entire Royal Family would be in attendance. I had been chosen to do all of the vocal and dancing solos – halfway into our run, the director had learned that I could dance as well as sing, and they assigned me the dance solos in addition to being the headline singer. I came out on stage, and there at the front center table was Prince Albert, along with his father, Prince Rainier III, and his sisters, Caroline, Princess of Hanover, and Princess Stephanie. He stared at me all night. I was a little rattled but not too much. This is where I shined, and I didn't let his attention deter me at all! After the show we went out front to watch Lionel's show, and all of a sudden George, Albert's bodyguard, grabbed me and planted a kiss on me! This was one crazy place. They opened up the roof after the evening shows and had a fireworks display. What a great way to start winding down our time in Monaco – we were scheduled to leave June 26th, and a new set of girls would be flown in to take our place.

Melinda and me, and a couple of the other girls, decided to take a road trip to the Cannes Film Festival. When we arrived, it looked a little like Ocean Avenue in Santa Monica, with Rodeo Drive on the beach. We really weren't too impressed. It was one of the biggest hustler joint experiences that I'd ever seen. It definitely shattered my dreams of Hollywood, and the façade that it truly is. Everyone there claims to be a movie producer of sorts. They would come up and say, "Hi, I'm a movie producer." And I would say, "Yea, you and a million other guys here, too!" We sat and had drinks with Sylvester Stallone's brother, Frank, and his agent as we watched movie starlets vying for attention on the red carpet while everyone was peddling their movies. The life of glamour that I thought I wanted was being revealed for what it really was as

I saw industry people pushing their projects with hopes it would be financed and given good reviews in the States. My eyes were being opened on levels that only God could have targeted, and His timing was perfect.

The Lord had been working on my heart so much during this concentrated time of exposure to life in France. I was watching these ultra-wealthy people searching for exactly what I was searching for: a purpose, a meaning to life, and a significance far beyond that which a temporal lust of the flesh could deliver. I had a conversation with Amad once, asking him if he ever felt satisfied with everything that he had, or was he always wanting more. The answer was, of course, that he always was going after the next thing. His answer left me wanting, searching, confused, and desiring to continue down my spiritual journey like never before. They also had a vacuous hole in their heart – just like I did. If these people hadn't found contentment and happiness on the highest levels that life could offer them, then what else was there? Though I couldn't know it then, this was a question that was about to be answered within three months after returning to America.

Our den mom was a practicing Buddhist, and she would chant for hours before our shows and at various times during the day. Melinda and I would always joke that she looked like a zombie, in some sort of trance after every time she would chant. However, behind the scenes she was also trying to get us all to convert to Buddhism while we were there. The spiritual warfare was

> **If these people hadn't found contentment and happiness on the highest levels that life could offer them, then what else was there?**

intensifying. Melinda's mom, Jean Phelps, and her sister, Jamie, came to Monaco before the last weeks of our contract. We had a few days off, so we all decided that we would go on a mini-vacation together before the show's contract was over, touring from Monaco all the way down the Cote d'Azur to St. Tropez. Jean was an outspoken, born-again Christian, and was very vocal in asking me questions about where I was in my walk with the Lord. She was sweet lady with such a mild demeanor that when she asked these questions it really wasn't offensive. She modeled the love of Christ to me in a way that was kind and loving, and my ears were listening.

We rented a car and started driving down the French Riviera, and it was magnificently beautiful. We stopped at a lovely hotel between Mirimar and Theoule. You could take a monorail down the side of the cliff that the hotel was situated on to a private beach below. The hotel provided towels, drinks, and lunch, and we sunbathed that afternoon. Jean tolerated us girls the entire trip, all the way to St. Tropez, as we experienced everything and sampled the freedoms that France had to offer. She continued asking me about my journey with Jesus, and when it was that I decided to walk away from Him for this season of my life. She was gently being used by the Holy Spirit to get me back to my roots, to reopen my eyes to the truth, and stir in my soul a desire to once again search for Jesus – the only One who could fill that hole in my heart that I had been desperately trying to fill with the lust of the eyes, the flesh, and the pride of life.

I had been seeing Matthew during these dates with all of these men, and had actually developed feelings for him. We were coming close to the end of our run of the show and had once again gathered at Cristal's for a good time. Stephan showed up with his usual entourage, thinking that I would drop Matthew again as I did in the beginning of our tryst. I preceded to let him know that I had no intention of going with him this evening, or any evening for that matter, and I told him that I didn't even know who he was before coming to Monaco. That was enough to put the cap on that relationship forever.

The show was getting ready to wrap. We had made new friendships, and each of us was wondering what was ahead. Our lives would never be the same after what we had encountered over the past three-and-a-half months in the French Riviera. We had arrived as girls, and we were leaving as women. My journey was really just beginning, and the Lord had made an indelible imprint on me while in this far away land. The Lord had loved me enough to chase me down, even to Monte Carlo, and send a lovely woman who would steer me back into asking questions of the Lord of the universe, who I knew was Jesus Christ.

> *"What good is it for a man to gain the whole world, yet forfeit his soul?"*
>
> — Mark 8:36

After one of my last shows, I took my usual walk home through the gorgeous park in front of the Casino du Monaco. It had priceless Picasso bronzes sitting on the grass and beautiful sculptures of art with benches next to them, and there I would sit. This night would be unlike any other I'd experienced while there.

I went and sat alone on the park bench. It was a clear, star-laden night, and the air was crisp and cool, and I looked up with tears streaming down my face. I uttered a quiet prayer that today, so many years later, I know my God answered. I asked, "Lord, there has to be more to life than this… Isn't there?"

It was that simple prayer that led me onto the path where I am today.

God indeed answers prayer.

Chapter 8

THE BLIND DATE

"**I** met your future husband at a party last night," Melinda said on the other end of the phone. "You're the only one who I know who could handle this guy," she chuckled. The thought of a blind date was really unappealing to me; I'd had some pretty unsuccessful ones in the past. I was stalling on the phone, not really wanting to go, but Melinda insisted and decided to drive from her place in Hollywood all the way to the beach in Santa Monica to pick me up at my apartment. She was convinced I was going to marry this guy, and she knew that I wouldn't go unless she came to pick me up.

Melinda had met Michael at his ten-year high school reunion party – and he was wild! She thought we would be a good match because we both were kind of "out there," with Michael being more over the top than even myself. Unknown to me, on the other end of this equation to get us together, Pete, Melinda's boyfriend, was trying to convince an unwilling participant to go as well. I found out later he had to use some enticements such as, "she's a former Miss Georgia," to coax him into going. Michael thought that I was worth "taking a look at." As Melinda drove up in her Porsche to pick me up, it felt as though she and I were going on another adventure, just as we had numerous times in Monte Carlo a few months prior. Little did I know that this adventure would alter the course of my life.

As we exited off Chapman Road in Orange County, California, heading to a local baseball game, we drove into the parking lot. As I got out of the car, I spotted a strikingly handsome, dark-haired man with thick eyebrows and a magnificent full head of hair! I was dressed in a really tight pair of jeans, wearing pumps with three-inch heels and white body suit with a fitted short black blazer. I was strategically dressed to kill, to allure the not so faint of heart. I figured I would scare away any man that wasn't secure in himself and draw out the ones that were confident.

> "You might want to move and let me sit here because she's going to be my wife."

From the moment I stepped out of the car, we were drawn to each other like moths to a flame! I was captivated with this dark and handsome man, well-groomed and dressed in a Cavarruci Italian suit. He was stylish, confident, engaging, and gorgeous!

Michael and I had an immediate attraction to each other and struck up a conversation. We had mutual interests and were not at a loss for words. We even had a mutual friend, Markita, one of my many hairdressers who did my wigs when I performed in *42nd Street* at the Shubert Theatre in Los Angeles. She had been a hairdresser on Regent Air, the same private airline Michael worked for when he flew in the early eighties, though he had left the airline by the time she started with them.

While we were talking, it was as though no one else was there, the world consisted of just Michael and me, and all of a sudden I saw Melinda jumping up and down behind Michael, pointing at him and mouthing the words, "That's him! That's him!" I was stoked that this was my blind date! I was really glad I came, and the rush of it all was exhilarating!

We were both extroverted, gregarious, with large personalities, and the electricity between us was palpable. My heart was pounding out of my chest. Could this be the man for me?

I wasn't looking for a relationship. I had just left Monte Carlo where I'd had experienced a couple of exciting, but carnal, relationships. So I had resigned myself to the thought that I could be happy single and on my own. Mind you, I was still severely backslidden at the time.

But with this new man came a variety of possibilities. Could he be "the one" for me? Would I be able to share my life, expenses, and experiences with someone after all? I could tell that this man had a large giving heart, but I also sensed a hint of danger within him. The "bad boy" type had always attracted me, much to my chagrin. There loomed a sense of excitement mixed with the thrill of the unknown.

We continued to talk throughout the baseball game and at the conclusion of it, Michael suggested that we all go to eat somewhere, and it was decided we would go to a local pizza hang out. Melinda and I arrived before Michael and Pete, and I found myself surrounded by many male suitors while sitting on benches and picnic tables at the pizza restaurant. When Michael arrived, he found me immediately and came up to a guy that was sitting next to me and said, "You might want to move and let me sit here because she's going to be my wife." I thought that this was the best pick up line I'd ever heard! So the guy looked at Michael and with a sheepish, "Okay," he got up and moved, and Michael sat down. Deep down I was thrilled he had said that, because in my heart I was already thinking, even this early on, that this indeed could be my future husband!

The evening continued with us deciding to go over to Pete's home on the water to hang out and get know each other better, and to continue with this magical evening. Michael suggested I ride with him over to Pete's. I gladly obliged and I hopped into his lipstick red Targa Porsche with a tan interior. When I got in the car, in between us on the console was a bottle of Moet Champagne on ice, chilling in a bucket! Michael was indeed a smooth operator. I was impressed, especially after what I had just experienced in Monaco. It would take someone like Michael to hold my attention after experiencing such decadence and opulence and the finest things that this life has to offer just months prior. When we arrived at our destination, we continued to talk until the wee hours of the morning, with me getting comfortable enough to lay back onto Michael's lap on an outdoor chaise lounger while we shared our hopes, dreams, and future goals. This was turning out to be a dream date.

Michael offered to take me home all the way from Orange County to the beach in Santa Monica, which was about an hour-and-a-half drive with no traffic, even though he had to get up to go to work really early the next morning. Michael was working as an internal wholesaler for a firm called August Financial there in Orange County. I took him up on his offer. I could tell that through his quirks he was a diamond in the rough. The deep feeling inside was that Michael had a beautiful heart, even if he had a lot of work ahead of him.

Although I wasn't walking closely with the Lord, I felt a presence as we were driving to the beach, a voice telling me this was going to be my future husband. I just knew it in my heart. When I was younger, my mom had always told me that I would just know when I met my future husband – and I was thinking that this was that very thing that she was talking about.

As the next couple of weeks progressed, we talked on the phone many times a day – and saw each other every day! I couldn't wait to see him and see what adventure awaited us as each day came. It is really easy to put on a good front for a few weeks after meeting for the first time. Those are the classic throes of new love.

Michael wined and dined me every day for the next two-and-a-half weeks. When I had to go and do a weekend cruise as a headline entertainer for two weekends to the Mexican Rivera, I would return to a minimum of twenty messages on my phone machine from this mystery man who I was growing to love more and more as each day passed. At first, I thought it was really sweet that he would pay that much attention to me, not even considering that this might actually be over-the-top behavior!

He took me on a double date one evening to the Bonaventure, the revolving restaurant in Los Angeles, and he would periodically get up and go to the bathroom and come back with a bit of white substance on his nose, which he was continually rubbing. He had an inordinate amount of energy that I attributed to hyperactivity. I didn't have experience with drugs. I figured that he was doing cocaine, but I really didn't think much about it. We are so blind when we are first falling in love. I should've seen the warning signs, but I chose to ignore them. I would've saved myself a lot of pain had I chosen to pay attention – not saying "no," but "go slow" instead. Little did I know that he had been a drug dealer for some time before I met him, and he had delved into that dark world.

> We are so blind when we are first falling in love. I should've seen the warning signs, but I chose to ignore them.

Since I had purposed in my heart that Michael was going to be my husband, I decided I wasn't going to sleep with him or live with him before marriage. While this should be a given as a Christian, I wasn't walking with the Lord. Rather, I took on this view to nab a husband. It would be an unspoken deal breaker if I slept with him. I needed to make him work for me. I knew the old cliché, "Why buy the cow when I get the milk for free?"

I was doing another company of the show of *42nd Street* in Anaheim playing Dorothy Brock, the leading lady role. Behind the scenes, Michael had approached my stage manager to see if I could have the weekend off during the rehearsal period to get married! I will never forget, three weeks into our whirlwind romance during Friday rehearsals, Michael arrived at the rehearsal hall with two dozen red roses and two plane tickets to Las Vegas. He entered the hall and stopped the rehearsal, declaring in front of the whole cast: "Pam Souders – will you marry me?" I screeched loudly, "Yes!" and the whole cast erupted with screams and wild applause.

Three weeks after we met, Michael Rozell asked me to marry him – and we were off to Las Vegas to elope and get married!

Chapter 9

THE ELOPEMENT

We arrived in Las Vegas on Saturday. Michael had reserved a suite at Bally's, a beautiful suite with a living room, wonderful master bedroom, and a bathroom fit for a queen. Michael and I proceeded to change into the clothes we had selected for our wedding. The white suit that I had chosen was actually the dress I had purchased in Monte Carlo to go on a date with Prince Albert. It was the prettiest and most expensive dress that I had bought myself to date – and it was white. Michael chose a shiny gray Italian suit that was obviously expensive, and which I'm sure he had worn on numerous drug deals. He was in complete control of everything we were doing, and I was certain that he was no stranger to Las Vegas. He had rented a limo for the entire afternoon and evening, and we got in and headed to the courthouse to get our marriage license. We were chatting with our limo driver, a really nice man who suggested the different venues where we could get married. Michael and I entered the courthouse, standing in a line with so many people that had also come to Vegas that day to tie the knot. We kept looking at each other and saying how crazy this was that we were doing this, and Michael finally asked, "Do you really want to do this?" I looked at him and said, "You brought me here, so you're going to marry me!"

We received our marriage license and got back into the limo, and our driver proceeded to drive us to the Silver Bells Wedding Chapel. A Church of God pastor and his wife met us with a big smile and a notebook that outlined what we could pay for our big day. We could have real flowers, a package deal complete with a video, or just a cassette tape of the ceremony. We chose the cassette tape and a sweet bouquet of flowers, and the pastor's wife played the organ for music. We asked our limo driver to be the witness for our wedding – a complete stranger.

This was not at all what I thought my honeymoon would be like.

As I started to walk through the small make-shift wedding chapel with neon lights, down a short aisle with an arch of fake flowers, I started to think about all the people that wouldn't be able to share in this joyous occasion with me – and especially my precious daddy, who I was so incredibly close to, not being able to walk me down the aisle. I drifted among my thoughts: I'd always wanted to elope somewhere, but then considered I could have a big wedding later on so I could have the best of both worlds.

We started reciting our vows to one another, and I started crying as I was saying them, realizing the gravity of what I was doing before the Lord. It was sacred – even though we were getting married in a rinky-dink Vegas wedding chapel. I remember Michael being distracted and nervous while he was saying his vows. Little did I know, he was really thinking about a parlay bet that he had placed before we had departed for the courthouse on three football games, which if they all came in winning would garner him thousands of dollars. This was a vice that I was unaware that I was marrying into – his gambling addiction, in addition to a rage addiction, a drug addiction, alcohol addiction, and four warrants out for his arrest for driving in excess of 130 miles per hour. Surprise, surprise!! That's what I get for marrying someone in three weeks!

After returning to the hotel after our wedding ceremony, Michael went straight into the sports bar off the lobby and sat down to watch and see if his games were going to pay off. I couldn't believe that on our wedding night he wanted to sit down to watch football games! This wasn't my idea of a great honeymoon. I resigned myself to the fact I would either have to sit with him and watch, or go shopping and decide where to meet later on in the evening. I sat down and proceeded to watch to see if his three football game predictions came in. This first won. Then the second. And when the third one came in, Michael let out a low screech and decided to buy everyone in the bar champagne. He started drinking right alongside everyone else in the bar, and his personality started changing right before my very eyes. He became raucous and loud and very aggressive, and a bit of an edgy, mean streak started to emerge. We went over to the cage to sign a paper for the IRS because he'd won over three thousand dollars.

We went up to the room to change clothes and it felt a little odd and anti-climatic after we had actually tied the knot. We didn't have anyone to share this momentous occasion with, and we even considered flying out his mom, Roberta, over for the weekend to enjoy this time with us. We ended up calling my Mom: "Mom, guess what?" She said, "You're married!" "How did you know?" I asked curiously. She said, "I know you, and when you called a few weeks ago and said you'd found the man you were going to marry, I figured that this is what you'd do." I heard my Dad groan in the background, a low guttural, "No!" After this, Michael and I discussed that we would definitely fly to my hometown of Thomasville, Georgia, to renew our vows in front of family and friends one year later. We really did want to share this with them, and I wanted everyone to meet the man that I had chosen to marry. After being Miss Georgia, everyone wanted to meet this charmed young man who stole my heart.

We went to a fancy dinner at the hotel, and as the champagne continued to pour, his demeanor continued to transform. Even his facial expressions were beginning to look extremely sinister and dark. I was starting to feel a bit annoyed – and a little scared – because I really didn't know this man very well or what he was actually capable of. Growing up, I had some experience watching people drink, watching how alcohol could poison the blood so much that it could change a person right before your very eyes. "What have I married? Did I do the right thing?" These questions were starting to loom heavily in my heart.

After dinner, we went back up to the room to consummate the marriage. I was taking a bath and getting ready to be with my new husband, and as I looked over at Michael getting out of his trousers, he fell over onto the floor, passed out in a drunken stupor. I was so angry and disappointed that I decided to leave him right there on the floor overnight! This was not at all what I thought my honeymoon would be like. I went to sleep that evening, wondering if my impulsiveness and free-spirited ways – which I let guide me up to this point – had led me astray and down a path where I had no idea it would lead.

Flying back on the plane to Los Angeles the next day, conversation was minimal. I was looking out the window, wondering in my heart, "Did I just make the biggest mistake of my life?" Only time would tell...

Chapter 10

THE PRODIGAL

For three Mondays in a row, Steve Savage had been calling Michael to come to a church with him to hear guest speakers at Calvary Chapel Costa Mesa. Steve was a friend from the old neighborhood who was still in Michael's life – and he had gotten "on fire" for the Lord. Michael had put him off, saying "no" each week. But after our impetuous weekend of a distressing elopement, he was much more open to the thought of going to church with Steve. When he got the call he said, "What time are you picking me up?"

Michael went to church with Steve and another childhood friend named Danny Rivas. They were excited to find out that the guest speaker that evening would be Pastor Raul Ries. He had a radical testimony, and they knew that this particular evening was ordained by the Lord for Michael to relate to a man with a testimony more radical than any they'd ever heard.

Michael walked into the sanctuary and felt like a fish out of water. He was comfortable in a corporate setting, but here with different types of people, from all walks of life, he was anxious and nervous. He saw bikers for Jesus with tattoos standing beside little old ladies with gray hair, and they were both worshiping the

Lord together in harmony. What was this? He felt like it looked like that first *Star Wars* movie in the bar scene where all the weird looking characters were getting along. He brought along his brief case because it was his stabilizer, allowing him to walk into foreign territory with his prop. He laughs today because we've attended Costa Mesa so many times and we've still never seen anyone come into the sanctuary with a brief case!

Pastor Raul started talking about Hell as a real place, that people would actually go there for eternity, with weeping and gnashing of teeth, and living in fire if they rejected Christ as the Son of God and stayed in their sinful lifestyles, and for those that accepted Jesus Christ as Lord and Savior they would live in a mansion in Heaven forever. Michael was weighing his options, and much preferred living in a mansion to a place called Hell. When the time came for the invitation, Michael went forward half-heartedly, giving his life to Jesus.

> "Happy Birthday Mrs. Rozell – P.S. – I got saved tonight!"

I was back to work in the company of *42nd Street,* and our schedules were the complete opposite. He went to bed earlier than I did, and that evening I didn't get back until about midnight. It was September 28, 1987, three days after my birthday – and we hadn't even spoken since the fiasco over the weekend. We got married one day after my birthday on the 26th. I went into the kitchen and there were a dozen red roses on the counter with a hand-written note which read: "Happy Birthday Mrs. Rozell – P.S. – I got saved tonight!" Oh my! I knew what that meant! I was happy, but also a little apprehensive. What does that mean for me?

On Wednesday, September 30, two nights later, Michael invited me to go with him to Calvary Chapel Costa Mesa. I walked into the large sanctuary and voices were resounding with the praises of Jesus. The restrains were so beautiful, and I felt love enveloping me as if I was being embraced by something supernatural, accepting me and welcoming me into a place that I had longed for so deeply since I was a child. Tears were streaming down my face immediately. I felt the presence of the Holy Spirit, and I knew that I was "home." I felt the love of Jesus Christ through worship like I'd never experienced before. This is what I had been looking for my entire life on my spiritual journey! These people didn't "play church," they knew Jesus! They had the answers I'd been looking for since my days in Georgia.

When the Pastor got up to speak, his bald head and a bigger and brighter smile than I've ever seen was radiating from the podium. When he spoke, I felt the love and the grace from someone who has spent time with a personal friend and Savior. This was the first time I ever saw or even heard of Pastor Chuck Smith. At the end of the service, I knew that the Lord was calling me back into His sheepfold to serve Him for the rest of my life. I went forward to rededicate my life to Him. I needed cleansing from the sinful life that I'd been living for the last seven years. Afterward, I waited to speak with Pastor Chuck. I introduced myself and gave him a brief summary of my life and how I'd fallen away the past few years, and that over the weekend that I had eloped in Las Vegas. He ministered to me, explaining to me that Michael would become my ministry for however long it would take over the coming years. He told me that after you say "I do," then you are mysteriously and inextricably tied in matrimony as "one flesh" for the rest of your life; that God sees us as one. I knew that whatever it took, I would allow God to solidify our union as husband and wife. This began a wonderful friendship, and a loyal, respectful following of this man in learning about Jesus from 1987 until his death on October 3, 2013.

During the next three months, I cried endless tears of repentance as I would think of where I took the Lord in my days of debauchery. I couldn't believe that I had taken Jesus to such dark places and down a path that I never thought I'd be capable of going. Michael was concerned that he had done something wrong because I was crying so much. I kept explaining to him that it had nothing to do with him, but what I'd done over the past years, and how sorry I was that I dragged the Lord into places I should've never gone. I was truly sorrowful over my sin. It was repentance. I was turning around and going in another direction. It was a time of cleansing in the deep recesses of my soul.

Once, while I was in our apartment, I had a "waking vision" of sorts where I saw Jesus standing in a white robe, and the light and love that was emanating from His face was radiant, tangible, palpable… His arms open wide, welcoming me back into the fold and holding me. I was on my knees weeping and He was fully accepting me back. I knew that I was truly forgiven! The humility I felt, and the overwhelming thankfulness, flooded my soul. I couldn't believe He would take me back after what I'd done to Him and where I'd taken Him. I felt clean and pure again. I totally surrendered my whole life to Him to do whatever He had in store for me. Words can't describe how amazing our Lord Jesus Christ is!

That weekend we heard that Calvary was doing baptisms. Michael and I planned to get baptized at Corona del Mar. We waited in line for Pastor Chuck, but the line was so long so we decided to let Pastor Dave Rolph baptize us. So we both had encounters with the Lord that same week, and by that weekend got baptized together holding hands as a married couple in the Pacific Ocean. I'm sure that the angels in Heaven had to get hold of us fast so we could get on track and do what He had planned for us. The prodigal daughter had come home. The Father had put a robe on me and a ring on my finger and was rejoicing that I had finally come home! His patience and love He has for us is mind-boggling.

The next few weeks, Michael and I found ourselves wanting to clean up our lives. It started with me taking all the occult books and Buddhist paraphernalia that I'd been dabbling in for the past few years and burning the books and throwing away the Buddha box that I'd been chanting to on the wall. We decided to start taking care of the four warrants that Michael had out for his arrest. We went from court to court and prayed before standing in front of each judge that the Lord would take care of each of them. He miraculously did, and when we got to the last one – for driving in excess of 130 miles per hour – we were on our faces praying to the Lord that He would intervene, because he could actually go to jail on this one and possibly pay a high fine, and we didn't have a lot of money. We sat in the courtroom together praying under our breath as the judge called

> Michael and I started having problems right away in our marriage. His rage reared its ugly head, and it wasn't pretty.

Michael to the stand. He said, "Mr. Rozell, how do you plead?" Michael replied, "Guilty judge, with an explanation." The judge said with a half smile, "This should be interesting. Go ahead." Michael went on to explain that he was a Christian now, and was married to a Christian woman – and he pointed to me. "I used to be addicted to drugs, and I have been delivered, and plan on cleaning up my life, and I promise never to drive that fast again. I apologize to the court, and to you, Judge." The Judge immediately responded, "I hope what you are saying is true, Mr. Rozell. Pay the court fifty dollars, and I hope to never see you again in this courtroom!" He slammed down the gavel and we were out of there. Michael and I couldn't believe it! This was the first of many miracles that he and I would witness throughout our married life. God was so gracious to us.

Michael and I started attending Calvary Chapel Costa Mesa three times a week. It was a one hundred-mile round trip for me to go from the beach in Santa Monica to Orange County. I would meet him at his work in the OC and we would go together from there. We were so hungry to learn God's Word. We couldn't get enough. I would hop on the freeway and would put in the worship CDs that someone gave me right after I rededicated my life to him – a worship leader named Morris Chapman. I'd open my car windows and stick my hands out, raised up to heaven and belt out worship songs to the Lord right along with Morris. I had never worshiped like this before. I uttered a silent prayer in my heart that one day I could sing with this man who knew Jesus on such a deep level – and oh, his voice was rich and divine! Jesus doesn't forget our prayers.

Michael and I started having problems right away in our marriage. His rage reared its ugly head, and it wasn't pretty. It would shake me to the core, frightening me to where I would tremble in a deep place inside my being. In his rages, he would often yell out truthful accusations at me that cut like a knife. Although what he said might have been true, the way he said it would hurt so deeply that I shut him out. I had never before been spoken to with such unkindness on an ongoing basis. I had experienced some of this in my family growing up, but not consistently, or anything like this. Michael's aunts on his mother's side, Vernette and Lucy, were definitely put in our lives to help guide us early on. They are both petite little gals under five feet tall, but they are powerhouses for Christ. They know how to intercede in prayer and fight spiritual battles. Aunt Lucy would take Michael in one room, and Aunt Vernette would take me in another, and counsel us in what it looked like to be married and to love one another. We just recently celebrated Lucy's going home to Heaven, and Vernette, still with us at ninety-one years old, is constantly praying for everyone in our families.

> "You are acting like a baby. Go and read your Bible for the next thirty days and minister to your wife and love her!"

One day Michael and I had a particularly bad fight, and I wasn't going to let him verbally push me around or give me ungodly advice. He decided he was going down to Calvary to meet with Pastor Chuck – I told him to go. He went into the office and asked to meet with Pastor Chuck, and they asked him what it was about. He told them that his wife wouldn't submit. They promptly went into the office and returned with Pastor Romaine. He was a former Master Sergeant in the Marine Corps and was Pastor Chuck's rear guard. Any hard cases were given to him. They went in the sanctuary, and Romaine asked Michael what the problem was. He told him that his wife wouldn't submit. Pastor Romaine started rubbing his face up and down, then proceeded to tell Michael that he'd been married for "forty years today." He told him that he really hadn't learned to love his wife properly until the last twenty years, and that saddened him. He said, "Since it's my anniversary, I'm not going to address this how I normally do." He held up a set of keys and asked, "But do you see these keys?" "Yes," Michael responded. "These keys open a door around the corner into the children's ministry. Now I'd like you to go into that room, and take this other key," he said, pointing to another spot on the ring.

"Okay…" Michael confirmed, wondering where this was going. Romaine continued, "And I want you to open the cabinet that this key opens and take out the Pampers inside – and put one on. You are acting like a baby. Go and read your Bible for the next thirty days and minister to your wife and love her!" He got up out of the pew and started walking away. Michael called out to him, "I'm going to tell Pastor Chuck on you!" He kept walking and shooed Michael off with a hand gesture as the door closed behind him.

Our first New Year's Eve together, Michael got a call from his dad asking if we would come with him and his wife to Las Vegas, all expenses paid, to ring in the New Year. This was a temptation straight from the devil himself! I told him that I was going to attend Calvary Costa Mesa to pray in the New Year with the Aunties. "I really want you to come honey," I said. As we went throughout our week, I could tell that Michael was struggling with what to do. He would vacillate between thinking it was a good idea to go to church on New Year's since he'd never done that before, and wanting to go and gamble and party in Vegas. I told him I was going to church, and he could go with his dad if he wanted. I was praying fervently that he would choose the Lord over what he was used to. Wholeheartedly, he chose to go to church to pray in 1988 with me and the Aunties. He couldn't believe what a great time he had, and what a great way it was to bring in the New Year together as a newly married couple. It was the first time in his adult life that he hadn't gotten wasted on this holiday. It would be ten years later that Michael and I would present our ministry at this very same church, bringing in 1998.

Michael and I are a truly unique couple in many ways. One is that we both found out after a few months into our marriage that we both rode unicycles. He was on a cruise with me to the Mexican Riviera and a juggling act opened for me. The juggler happened to have a unicycle in his act and I asked him if I could ride it on the boat deck one day. We all met up on the deck, and I hadn't ridden one since my junior high years, back when I used to ride one, complete with tricks, for basketball halftime shows, as well as riding in parades. Michael said that he wanted to try, so he got up and started teetering back and forth – complete with the "Whoas" and such – and then started riding like a champ. I was shocked! I couldn't believe he got up on the first try. Then of course I found out that he was playing a joke on me and that he had also learned to ride in his early teen years. This is one of many jokes he has played on me through the years. I'm not as gullible today. Michael bought us matching Schwinn unicycles for our first Valentine's Day together. We would take them down to Venice Beach and ride them on the boardwalk, and of course we would draw a crowd.

One day after riding our unicycles, Michael saw a pottery shop and we parked our cycles and went in to view the wares. He was walking around like a kid in a candy shop, excited and looking at each piece. He picked up a tall large cylinder and turned it over to see what it cost – and it had a price tag of six hundred dollars. He exclaimed, "Wow, pottery has come a long way since I was a kid." I didn't know what he meant, and he turned to me and said, "I can do this." I replied, "What do you mean?" He explained, "I can throw pottery." I was amazed and asked, "You can make pottery?" He replied in the affirmative. I couldn't believe he wasn't doing this if he really was able to! I had always made a living at what I loved to do. He was working a job that he didn't love, but could do something he truly did love. I was confused.

When we got home that afternoon I found the yellow pages and started looking for a pottery studio where Michael could start working on his art again. I found a place a few blocks from our apartment called, The Clay Pen. It was a co-op where you could pay forty dollars a month and have unlimited access to the studio, complete with pottery wheels, kilns, and glazes. I signed him up immediately!

He couldn't wait to get back into the studio. It had been ten years since he'd thrown. His dad told him that he would be a bum if he chose to do pottery for a living – that he needed a "real" job. The next day, which was on a weekend, I drove him down to the studio and dropped him off, telling him to call me when he had made a pot. I went home and got a call ten hours later. "I made a pot, come down and see," he spoke proudly over the phone. I drove down and was so excited to see what he had made. I walked into the studio and there were twenty wheels with twenty gorgeous vases of all shapes and sizes! He was covered head to toe with clay, and he stood there like a little boy and asked, "What do you think?" I was so moved and overwhelmed by the display of beauty before my eyes that I dissolved into tears as they streamed down my face. "Why aren't you doing this?" I exclaimed. "This is what God has designed and created you to do! I've always made money doing what I love, why don't you?"

This was the first time anyone gave Michael a chance to dream...

Chapter 11

LED BY CLOUD BY DAY
AND FIRE BY NIGHT

Marvelous things He did in the sight of their fathers, in the land
of Egypt, in the field of Zoan. He divided the sea and caused
them to pass through; and He made the waters stand up like a
heap. In the daytime also He led them with the cloud, and all
the night with a light of fire.

— Psalm 78:12-14 NKJV

One year after Michael and I eloped, we went back to my hometown in Georgia to throw a big wedding. I really wanted my daddy to walk me down the aisle, and my mom to put it all together (which she did beautifully while I was on a cruise in Bermuda with Michael for three weeks), and for the people in Thomasville who loved me to meet the man I married. Of course Melinda, who introduced us, was a bridesmaid, as well as Deborah, my bestie, Cayla, my next-door neighbor growing up, and my sister-in-law, Patricia. On Michael's side he had his brother, Steve, my brother, Greg, his first cousin, Kevin Hanks, and his "groomswoman," Teresa Lee. The town was up in arms over the fact that a woman was on his side wearing a tuxedo. Michael really loved my friend Teresa and wanted her on his side. She also sang beautifully.

During our first year of marriage, Michael had watched an episode of *The 700 Club* that featured Steve Howe, a professional baseball player who was a super-talented, left-handed relief pitcher. He had been Rookie of the Year in the early eighties with the Los Angeles Dodgers, and he had just been kicked out of baseball because of his cocaine abuse. Michael made me come in the living room and watch the show. He told me that he'd been praying for him since he had heard that he got kicked out. Steve was playing catch in the backyard of a nice home with his daughter, and it also showed scenes of him painting the Foursquare Church in Whitefish, Montana. Michael told me that he related so much with this guy because he totally understood how hard it was to kick the cocaine habit being a former addict himself. Right then and there, Michael told me that we, as a couple, were going to consistently start praying for this athlete, that he would be delivered and restored back to baseball. I didn't really care about any sports, to be honest, but I agreed to start praying for this man that my husband felt a burden from the Lord to faithfully pray for. I was happy that Michael was taking the initiative to try to lead our family spiritually for the first time. Although I had started out in our marriage being the spiritual leader in our home, the Lord told me that one day I would be scrambling to keep up with Michael.

During this time, I was doing a lot of cruises to earn money to make ends meet. This put a strain on our marriage. We were like two ships passing in the night. There was still quite a bit of fighting, and his rage would continue to pop up unprovoked from time to time. Michael got an opportunity to interview for a position as a regional marketing director for a Wall Street firm, and his territory would be the southeast region with an emphasis in Florida.

Since I was already flying cross-country twice a month to the port of Miami from Los Angeles, I suggested that he interview for the position. I was working with seven major cruise lines and could get booked anywhere in the world, but I was mostly doing Caribbean cruises at the time.

I was starting to feel a major tug from the Holy Spirit to not do cruises as much. We needed to work on our marriage, and I wanted to become a good wife. I knew if our marriage was going to work I would eventually have to stop altogether – but this always put fear in Michael when I would talk like this because he relied upon the considerable cash income I earned during the weeks I booked cruises. So I was submitting to my husband, still doing cruise shows, even though my heart was no longer in it. I wanted to consecrate my gifts and talents to the Lord alone. I didn't know how that was going to happen, but I trusted in Him that if He gave me that desire, then it would come to pass in His timing.

Michael and I were on a Disney Cruise one week – he came for free as my guest – and we had one of the biggest fights that we'd had to date. He had been coming unglued on me quite a bit, and I had just about had it. I was reclaiming my voice, not allowing him to crush my spirit as much as he had been. I was becoming a prayer warrior, getting calluses on my knees praying for him each day and night, hoping that his explosive anger would get under the Lord's control. The walls were very thin on cruise ships, and I'm

> "Pam you are now married and one flesh in the sight of God. Michael will become your ministry now as you walk out living for Christ before him."

sure our neighbors were quite entertained listening to us yell at each other throughout the week. When he left to go home, I still had another week on the ship. He was still trying to control me and was yelling at me as he was exiting the ship's gangway. I was so incensed with him that I actually couldn't believe the words that spewed out of my mouth: "I hope you get in an accident and die on the way home! Better yet, that you have an affair and then I can leave you!" I hollered.

How could I let myself get to this point? I needed to regroup and get my heart right with the Lord. I remembered the words of Pastor Chuck Smith right at that moment, "Pam you are now married and one flesh in the sight of God. Michael will become your ministry now as you walk out living for Christ before him." The rubber was meeting the road in my Christian walk, and I had a choice to make. Either allow the Lord to use me as an integral part of Michael's healing process, or yield to my flesh and let another Christian marriage bite the dust. Sadly, the divorce statistics are the same for Christian marriages as secular ones. Fifty percent of all marriages fail today.

Michael got the job with the Wall Street firm and we decided to move to Boca Raton, Florida. It would be easier for me to hop on a ship, and he was starting a new job that paid extremely well – with full benefits and incentives galore. It seemed as if our lives were on the upswing. Michael was moving and shaking in his job and set his sights on a "big elephant" client, that if Michael could bag him, it could put him on the map with his new firm. Michael was relentless in his pursuit, and he phoned in every week until the guy took his call. He was given three minutes on the phone to sell himself and his product. Michael told him he was married to a Miss Georgia from Thomasville, and as soon as he heard this, he was hooked! He had friends in Thomasville, and that opened up a dialogue between them that eventually blossomed into a friendship, and this man being one of Michael's largest clients.

This man attended a large Presbyterian church in town called Spanish River Church; he was an elder and on the Board. Michael had shared with him that I was looking to stop cruising as much as I had been, and he told Michael about a position that was opening up at his church for a Program Director/Worship Leader, suggesting that I interview for the job. I would have to put on two major productions a year, one at Easter and one at Christmas. I would be in charge of worship and anything to do with the running of the services on Sundays. This sounded great to me. I could stay home, make money, work on my marriage, and I could put a clause in my job description that I could still cruise and make money a few weeks during the year. I interviewed and got the job with the salary I asked for, along with six weeks off during the year so I could go and do cruises or whatever else I wanted. With the Lord's help, I had a successful run at Spanish River and put on some elaborate productions.

In 1990 we visited Southern California, and Aunt Vernette's daughter-in-law, Phyllis Swanson, had heard of a wonderful music producer named Walt Harrah. She actually found his phone number and boldly called him, telling him he had to meet me and produce an album for me. She set up an appointment and we went to his house to meet him, and he asked me to sing for him and his wife, Sherry, there in his living room. Walt was a producer/songwriter and arranger, as well as being an accomplished singer himself. After I sang, he said, "I'd like to produce your album!" I was so excited! Now Michael and I just had to figure out how to pay for my first album.

While Michael and I were on a Royal Caribbean Cruise, he met a man after one of my shows named Noel Robbins who owned

Robbins Pharmaceutical, an older gentleman who invented the tools that are used today for liposuction. He and Michael were talking about how great the singer in the show the night before was, and Michael was kind of playing with him and said, "What if I could introduce you to her?" He was intrigued and said, "Really? She was a great singer!" He said, "She's my wife!" He couldn't believe it, and soon after their conversation I came out with no makeup on…and he didn't recognize me! He told me how much he loved my show the night before. We struck up a conversation – and subsequently a friendship – with this man and his wife, Hope, and they wanted to contribute to my first album. He ended up providing half of the funds, and my dad loaned us the other half – which we ended being able to pay back within six months.

Walt produced that album in 1990, which was called *Let All The Earth Hear His Voice*. Michael and I didn't have a ministry together yet. I was being wooed by the Holy Spirit to leave the secular world and to start doing Christian concerts, and the Lord was opening doors for that to happen.

Claire Cloninger, an author and six-time Dove Award winning lyricist, was coming to speak at Spanish River Church, and she needed someone to sing her songs. She wrote wonderful songs, but she couldn't sing them. The pastor asked if I would sing for Claire when she came, and I jumped at the chance. She came to speak, and I sang her beautiful songs which had been recorded by such artists as Sandi Patti, Wayne Watson, and Amy Grant. We hit it off – being southern girls – and this started a lifelong friendship with her and her husband, Spike. I co-wrote songs with Claire and Walt for years, and they are some of the best songs on my ten recorded CDs. Walt also ended up producing many of my CDs. He has recorded so many worship songs on the Maranatha Worship Series, and he was a member of the renowned Haven of

Rest Quartet. Walt and Sherry became lifelong friends of ours as well. I ended up singing for Claire's events on numerous occasions at different venues – she and I just clicked. I started my Christian concert career at Spanish River Church with a really large concert, and it grew from there, doing a few churches in south Florida in between cruises.

When Michael would go on cruises with me, he had his first experiences with being an evangelist, and me the singer. We would go down into the bowels of the ship where all the workers were; they were mostly Filipinos. We would put up on the staff bulletin boards in the crew mess that he would do a Bible study, and I would bring special music. We'd have a good-sized crowd, and people actually got saved on these trips. I took my last eight-week world cruise on the Five-Star Line, Royal Viking in 1990.

Michael's Wall Street firm wanted him to take on more territory, and he was traveling quite a bit. We decided that he didn't want to do that so he gave his notice to the Wall Street firm, and his "elephant" he had bagged, the man that got me the job at SRC, wanted to hire him at Prudential Bache. He took the job, and we were both now planted in south Florida where the Lord continued His process of cleaning the both of us up.

One weekend when I returned from a cruise, Michael was particularly excited when he picked me up at the port. He said, "I found a new church behind an Albertson's grocery store that I think is like the Calvary we came out of in California. I'm not sure, but it's just like it – and I love it." I knew that Michael wasn't so thrilled with the Presbyterian Church we'd been attending, so I took a Sunday off at SRC to go and check it out with him. If my husband was actually excited about a church, I would oblige. I went and it was indeed a Calvary Chapel affiliate! Michael started going on a regular basis, even though I still had to lead worship and work at SRC. I was so happy that he found a place to learn more about Jesus and grow and plug in. We started talking about me quitting at SRC and we could go full-time to this new Calvary. I gave my notice, and we started attending Calvary Chapel Fort Lauderdale, which would be our church home for the next seven years. This is where my husband was held accountable to grow and learn the Scriptures like never before. He was hungry and devoured the Word. We both couldn't get enough of Jesus. I became heavily involved on the worship team – leading worship every time the opportunity arose. I was the worship leader's "go-to" gal, and I was loving every minute of learning how to really worship our Lord.

My first experience seeing an actual manifestation of the moving of the Holy Spirit was when I was Miss Georgia at eighteen years old. One of my chaperones took me to a church in Atlanta called Mount Paran Church of God. I stood during worship, and a number people started speaking in tongues, followed by the interpretation of what had been said. This fascinated me, as I had only heard negative things about this while growing up, mainly because of the "snake charmer" backwoods churches that you heard about in the south. What I was witnessing and feeling at this church was the real deal. I felt the Holy Spirit come upon me, and I started crying, full of the joy of the Lord. The next time that I experienced this type of moving of the Spirit was while we were touring in Kentucky at another Church of God. I was worshiping, and surprisingly, the Holy Spirit fell upon me and I started uttering an unknown tongue. It truly was an amazing experience, and afterward, I couldn't stop praising our Lord in English either.

Some of my sweetest times of worship were on Sunday nights at Calvary. The people who were really serious about knowing Jesus would come to this service. It was intimate and felt like family. There was a supernatural movement of God happening in this church, and it was growing each week, and we ended up moving into a new, larger building soon after we started attending at the Albertson's property. It had a congregation of about three hundred fifty people when we first started attending, and before we left to move to Montana it had grown to over five thousand. Calvary Chapel Fort Lauderdale is at nearly twenty thousand today.

The Lord started restoring my songwriting during this honeymoon time with Him – He was trusting me again with such a sacred gift. I would have dreams of songs and get up the next morning with the strain of the tunes resonating in my head and heart and would write them down immediately, pounding out the melodies on my grand piano, my wedding gift from my husband. We didn't have an engagement, so instead of a ring I asked for a piano instead. I did, however, get a ring twenty years later, and it was well worth the wait! I would sit quietly during my time with the Lord, and He would give me lyrics that would effortlessly pour out of me.

This season with Jesus was such a sweet, intimate time. Most of the time He would give me songs that would minister to my own heart, to keep fighting the good fight in the midst of Michael not being completely healed. He would rage on me, and I was fervently praying for his deep healing. I knew the Lord wanted to heal him, and I knew none of his actions were my fault. The Lord reassured me of these things daily through His Word. One day, He asked me in that still small voice if I would be willing to be a vessel of healing through which He could pour out His Holy Spirit to touch Michael in the recesses of His soul. "Of course I will Lord," I responded. I had no clue of the depths of dying to myself that my promise to Him would require. After a particularly vicious fight one day, I sat down and through my tears, wrote a song called "Faithful Hearts":

Faithful Hearts

Lyrics by Pam Rozell

Music by Pam Rozell & Clay Hecocks

I don't know how you're hurting – But I see it in your eyes
The lonely conversations, unwilling compromise
But by His grace we'll run this race – The Lord will see us through
And shine His light into our hearts – And show us what to do

CHORUS
Faithful hearts, bound together by His love
Faithful hearts, two are beating now as one
We'll look beyond our words and see
Forgiveness, love and harmony
His love alone will set us free
Faithful hearts

I promised you so many things – And on that special day
I'd never thought I'd feel alone – how did love slip away
But by His strength and not our own – We're sure to make it through
He'll shine His light into our hearts – Our love will be made new

BRIDGE
With faithful hearts, we'll serve each other
With faithful hearts, we'll love each other
Through God's eyes

While still attending this church, I recorded my second CD, *On The Potter's Wheel.* They fronted the money to pay for production, and after my first concert at the church, I nearly paid back the entire loan. And after only a few bookings at other nearby churches, the complete loan was paid back. I also recorded a number of solos on other worship albums while I was here, coaching the singers on the records and the worship teams.

At our stadium events during Easter and Christmas, I always did special music. On one particular Christmas Eve service at the NY Yankee's Training Stadium, I sang "O Come, O Come Emmanuel." My parents and mother-in-law, Roberta, were in attendance. It was a sweet time of worship followed by a powerful message. At every Christmas Eve service we were given candles as we came in, and at the end we would all light them. This night, a quiet hush came over the stadium as we all looked around and saw thousands of beautiful lights illuminating the stillness of the night. Then the pastor said, "Happy Birthday Jesus!" and we led a chorus singing, "Happy birthday to you…dear Jesus…happy birthday to you!" All of a sudden, when the last refrain was sung, out of the stillness came a whooshing sound that started to roll through the crowd, and a great rushing wind, seemingly from nowhere, came through and blew out every one of the thousands of

> I looked down and saw my precious daddy standing at the front of the stage, rededicating his life to the Lord!

candles! The pastor started laughing and said, "Jesus just blew out His own candles! Thank you Lord!" He did an altar call right after this supernatural event and the response was overwhelming. As I was singing the invitation song, I looked down and saw my precious daddy standing at the front of the stage, rededicating his life to the Lord! My mom was standing by his side, and just a few people away, there was Roberta! I jumped off the stage to go and embrace my family. Oh what a day of rejoicing this was! My family would never be the same. Their lives truly turned around after that special night.

There have been a handful of times that the Lord has allowed me to see in the natural realm the things He's doing supernaturally. I don't take this for granted – or lightly. It is an honor and a privilege, and I can always look back on these things to draw strength from in times of weakness in my daily walk with Him. I remember well the exact evening that the Lord anointed me for service and touched my lips to sing for Him. It was at one of the Sunday night worship services. While I was singing, I was allowed to see a thick white cloud, a mist, hovering over the congregation. I even wiped my eyes to be sure they weren't playing tricks on me. It was just me singing, with the worship leader, Clay, playing the piano that evening. The Holy Spirit was manifesting Himself. As I was singing, I started feeling electricity pulsating and coursing throughout my body. During the last couple of songs, this vibration intensified to a fevered pitch, and my lips were buzzing, vibrating at such a fast rate…what was happening to me? I just knew in the core of my being that I was standing on Holy ground, that I was in the presence of holiness, and could no longer stand because of the sheer power of His presence. I fell to my knees with my face on the floor and worshiped my Savior like never before!

After the worship set concluded, I went backstage and asked Clay, "Did you feel that? Did you see that?" as I was trembling and crying uncontrollably. The electricity was still heightened, and powerfully resounding through my entire being. He said he hadn't felt anything. This lasted fifteen minutes after I exited the stage. I know this is the night that the Lord touched my lips and anointed me to sing for Him. Only He knew what was around the corner for Michael and me.

"...For I am a man of unclean lips, and I live among a people of unclean lips, and my eyes have seen the King, the Lord Almighty." Then one of the seraphs flew to me with a live coal in his hand, which he had taken with tongs from the altar. With it he touched my mouth and said, 'See, this has touched your lips; your guilt is taken away and your sin atoned for.' Then I heard the voice of the Lord saying, 'Whom shall I send? And who will go for us?' And I said, 'Here am I. Send Me!'"

— Isaiah 6: 5-8

Over the last twenty-five years, similar things such as this have happened where I've been allowed to see right before a mighty movement of God. I've seen the cloud of the Holy Spirit over congregations a handful of times, and have felt His electrifying power during times when I needed an added measure of His Spirit, but never to the intensity of that first time. Last year, I was singing at an outdoor event in Delaware County, Pennsylvania, and the only way I can describe it is that I was caught up into the heavenly realms while I was singing. I'd never sung so effortlessly, where it was just pouring out of me with clarity and perfect pitch, and I knew I was singing through His power – not any of my own. I was standing at the bottom of His Throne, singing right to Him. I was transported, unaware of the thousands of people in the crowd. It was just Him and me, and I was bringing my sacrifice of praise, purely before His Throne. This also happened when we first did our ministry, the events which I will describe in a few chapters.

Michael and I went to a Christmas party that his boss was throwing at his home. He and his wife had become pretty good friends, and we liked to get together periodically to go to dinners and talk, or go to their home to play board games. This night was typical, with a few couples that they had invited who we used to go to Spanish River with. As the night progressed, things got a little weird. Michael had asked me to go out to our car to get something that he wanted to give to someone. Though I was unaware, his boss had followed me outside, and as I was coming back in through the dark, pitch black garage, he lurched out at me, grabbing me by my waist and pulling me into him, holding mistletoe above our heads. He firmly planted an inappropriate kiss onto my lips as I was fighting to push him off of me. I was stunned, and was trying to wrap my brain around and process what had just happened. I went back into the party, trying for the rest of the evening to act as if nothing had happened, but thoughts were racing through my head. "How can Michael continue to work for this guy? How can I tell him? He pays our paycheck." After this incident, as the week progressed, I was holding this in and had no one to tell or talk to about it. I was bottling up feelings inside and taking it out on Michael. He knew something was wrong, but didn't know what it was. I was praying that the Lord would show me a way to tell him, but I didn't know what it would mean for our livelihood. The Lord told me to tell him and leave our livelihood up to Him.

> If you could do anything in the world that you loved and make a living at it, do you know what it would be?" Michael answered, "I do. I'd be a potter!"

We had a trampoline in our backyard, and Michael and I would jump on it now and again, but it was also a place where he and I could just go and lie and talk to each other. We ended up on the trampoline talking one evening, and I decided to tell him what had happened. When I told him, he took it so much better than I thought he would. Michael said he knew he couldn't work for this man anymore, but had to be strategic on the timing of when to confront him. Since his wife was my friend, Michael said we would have to tell her, too. I knew he was right. Michael confronted him at his office the very next day, and they made an afternoon appointment to meet his wife at their house to let her know what had happened as well. It went much better than I thought it would have, even considering she was a licensed psychotherapist and had better tools than most to deal with these problems. His boss truly showed repentance – to us and to his wife – and we all forgave each other, trying maturely to process what had just happened in a godly manner.

Michael made an appointment with the pastor at Calvary to meet for lunch during that week. They met at a Friday's and Michael started telling his story, how he hated his job, and that he was compromising, putting old people into investments they should never be put in. He felt he couldn't be a good Christian in his present job. And then he told him about what his boss had done to me. The pastor told him he couldn't stay in his job. Michael was a little fearful of this, considering he needed to make money to take care of us. So the pastor said, "For the sake of this meeting, let's not worry about money. If you could do anything in the world that you loved and make a living at it, do you know what it would be?" Michael answered, "I do." The pastor exclaimed, "Well I could ask that to twenty men and they wouldn't have an answer, so this is good. What would it be?" Michael calmly replied, "I'd be a potter!" "You mean like on a wheel with clay?" asked the pastor. "Yes," he responded. "Do it man! What a noble profession! Working with your hands!" This started the wheels turning in Michael's mind.

He came home after his lunch with the pastor, and I was lying out in the sun reading a great book called *No Compromise*, by Melody Green. It was the life story of Keith and Melody Green. He was an incredibly anointed, prophetic, touring singing artist back in the late seventies and eighties who died in a tragic airplane accident, along with two of their children. He preached with fire and conviction. I was enthralled and riveted reading about this man and his wife and how they ministered with such power and truth, and their reliance upon the Lord was amazing, and their call to holiness for the people of God was contagious. Before Michael came home, I uttered a prayer under my breath, "Dear Lord, please give Michael and I a ministry like Melody and Keith." When Michael got home, I asked him how the meeting went. He told me that the pastor had snapped and told him to become a potter. I told him, "That's the Lord! I've always thought you should be doing what you love to do, and doing what the Lord has gifted you to do!"

> "You are never going to believe who's sitting at my table tonight! You know that guy that you and I have been praying for the past four years? He's sitting at my table."

Michael didn't want to work for a boss who had made a pass at his wife. When he had confronted him about it and had told his wife as well, my respect for Michael had skyrocketed as he picked up the mantle to defend me and my honor. Strand by strand, this incident started knitting our marriage together like never before. We were communicating on a deeper level, and becoming a team instead of two separate individuals living under the same roof.

Michael decided to move on and start a pottery business. I promised to book some cruises to pay the bills while he tried to get the business off the ground. He enrolled at Florida Atlantic University where he learned new glazing techniques, and he entered several fairs and exhibitions for his art. Although he sold some, it wasn't enough to pay our bills.

He needed a job that would pay, so he searched for a five-star restaurant in the area and found one called The Down Under. It was on the intra-coastal waterway in Fort Lauderdale. He went down to interview and he was met with a four-page test on sauces, dishes, and wines. Though he hadn't done this sort of work in a long time, he scored one hundred percent on the test! He was so excited that he'd retained everything from his past. He got a job as a captain right away. It paid well, and Michael was a great captain because he's so professional and personable, with finesse at tableside dining, selling the most expensive dishes with just a suggestion. He never came home with less than a hundred dollars a night, and on the weekends it was a few hundred.

He would work long hours into the night, and would have to work on Thanksgiving and Christmas – but we didn't complain and made the best of this job that we knew was from the Lord. When he got the job, the Lord told him not to tell anyone what he did in his former career. He was to be only a waiter to everyone at work. This is where the Lord started humbling him and teaching him how to be a servant, and how to walk out his faith through his actions without ever saying a word. But when asked, he would share his faith. So many of the people that he worked with made their way to the church; they made professions of faith and their lives were changed. Michael's life was the only Bible most of these people would ever read. We would hear about them coming to the church, one by one, as we started venturing out in faith. This was Michael's preparation for what was ahead.

One night I got a call. Michael's voice was at an excited pitch, saying, "You are never going to believe who's sitting at my table tonight! You know that guy that you and I have been praying for the past four years? He's sitting at my table and I'm waiting on him. He's with his agent, and they are trying to get him to get signed by the New York Yankees at their spring training camp down here this week!" After the former baseball commissioner had died, and by another miracle of God, the new commissioner accepted him back – Steve Howe had been reinstated to baseball. I couldn't believe it!

Michael bounded into the dining room and up to their table exclaiming, "Steve Howe, I've been praying for you for the past four years!" Michael's boldness got the attention of his wife, Cindy, and she took him aside and told him not to stop praying…they were there to see if any team would take him. Michael invited her to an upcoming concert that I was giving at Calvary Fort Lauderdale. She said that she would try to come, that all the wives had been going to that church since they had been there. Michael was thrilled that by our praying for this man, it had materialized into a real-life miracle of how God connects the dots through the power of prayer.

As I started my concert with my band that evening at Calvary, the Yankee wives were sitting off to the left in the front rows. I'm glad that I didn't know they were there until afterwards. Michael had found them and struck up conversations with several of them. He made plans for us to get together with Cindy and Steve. Over the next years we would become close friends with their family. They would fly us up every winter for two weeks for an all-expenses-paid vacation to Whitefish to snow ski, since Michael loved skiing so much.

That particular night after my concert, as we were leaving with some friends, a lady came running by us shrieking in unintelligible tones and sounds, hissing and spitting as she scurried under a van convulsing. I had never seen anyone actually possessed by a demon until this night. Of course this would happen after such a spiritually-infused evening where so much ministry had taken place. I asked Michael to run and get Pastor Gennarino, the assistant pastor, to come and help since he would know what to do. He came running, and started getting her out from underneath the van so she wouldn't be in harm's way, rebuking Satan in the name of Jesus. Since Michael still didn't have complete victory with his rage issues, and I still wasn't quite sure if his "going forward" to profess Christ back in California had truly taken root yet, I found myself partially concerned but still halfway kidding as I shouted out to him: "Run, Michael, run! The demons might come out of her and go into you!" as we all laughed hysterically.

But the spiritual battle and warfare was just beginning…

Chapter 12

THE DARK SIDE

Michael had the kind of past that I had only read about in books or seen on TV shows like *Miami Vice*. He cavorted with Columbian drug dealers. He had parties full of debauchery. He dated mud wrestling girls. In short, Michael had no boundaries. His bad boy, exciting, adventurous side was part of the charm that drew me to him in the first place. He was hilariously funny and the life of any party. But with his past came a spiritually dark, demonic side that he had opened himself up to. Michael used drugs, pharmaceuticals – a word derived from the Greek word *pharmakia,* which in the original language of the New Testament translates to the word "witchcraft," and that can bring demonic oppression into one's life.

I had also opened myself up to the dark side by entertaining psychics and mediums when I wanted to have insight into my future. I would participate in "free writing," where in response to our questions, someone would channel a "spirit" to take them over while writing down the answers – or whatever else the spirit would tell them to write. I had also dabbled in some eastern religions, mainly Nichiren Buddhism, because the den mom from Monaco had lured me into her world, taking me to meetings during my times of searching after I got home from France, before I met Michael. She was choreographing my ship act, and while we were spending a lot of time together, she took the opportunity to introduce me to "chanting." I would chant to a Gohonzen (a box on the wall that you would offer fruit sacrifices to), not knowing what I was saying. I could've been conjuring up spells for all I knew.

Michael and I were both coming into this relationship with some spiritual baggage that the Lord needed to take care of. We needed to clean house – literally and figuratively. In the weeks after our wedding, I got rid of all of my Buddhist paraphernalia, and any other book or trinket associated with or tied to the occult.

> We were indeed in a spiritual battle for our very lives. Many supernatural things were taking place, both demonic and divine.

I do want to make it clear here that Christians cannot be possessed. His Holy Spirit dwells in us, which protects us from demonic possession. However, Christians can be attacked and oppressed by the enemy. In the early years of Michael's faith, the anger issues and excessive drug use from his past made him a prime target for being relentlessly attacked. He had gone forward to make a profession of faith, and he was seeking the things of the Lord. But in his young faith, and without one-on-one spiritual guidance, he lacked the tools to stand against attacks, and he would allow himself to give into the flesh and cross boundaries into an inappropriate level of rage. It would be four years until these roots would begin to take hold, and the Holy Spirit would be the one to eventually deliver him and set him free from the bondage that held him prisoner.

Finally, my brethren, be strong in the Lord and in the power of His might. Put on the whole armor of God, that you may be able to stand against the wiles of the devil. For we do not wrestle against flesh and blood, but against principalities, against powers, against the rulers of the darkness of this age, against spiritual hosts of wickedness in the heavenly places. Therefore, take up the whole armor of God, that you may be able to withstand in the evil day, and having done all, to stand.

— Ephesians 6: 10-13

We were indeed in a spiritual battle for our very lives. Many supernatural things were taking place, both demonic and divine. The spiritual warfare had begun while we were living in Santa Monica, California.

My dear friend, Teresa Lee, who I had done shows with every summer throughout my college years at Opryland USA in Nashville, Tennessee, was still in my life – she is one of those "lifer" friends that are a gift from God. When Teresa and Michael met, they hit it off immediately and they were instant friends. Because she was so innocent, and somewhat gullible or too trusting, he would mercilessly tease her and play practical jokes on her. One incident in particular we still chuckle over today. We were in Southern California, on our way to attend a Wednesday night church service to see Pastor Raul Ries at Calvary Chapel West Covina (now called Calvary Chapel Golden Springs), and we took her to get her first In-and-Out burger. As we went through the drive-through, he proceeded to tell her that when she ordered her burger, she would have to ask in a whisper for the "secret sauce." He told her that it was a well-kept secret, but they would comply if she would ask for it. So we drove up to the window to order and Teresa says, "I will have a double-double…," then in an almost inaudible whisper, "with the secret sauce." The man said, "Excuse me, ma'am?" She repeated, "I want the 'secret sauce,' please." And he responds, "I'm sorry ma'am, we don't have any secret sauce." By this time, Michael and I were laughing so hysterically that tears were streaming down our faces. Teresa was such a good sport, and would endure many more jokes in the years to come. But she would also endure – and be an active participant in – helping to lift the demonic oppression that was plaguing my husband in that crucial first year of our marriage.

I knew that even apart from the supernatural battle swirling around us, there were serious issues in Michael's life that needed deep healing and a touch from God.

One day while Teresa was visiting us at our apartment on Fourth Street in Santa Monica, everything was going great until one of us managed to touch one of Michael's "triggers." Neither one of us knew or understood what was causing him to have one of his "rage fits." They would come seemingly out of nowhere. We would be having a good time and then all of a sudden something would set him off. It may have been that he felt disrespected, whether or not what was said was intended to be so. Or, right out of left field, he would get instantly angry, and it would escalate into rage. It would always scare me, and I would tremble inside, and it would put me off-balance not knowing what I had said or done to elicit such a response. He started flying into a rage in front of Teresa, saying to me that he wanted me out of his life, and he started taking my clothes out of the closet and throwing them on the floor and on the bed – and his behavior continued to intensify. I saw the terror in Teresa's eyes, and my mouth became really dry with the fear creeping up inside of me, as well. I knew that we weren't dealing with anything of this world during this episode. Michael's face was distorted, with his veins popping out around his carotid arteries, and he was spitting while he was yelling, actually screaming in a guttural tone. I saw that his eyes had become elongated and menacing. I wasn't dealing with the natural or physical – this was "other-worldly," and not from the good place. I knew that something demonic that was overcoming my husband, and at the very same time, Teresa and I both started rebuking Satan in the name of Jesus! We were pleading the blood of Jesus over Michael, commanding whatever evil thing had taken hold of him to leave him at once! After about a minute – which seemed like an eternity – Michael started to calm down, and his features started to come back to normal. This was the first of many rages that my husband would fly into over the next seven years of our married life.

I knew that even apart from the supernatural battle swirling around us, there were serious issues in Michael's life that needed deep healing and a touch from God. The Holy Spirit would comfort me, telling me in my core that his behavior had nothing to do with me, that He wanted to touch and heal the deep places in Michael's heart where he had been wounded. That I had a diamond in the rough, and if I would trust in Him, He would heal Michael in His time. This started my journey to becoming a prayer warrior, interceding for Michael on a daily basis. Praying on my knees, I was going to war for my husband's soul. We were in a battle, and the forces of evil were working overtime to split our marriage in two. I was standing on my vows – that we were irrevocably "one flesh" when we said, "I do." I didn't know why we were being so mercilessly attacked, and it wasn't until later that I truly understood why. Satan wanted me out of the way, and he wanted our union dissolved. Jesus had a plan for our lives that we couldn't even fathom.

> *Therefore, my beloved, as you have always obeyed, not as in my presence only, but now much more in my absence work out your own salvation with fear and trembling.*
> — Philippians 2:12 NKJV

Once, after we moved to our condo Florida, Michael had gotten so out of control during an altercation that he broke every hand-thrown vase he had made at FAU that was going into his art show the next week. They were really beautiful pots, too. I loved one in particular, and he smashed that one into a thousand pieces thinking it would hurt me badly. I looked at him and said, "You're an idiot!" Later on, after he had cooled down, he agreed that was an idiotic thing to do. He had only hurt himself. Luckily, I took a picture of that one, so at least I have a memory of it.

After moving to our home in Boca, the warfare rose to new heights. God gave me a mysterious amount of faith, and the strength to withstand and endure all that was happening to us during this time. Michael and I would have crazy fights where we would have such anger towards each other. One time we threw peanut butter at each other, and it ended up all over the cabinets, in drawers, and all over the kitchen.

While all these things were going on, Michael's dad tried to sabotage his new job with the Wall Street firm. He received a frantic call from his supervisor saying, "This man called so upset that you missed your appointment with him. Why did you do this? He's so mad that you didn't show up." Michael was up in arms thinking that he had missed a critical client. The man on the other end of the phone had presented himself as a big guy in the financial industry, and couldn't believe that this company would put up with someone blatantly missing their appointments. Knowing he hadn't missed an appointment, Michael was looking at the number, he knew that something was askew. He said, "Have you looked at the area code?" It was a 714 area code. "It is a Southern California number, and all of my clients are in Florida." His supervisor got off the phone and called the number and found out that Michael's dad was calling from his firm in Orange County trying to get Michael in trouble. He felt so badly for Michael, and he kept saying, "I'm so sorry man." Michael could've lost his job over something like this, and it hurt Michael very much. It was like pulling the scab off an old wound.

> My body was paralyzed and I couldn't move, and I had the weight of two invisible hands on my mouth trying to suffocate me.

Calling his dad, he confronted him. His dad tried to make light of it, but Michael stayed the course. He started hurling loud curses at Michael; I overheard and told him, "Hang up the phone. We don't need to listen to such vitriol." That was the last time Michael spoke with his dad. He died not too long afterwards of a massive heart attack, sitting on a bar stool in a local bar across from John Wayne Airport.

When Michael changed jobs and worked for the boss that had later made a pass at me, we had a plague of fleas that were everywhere in our home. Our poor cocker spaniel, Katie – they were on every part her body, and they almost killed her. They got into our carpet, and they would jump up on our legs and clothes, they were even outdoors in the yard. No one could figure out where the fleas came from, and we had to hire a professional to kill them.

Through prayer, I was actively fighting the menacing forces that were pursuing us with a vengeance. At night, while Michael was sleeping, I would gently lay my hands on him – hoping I wouldn't wake him up and make him mad – and I would go into battle, praying over him. I would pray for the deep places inside of him to be healed, for him to get on fire for Jesus, and then I would pray in my prayer language, knowing the Lord knew what we needed.

Right before we were called into ministry, I had actual, physical manifestations of demons present themselves to me. I wasn't sure if this was intended to intimidate me, or scare me so badly that I would back down from the battle I was fighting, but I would speak scriptures out loud to whatever forces were bothering me. *"He that lives in me is stronger than he that lives in the world!"* I was literally in a fight for my life, and they knew God was giving me the faith to stand against it. Waking up one morning, I turned over, and there, standing at my bedside was a short, brown, demonic apparition that appeared covered in scabs. I rebuked it in the name of Jesus! I told Michael about it, and he didn't seem to be that moved by it, or perhaps at the time he just didn't believe me.

I was heavily into the Word, seeking the Lord at every turn. What put the icing on the cake was what happened on another morning. I was just awakening, and aware of everything going on around me, but my body was paralyzed and I couldn't move, and I had the weight of two invisible hands on my mouth trying to suffocate me. I felt intense pressure on my face and mouth, and I knew in my mind that all I needed to say was the name "Jesus" and I would be okay – there is power in the name of Jesus! It took every ounce of strength within my being to try to mouth those words. It took more than one attempt, for I was immobilized and trying to twist my head to get those hands off my mouth. I finally slurred in slow motion the name of "Jesus!" The hands instantly flew off of my mouth and the weight of them was gone!

Now I knew they wanted me dead...

> *Stand therefore, having girded your waist with truth, having put on the breastplate of righteousness, and having shod your feet with the preparation of the gospel of peace; above all, taking the shield of faith with which you will be able to quench all the fiery darts of the wicked one. And take the helmet of salvation, and the sword of the Spirit, which is the word of God; praying always with all prayer and supplication in the Spirit, being watchful to this end with all perseverance and supplication for all the saints – and for me, that utterance may be given to me, that I may open my mouth boldly to make known the mystery of the gospel...*
>
> — Ephesians 6:14-19 NKJV

Chapter 13

THE DREAM

The television screen flickered like a strobe light against the darkened walls in our Boca Raton, Florida home. I was channel surfing at two in the morning because, once again, I couldn't sleep.

We were living in our first single-family home together. We had lived in an apartment in Santa Monica, California, when we first got married in September, 1987, and in 1989 we rented a townhome condominium when we first moved to Boca Raton, Florida. The townhouse had started to get really cramped. It was a small two-bedroom, two-bath, upstairs and downstairs unit.

We bought Katie, our first dog together, while living in this condo. Michael gave her to me as our second Valentine's Day gift. She was a beautiful, black cocker spaniel, with a sweet face and large, kind eyes that reminded me of a seal; it was our first attempt at pouring ourselves into another living creature besides each other. We had been very successful in indulging in our own narcissism up until this point in our lives. She would become a buffer for me, used to show Michael how scary his escalating emotions would frighten Katie and me when he would come unglued in his rage fits. She would shake uncontrollably when he was yelling at me, and would press tightly against me to protect me every time these fights would ensue. She would growl at him if he came too close to me during these encounters. We would actually console one another. It was also here in this condominium that Katie would stand at the bottom of the staircase and look up, as if someone was standing in front of her, barking in fear at someone or something that we couldn't see – but she could! We know in the Bible that our war isn't against flesh and blood, but against principalities and things that we cannot see! This was the beginning of the tangible spiritual warfare that was going to take place over the next few years in our lives.

We made the move to Boca Raton after Michael had inter-viewed for a position as a Regional Marketing Director for a Wall Street firm. I urged Michael to interview for this job because I was flying cross country twice a month from Los Angeles to Miami to hop onto whichever cruise ship I had booked for that month. I was a headline entertainer on seven major cruise lines. An enviable job you would think, but I would only work one show per week as the main attraction, and the rest of the time I had to fill with whatever I chose to do. I would go on tours, get massages, pedicures and manicures, spent hours in the spas, read a lot of books, and learned how to crochet a lot of blankets. I referred to this experience as a luxurious jail. I was held captive at sea with a lot of time on my hands – and there is only so much sun, working out, and shop-ping and eating one can do while on board. It paid a great deal of money though, and Michael and I both needed to make big money to keep the lifestyle afloat (no pun intended) which we both had grown accustomed to before meeting one another. We both lived above our means, and wanted to present to the world that we were materially successful. After interviewing in New York, he landed the job in south Florida, and we loaded up everything that we had after two years of marriage to make the trip from California to Florida and start a new life.

After Michael had gone forward at Calvary Costa Mesa, he had nominal growth in his Christianity, but outwardly he would do things that made me think that he was changing for the better. He really felt the need to strip away a lot of our material possessions before we moved – like selling his beloved Porsche. He went into a Toyota dealership and traded it for a stripped-down little gray Toyota truck with no air conditioning. And we were moving to Florida! Needless to say, after being in Florida for a few months, we decided to add the air conditioner because when Michael would go on his calls to various offices, his suits would be drenched in sweat from the horrible humidity before he ever got out of the truck. While we were driving cross-country with everything we could cram into the small truck bed – a moving company did all the rest – I will never forget when I took over the driving responsibilities for a while so Michael could get some rest. I saw a sign that said, "All trucks pull over at next exit." Well, being the law-abiding citizen that I am, I dutifully pulled over and found myself in between two gigantic semi trucks! I started to think that I maybe didn't have to pull over. Michael woke up because we were stopped and asked, "What are you doing?" I told him that it said that all trucks needed to pull over. He looked in

> We were supposed to be happy...but we weren't. The single-family home turned out to be a money pit, and everything started falling apart – from the home to the marriage.

front of us, and then behind us, and started laughing so hard that he couldn't breathe! I realized that it meant "semi-trucks," and I started laughing hysterically, too. Sometimes I really do have "blonde moments."

We wanted the "good life" together, and Michael had heard quite a bit from his new firm about Boca Raton being where the wealthy and business-minded people would congregate. They thought it would be a good fit for him, and he could do a lot of business deals on the golf courses down there, too. That was a big draw for him; most of his cronies would work until two or three in the afternoon, then go and make big deals on the golf course while enjoying eighteen holes. He was a wholesaler selling direct investments and limited partnerships to brokers. Michael is such a social animal that he can make friends with anyone, and his business skills are such that he could literally sell ice to an Eskimo. Being a former beauty queen, I also present myself well. So together we – as this self-acclaimed "power couple," along with our dreams of upward mobility and the all-illusive happiness it accompanied – determined that Boca Raton was the place for us. Boca Raton literally translates "mouth of the rat," and we were indeed about to fall into a trap of materialism and ladder climbing to success that God never intended us to ascend. But it would all work into His divine plan for our lives.

After two years in our little townhouse, we decided we needed a larger place, and in 1991 we began fervently looking to move. What we found was a cute four-bedroom, two-bath, ranch-style home in a quiet Boca Raton neighborhood. It had a small backyard that was fenced in, and in the front it had an enormous beautiful banyan tree that framed the façade of the home. We were supposed to be happy…but we weren't. The single-family home turned out to be a money pit, and everything started falling apart

– from the home to the marriage. The community of Boca Raton was filled with upscale, pristine homes that looked great on the outside, but as we were soon to find out, on the inside they were another story. Michael and I both knew how to put on an outward display to others, even if we were ninety days from going upside down and losing it all should anything happened to either one of our jobs. But Michael and I wanted a nice home. We tried to buy no fewer than five houses or condos in this area over the course of a few years. The Lord shut the door on every potential acquisition.

When we first got married, Michael's credit score wasn't the greatest, and we both had substantial debt. Every bill he forgot to pay, including having the lights turned off, the Lord used to teach him fiscal responsibility and how to become the head of our household. I needed to relinquish the checkbook to him and surrender my control issues, allowing him to make mistakes in order for us to grow as a couple, and for him to grow into the man, and me the woman, that God intended us to individually become. We didn't know that eventually we would be leading countless thousands to the Lord, and Michael would become one of the most incredible, fiscally-responsible men I know in the ministry today regarding both money and integrity.

When the Lord closed the door on every home we attempted to buy in Boca, we, in our own fleshly attempt, found a home we liked and determined to make it happen. After much finagling, Michael persuaded the owners to agree to sign a lease option to buy contract. In many ways, this could even be paralleled to our "marriage contract." I was standing on my childhood convictions that when you married, you married for life – for better or for worse. And I really did mean my vows, even if the marriage did start out as a whim – a fun time to have over the weekend. Michael had no role models for marriage, or any convictions in his heart at this time on the longevity of a marriage contract. From the example provided by his Dad through the years, he had seen the institution of marriage as being disposable. In the early years of our marriage, the "D" word – divorce – was bantered around during every fight quite often by him.

The big banyan tree in our new front yard was a magnificent specimen, with an intricate root system that was fascinating to look at, the focal point as you drove into the driveway casting much-needed shade over our brick home. Over the course of the next two years living in this house, we started realizing that what you see is not always what you get. We discovered that the beautiful banyan tree I loved so much had such a deep root system that it was actually lifting the house off of its foundation! If the tree wasn't cut down and the root system removed, the house would be destroyed by the roots of the tree. We had no extra money to take on the removal of a giant tree. Michael had no desire to deal with heavy problems at this time in his life. It would infuriate me that he would slough off what I perceived as huge problems, that if not addressed would cause even more destruction down the road. The ease with which he would ignore issues, or go from room to room to fix only the obvious problems, or just apply "another coat of paint" was foreign to me. I knew we needed to deal with hard things now, or later they would just get compounded, fester, and

> My love was beginning to erode and show signs of deterioration, waning with every fight and every cross word that we would speak, yell, and hurl at one another.

cost more in the end...or worse, the home would totally break down and fall apart.

I had endured a lot of wrath from this man who presented himself one way on the outside, but underneath had many issues in his life – issues he had not yet peeled back one layer to get to the root problems causing the rage that welled up inside of him. I knew that if both of our "root systems" were not removed and rejuvenated and resurrected by the power of the Holy Spirit in our lives, our marriage didn't stand a chance.

My love – which I had been so full of when we initially eloped – was beginning to erode and show signs of deterioration, waning with every fight and every cross word that we would speak, yell, and hurl at one another. I wasn't a picnic to live with either. The Lord needed to strip me of my self-centeredness, stubbornness, and unwillingness to yield to anything or anyone. He needed to strip me of the fierce independence that I had once prided myself on, shattering it into a million shards so He could make me into a new vessel, totally dependent upon Him, to use as The Potter saw fit!

We took on each room one by one, stripping off old wallpaper and putting up new, painting, buying new carpet by the thousands of dollars throughout the home, pouring money endlessly into a home that was falling apart at the seams. We replaced the air conditioner after the old one flooded, almost ruining the brand new carpet we had just laid. Then there was the fear of mold growing in the humid Florida climate – and I was deathly allergic to mold. We would have random power surges throughout the home and learned that the entire plumbing and electrical systems had to be replaced or else the possibility of a fire was imminent. It would cost thousands of dollars to get this home to a livable state.

I remember my dad suggesting we run from this house. What a metaphor of our marriage! I know that secretly, my dad would've loved for me to flee this abusive union – secretly, I wanted out as well. Everything in our marriage, personal lives, the things we had subjected ourselves to, as well as who we had become separately, needed to be uprooted right down to the foundational level, the "old becoming new," and to start over in Christ Jesus!! *"Therefore, if anyone is in Christ, he is a new creation; old things have passed away; behold, all things have become new"* (2 Corinthians 5:17 NKJV).

As we began the physical labors of trying to save our house, God started working in our hearts and marriage. He started cleaning up our thought processes – from room to room, in each compartment, and started putting up new paint and wallpaper while rebuilding, correcting, and replacing old patterns of behavior. He was in the process of unearthing and unveiling hard truths that we both needed to face and confront in the recesses of our souls. He was rewiring our synapses by letting the Word of God pour over and through us. The pruning process had begun.

It was going to be a long and arduous process, but sanctification and transformation takes time. There are no short cuts in the Christian race – that's why it's called the sanctification process. Our old "root system" needed to be dug up so our foundation wouldn't crumble and ruin. The new foundation needed to be laid and built upon the cornerstone of Jesus Christ in order to withstand any hardships, winds, rains, and storms that would come to pass through the years. This would take time, money, fortitude, counseling, communication, change on both our parts, yielding and submitting to one another, two willing hearts and the blood, sweat, and tears to fight in order to keep what I believed was God's intention for us: *"What God hath joined together, let no man separate."* The Tree of Life was breaking up our artificial structure that was built on shifting sand. We needed to build our foundation on the Rock – Jesus Christ!

I don't think that either Michael or I would've had the ability to acquire the tools necessary for change without guidance early on in our marriage from some really great Christian counselors. The Bible is very clear on the outline for godly marriage, but we needed some coaches with strong godly credentials and solid healthy marriages to help us in our blind spots, with one another and with ourselves individually. It is far too easy to deceive yourself, both in marriage and in life, if someone you trust isn't there to help you along the path.

I know that if Michael and I hadn't had wonderful godly couples who were mirroring and walking out their faith, refereeing our disagreements and fights, along with providing Christian counseling, we wouldn't be together today. We learned invaluable communication and

He had a fuse so unpredictable that it left me off balance and never able to relax within the relationship.

fair-fighting skills, and how to deal with conflict resolution within a marriage. These are skills that we use even today as we now counsel other Christian couples.

Wherever Tim Mooney is today, we are indebted to him for walking us through some deep issues regarding our upbringing, showing us how we had carried those bad behaviors and habits into our marriage relationship, and giving us practical ways to change our behavior.

We also owe a debt of gratitude to John and Connie Chinnelly of Calvary Chapel Fort Lauderdale, who not only helped us to understand our individual personality types and how to cope with them, but also lived out godly principles in front of us on a daily basis while we attended that church for seven years. One time John had given Michael and me a personality test, and after reviewing the results, he shared that over the course of his years of counseling only one other couple had a test which revealed they both had the exact same personality! Well, the Lord showed me something so ugly about myself through this fact. He told me "that I loved myself so much that I married myself!" Yuck! Ouch!!

Roger and Traci Gales were another wonderful couple who helped us from day one. Roger had worked with Michael in the finance industry, before he had come to Christ. They have been in our lives for well over thirty years, as dear precious friends and mentors, still modeling a godly Christian marriage, with four grown boys. Roger has been a Board Member for Potter's Field Ministries for years now, and still sits on the Board to this day.

I wondered how long I could stay in this scary, unhealthy union and take Michael's unending verbal abuse. He had a fuse so unpredictable that it left me off balance and never able to relax within the relationship. However, I found that I had a deep resolve within my spirit that God could – and wanted to – save this miserable marriage. I wasn't a quitter. I was raised by a Master Sergeant in the Marine Corps and I was going to pull myself up by my bootstraps and fight like any good daughter of a soldier would. Perhaps it was just my own stubbornness and unwillingness to lose that made me want to fight, or my deeply held convictions from my childhood about marriage being a life-long endeavor. But I was being given a spiritual fortitude that only God and His Holy Spirit could endow me with, and I would stand on the covenant of the marriage vows that I had made within myself and before Him. No matter what it was, I was staying and fighting to the death for this marriage.

From the moment I met Michael, I knew down deep within my soul that he was supposed to be my husband. Of course, when you're in the throes of new love, you choose to not see the "warning signs" that are glaringly staring you in the face. Your hormones are raging so much that even if he wasn't a good person, your raw emotion takes precedent over reason. And your flesh wins, especially when you're in a backslidden state, not walking with the Lord in the way you had in the past.

Since I received the Lord, I have always known when He was speaking to me. It was always a really clear "voice" or conviction, speaking loudly in the core of my soul, that something significant was taking place. This was one of those life moments – I needed to take heed and listen. It was one of those times that, if I didn't listen, I would regret it. I knew underneath all of the obvious problems that Michael had a good precious heart, and that, as God had already spoken to me, I had a diamond in the rough. Maybe I was crazy. I certainly didn't know the depth of spiritual warfare that was down the road for the both of us. But I knew deep inside that God had a plan for the both of us, and I would stand on that promise by faith. I certainly couldn't see it in the natural world, but we are called as Christians, to *walk by faith, not by sight*" (2 Corinthians 5:7 NKJV). Also I was given this verse:

> *For I know the plans I have for you says the Lord...plans to prosper you, not to harm you...to give you a future and a hope."*
> — Jeremiah 29:11

But how realistic was I being to really believe this promise amidst the erosion of this rocky union? Every bit of love that we had for one another was numbed and dying daily through reckless words, rage, and skirmishes on this battleground, with neither one of us willing to wave the white flag in surrender. We were in a battle for sure, an unseen war raging around us since day one of our marriage, a spiritual assault on our souls.

It was two in the morning in our Boca Raton home – the home that was pretty on the outside but falling apart on the inside, ready to catch fire, badly in need of repair, and damaged at its very foundation, the home that sucked out our energy and resources, and that silently, metaphorically, and mercilessly mocked our marriage. Michael was asleep next to me in bed. He had been asleep for hours. I was wide awake.

This bewitching hour was the only time during my day that I was truly alone, stress free from the possibility of Michael coming unglued on me never knowing when I would push a button – a trigger if you will – that would make Michael fly into a verbal rage, stirring up in the pit of my stomach such a nervousness and a deep fear such an animal might associate with "fight or flight." I was lying in bed, mindlessly watching the television screen and thinking, my mind was playing over and over, "What I had gotten myself into?" Staring blankly at the channels flashing before my eyes, I was simply trying to pass the time until another day could arrive…another emotionally-exhausting day filled with fighting, screaming, and vying for position in the marriage, another day that the love that I had for Michael continued to die inside of me like a withering rose. Every verbal assault he would hurl at me was an attempt to make me leave. He was doing a good job. My unwillingness to forgive him – and not even having the tools to do so – was also playing a part in this volatile relationship. These were the things that abandonment and rejection issues were made of: subconsciously pushing the one you love out of your life before he or she could find out who you really were and leave you. This is self-sabotage at its best.

Three years into the marriage, and the battle scars were already as wearying and draining as if we'd been married for decades. I was the closest I'd ever been to leaving this union. While sitting in that home and watching that television screen, I closed my eyes and whispered a prayer to the God of the universe: "I need a sign, Lord. To stay in this marriage, I need a sign."

> *Show me a sign for good, that those who hate me may see it and be ashamed, because You, Lord, have helped me and comforted me."*
>
> — Psalm 86:17 NKJV

In my desperation, I cried out to the mighty Lord, and in resignation of body, soul, and spirit, I waved my white flag to Jesus in my heart.

I finally surrendered.

He could now work in my life.

All of a sudden, completely unprovoked, Michael sat up in the bed in a dead sleep – his eyes closed shut – and muttered these words, "I know what we are supposed to call our ministry. It's supposed to be called Potter's Field Ministries!" Then he fell back into the bed and went to sleep!

I was thinking, "What was that? We don't have a marriage, much less a ministry! And what was he talking about?" Could this indeed be the sign that I had just moments before asked the Lord to perform? I believed with a childlike faith that it was!

This would mark the beginning of a season of walking in the promises of God. It would become the cornerstone of faith upon which we would stand during the tumultuous times that were still to come as we walked ahead – together – into our future.

Chapter 14

THE POTTER'S FIELD

The next morning, my head was whirling. I couldn't get the words out of my head that Michael had uttered while completely asleep. "I know what we are supposed to call our ministry. It's supposed to be called Potter's Field Ministries!" I don't even like this man, much less ever want to have a ministry with him! When Michael left for work that morning, I decided to get my Bible out and do some research on anything to do with potters or a potter's field. Now, I didn't know the scriptures very well, so I decided to play "Bible Roulette." I don't suggest you do this on a regular basis, but at that time it was really the only thing I knew how to do. I said a prayer: "God show me what this is all about. I believe this is the sign that I asked you for." I took my Bible and opened it up randomly, and it fell open on Isaiah 64:8 – *"But now, O Lord, You are our Father; We are the clay, and You our potter; And we are the work of Your hand"* (NKJV). I had chills from head to toe! Could this be the Lord speaking directly to me?

I continued on, and the Bible opened again to Jeremiah 18:1-6 – *"The word which came to Jeremiah from the Lord, saying: 'Arise and go down to the potter's house, and there I will cause you to hear My words.' Then I went down to the potter's house, and there he was, making something at the wheel. And the vessel that he made of clay was marred in the hand of the potter; so he made it again into another vessel, as it seemed good to the potter to make. Then the word of the Lord came to me, saying: 'O house of Israel, can I not do with you as this potter?' says the Lord, 'Look, as the clay is in the potter's hand, so are you in My hand, O house of Israel'"* (NKJV). Oh my goodness! Was God laying out His plans for us so clearly and this methodically? I knew something so special was taking place while I was sitting on my bed looking through my Bible. I was hearing God clearer than I ever had in my life!

> ## It was all making sense to me like never before! I understood my salvation in a deeper and more profound way.

I saw in my study Bible that the Hebrew word for "potter" meant *maker*, with reference to God. I didn't know what a potter's field and the Bible had in common, so I looked up what a potter's field was in the references in the back and it led me to Matthew 27, where Judas hangs himself. I was actually having a dialogue with God right there in my room, just Him and me. I knew that He was giving me new marching orders and promises to hold onto because the battle for our marriage was going to intensify. I began to read:

> *When Judas, who had betrayed him, saw that Jesus was condemned, he was seized with remorse and returned the thirty silver coins to the chief priests and the elders. "I have sinned," he said, "for I have betrayed innocent blood." "What is that to us?" they replied. "That's your responsibility." So Judas threw the money into the temple and left. Then he went away and*

hanged himself. The chief priests picked up the coins and said, "It is against the law to put this into the treasury, since it is blood money." So they decided to use the money to buy the potter's field as a burial place for foreigners. That is why it has been called the "Field of Blood" to this day. Then what was spoken by Jeremiah the prophet was fulfilled. "They took the thirty silver coins, the price set on him by the people of Israel, and they used them to buy the potter's field, as the Lord commanded me."

— Matthew 27:3-10

The Lord was speaking to me on such a deep level, taking me from scripture to scripture, now cross-referencing to Zechariah 11:13 to show me that thirty pieces of silver was the price a slave was bought for by the Israelites in ancient times. Jesus was being sold out and betrayed by Judas for a slave's fee. Since it was "blood money," it couldn't be put back into the treasury, so they decided to buy a potter's field with a name that literally translates to "field of blood." God spoke to me almost audibly, "You will call your ministry 'Potter's Field Ministries' because you are to never forget that you were bought for a price, the precious blood of Jesus Christ!" It was blood money to remind us that innocent blood was shed for our sins.

It was all making sense to me like never before! I understood my salvation in a deeper and more profound way. I knew that this ministry was something that was going to happen in our future, and I was privileged enough to have the God of the Universe letting me in on the foreshadowing of our lives. My faith was being strengthened and enlightened. He went on to tell me that we would be used as vessels to help put broken lives back together again by the power of His blood. A literal potter's field is where the potter throws all the broken shards and unused pieces of clay. Our ministry would go out to the broken, the weak, the discarded, and the forgotten, and He would put them back together again, and then He would shine His light through the cracks of their now-restored lives. He never throws the clay away!

As I excitedly continued searching the scriptures, listening to God on a broader level of hearing, I felt a compulsion to look up two verses that I was not familiar with. I felt that God was giving me two specific promises to hold fast to when things got rough. The first one, I enthusiastically looked up was:

> *Forget the former things; do not dwell on the past. See, I am doing a new thing! Now it springs up; do you not perceive it? I am making a way in the wilderness and streams in the wasteland.*
>
> — Isaiah 43:18-19

By this time I was weeping tears of joy, knowing my God hears my prayers and answers them in such a personal way. He was asking me to trust Him on a fathomless level, to walk completely by faith and know that He had our best interests in His heart. I was to forget my sins of the past that were keeping me in guilt and shame and remorse for wasting so much precious time, and to know that He would make a way for us even when it looked impossible. We do indeed serve a God of the impossible! My God would make an actual way in the desert and streams in the wastelands.

The other scripture I hurriedly looked up after this one was 2 Corinthians 5:17-20 (NKJV) —

> *Therefore, if anyone is in Christ, he is a new creation; the old has gone, the new is here! All this is from God, who reconciled us to himself through Christ and gave us the ministry of*

reconciliation: that God was reconciling the world to himself
in Christ, not counting men's sins against them. And he has
committed to us the message of reconciliation. We are therefore
Christ's ambassadors, as though God were making his appeal
through us. We implore you on Christ's behalf: Be reconciled
to God.

God was telling me that Michael and I would one day be ambassadors to the nations! We who are recipients of this divine reconciliation have the privilege and obligation, like Paul, to become the instruments of love in God's hands to minister the message of reconciliation to the world. We would one day be sent to be representatives to present Christ to all He would put before us.

Needless to say, this revelation ignited a new fire within my soul. I couldn't get enough of God's Word. I was excited to go to church and lead worship, and then to hear what He had to say to me with each new day.

I became so convinced that Potter's Field would come into existence, that I placed the Potter's Field name on my first album, *Let All The Earth Hear His Voice,* which I recorded at the Haven of Rest Studios in Los Angeles. In fact, it would be two more years before we would even do our first Potter's Field presentation.

One morning, I woke up to the sound of my own voice. I thought Michael was playing it on our stereo, but it was actually playing on Fort Lauderdale's largest FM Christian radio station! I heard strains of the bridge that my record producer and friend, Walt Harrah, penned to the old hymn, "Revive Us Again" —

Will you not revive us again, showing your love like before
Pouring out your spirit more and more
Hallelujah Thine the glory!

Hallelujah amen!
Hallelujah Thine the glory!
Revive us again!

My heart was thrilled! The DJ was saying, "That is local Christian artist, Pam Rozell singing 'Revive Us Again!'" I couldn't believe so many songs from my album were being played on regular rotation on the radio. God was using my gifts and talents to glorify Himself! And was this a prophetic anthem that the Lord Himself was trying to get through my thick skull? I knew deep in my heart that it was, that He was going to do supernatural things that seemed natural to rewrite our story and heal our broken marriage. I would stand on these promises for years to come, unwavering in "my God, my only friend in whom I trusted," who had promised me in His Word and in my heart that He would heal us, use us, and resurrect this decimated marriage relationship.

Shortly after this incident, God gave me back a precious gift that He had stripped from me while I was in my backslidden state. I started writing songs again! All the songs from *Let All The Earth Hear His Voice* had been written by Walt. I couldn't be trusted with this gift while I dragged Him into places and situations that I never should have taken Him to. But now, they started pouring out of me. The first song was a simple praise song called "A Hymn Of Praise." I then wrote an instrumental on my piano called "Streams In The Wasteland," followed by "Instrument of Love," and after a fight with Michael I wrote a song about marriage called "Faithful Hearts." Some of these songs that would appear on my second CD, *On The Potter's Wheel,* which I recorded in 1994. I was writing because the Lord was giving me songs, but I didn't even know I would have the privilege of recording another CD for four more years after these events.

A Hymn of Praise

Lyrics & Music by Pam Rozell

I lift my voice in humble praise
To You, I'll magnify, Your name I'll raise
To You I'll sing, Your name be praised
Exalt the Lord our God, Jehovah reigns

You're Lord of All, You reign on high
You are my Comforter, my El Shaddai
Lord God Almighty is my cry
My lips will praise Your name until I die

You reign above in majesty
Your works displayed around in all I see
You suffered shame and misery
Only to go prepare a home for me

A hymn of praise to You I sing
In God whose word I trust
Such joy you bring
You are my Rock, my everything
Jehovah, Yahweh, Abba, King of Kings

Our house in Boca Raton was falling apart, so we finally managed to get out of our contract and we moved to Coco Parc, an apartment complex in Coconut Creek, Florida. There was a pond behind our apartment. I used to fish in this pond and catch catfish, harkening me back to great memories fishing with my dad and grandfather while growing up. One day, I was sitting in front of this pond after fervently pursuing the Lord, and all of a sudden it was as if I was watching a Claritin commercial. The fog that was over the image of the pond started coming clear and into view with such clarity, as if I had just taken an allergy medication. The greens were greener, the pond was prettier, and the sounds of the birds and crickets and water lapping against the sides of the shore were so crisp and clear that I could almost feel them. All things were indeed becoming new!

This was a wonderful season for Michael; he was being mentored, taught, rebuked, corrected, encouraged, and directed by godly men who actually cared about him and saw his potential in Christ.

I was going about my life, trying to be a good wife, knowing that I wanted to quit cruising altogether and see what God had for us. I didn't know how God was going to change things, but I knew I needed to be faithful in what I was given day to day. I was still doing Christian concerts in such places as West Point Military Academy in New York, in North and South Carolina, Florida, and once even opened for Bryan Duncan in Fort Lauderdale. I wasn't sure how God was going to give us a ministry together, but I was sure He would one day.

Michael and I were still having our troubles, fighting and standing toe to toe, and hurling verbal assaults at each other, and he still having his rage issues. The love I had for him was dying a little more each day. I wanted to be obedient to God and love Michael, but I was finding it nearly impossible to do so. I prayed that God would restore in my heart the love I had for Michael because in my own strength I could not muster any feelings for him. I was still having a physical relationship with him because God gave me the conviction to do so, even though I felt nothing. I would pray through the whole ordeal while it was happening, because I knew that our physical expression was the glue – the gift that God gave us to make us one flesh and tie us together, despite my feelings. I knew if I stopped this altogether, it would've been even harder for both of us to overcome the "evil one."

One day, as I was looking at Michael, God answered my prayers as a wave of love towards him poured over me for about three seconds. It was as if a cold glass of water was thrown on me. This was a foreign feeling which I hadn't had in quite a while. A week or so would go by and another fleeting feeling of love would hit me, a little longer this time. It was a reminder of why I fell in love with him in the beginning. He had a beautiful heart underneath all of his calloused outside. One Sunday, I heard a sermon about love that explained how love was an action and not a feeling. So I started putting my love into action by doing small, loving things for him that I knew ministered to him, like cooking a meal or serving him, and waves of loving feelings would roll over me more often. During my devotional time one day, the Lord told me to hold on just a while longer, that even though I was more spiritually mature than Michael, a day was coming when I would be scrambling to keep up with this man. He assured me that Michael was like one of his potter's tools, a sponge, and when he got ignited for Jesus, he would drink in all he could about the scriptures – and it would happen fast.

Michael started getting involved in our new church which by this time had grown so large that we had to move into a larger facility, serving everywhere he could. He started by folding chairs after multiple services; after the men's studies he would cook hundreds of hamburgers for a bunch of starving men; and then he became an usher. One day as they were folding chairs, Gennarino, one of the pastors on staff, told him to go home because he was talking so much and distracting the other volunteers. He said, "Go home Michael. You don't want to serve, you want to be seen." He had never been talked to or corrected by another man like this in his life, and it took him off-balance. This was a wonderful season for Michael; he was being mentored, taught, rebuked, corrected, encouraged, and directed by godly men who actually cared about him and saw his potential in Christ.

Michael got a call one day from Jeff Denis, an elder of our church who is now the senior Pastor of Calvary Chapel Florida Keys, saying he wanted to have breakfast with him. Michael was so excited because in his thought processes, he thought they were going to make him an elder. I knew that this wasn't the case…yet. They met at a Denny's Restaurant down the street from the church. The meeting wasn't what Michael expected as Jeff proceeded to ask, "Michael, can Pam see Jesus in your eyes?"

Michael was blindsided by this question. He was suddenly thinking that this wasn't going quite like he thought it would. I had shared the state of our marriage with Jeff's wife, Kathleen, and the peril that it was in. She was one of the many women who was praying for our marriage, to help keep my arms up as I was walking down this turbulent road.

Jeff then said something that would change Michael's life: "Michael you're a phony! And everyone knows it." Michael's head was swirling. As he drove home, he was thinking, "Pull the honking redwood out of your own eye brother. You can't talk to me like that – I have an ushers badge!" This is one of the first times that a man Michael respected had actually spoken into his life. Even though it was painful, he had to take a look at what was said to him over breakfast. When he came home Michael was angry, and he started telling me some of what was said to him. He was negotiating and wanting to leave this church and go to another one. I asked him one question: "Well, was he right?" Michael knew that he had been called out by a godly man. He would have male authority and accountability for the first time in his life. He would either face the music and change – or run. I told him that he could go to another church, but I was staying, and I believed this was where the Lord had us for this season of our lives so he could grow into the man of God I knew he could become, and it was where I needed to stay to mature and gain more knowledge of God's Word.

That afternoon after I had left to run errands, Michael crawled under the piano after he had spent time pondering what was said to him at the breakfast, and he cried out to the Lord. He had an epiphany – he knew that he was playing with God and not serious about knowing who He was or loving his wife the way he should.

In 1991, alone in our apartment under the grand piano he gave me for our wedding, Michael totally surrendered to Jesus Christ. Through his crying out, the Lord heard him and took him seriously, and a new day dawned in the Rozell household. He truly repented; he had turned around and gone in another direction. It wouldn't come without its trials and tribulations, but his sincerity was real.

That afternoon, Michael surrendered his life to God in totality, giving his life to the Lord to do with him as He saw fit in the years to come.

Chapter 15

THE CALL

I was struggling really hard with who I thought I was and who I was becoming in Christ Jesus. I was fighting depression, because up to this point in my life, my significance was found in the things I did, and the accolades that I received from it. I was performance driven, and the Lord was trying His best to kill this in me. I needed to die to that part of my being because He needed a clean, emptied-out vessel to pour His Holy Spirit into as a conduit for His people. I was just a tool in the Potter's hands, of His making, and nothing of my own. The Lord needed to strip me of all pretense, performance, the ability to manipulate an audience, and to remake me into what He wanted me to be for His glory alone. He had allowed me to go through all the things I had early on to show me the emptiness and futility of living for myself. But going this route had left a stain of self-centeredness on my soul, instead of "others-centered." He needed to bring out His needle tool to cut away and prune this part of me that would hinder what He had planned for us to do. I would indeed endure the pain and the restructuring of who I thought I was in lieu of a better plan that had been set into motion before I was ever born.

Most people won't go though this type of searing, unvarnished truth to get to the core of whom you have become through the years. It's just easier to not change and live with the choices you've made in life. I knew that I would have a "good" life if I stayed who I was, or I could have the "better" life that Jesus talks about when He says He came so we might have "fullness of life." I wanted this life, but it would take death to get there. That is really the paradox of the gospel. Jesus had to die in order for us to have eternal life. And so must I die as well, and so must you. The Lord was asking me if I would die to the dreams and goals that I'd set for my life and allow the Master Potter to make me into another vessel that seemed best to Him, to be used as He saw fit, to serve His people, and to further His Kingdom. The question was: "Was I willing to pay the cost?"

My hopes had been dashed, and I was beginning to question if I had even heard from God about being involved with third world children.

I was still doing Christian concerts, and some large churches out in Los Angeles had booked me to sing in their Christmas productions. I was asked at one of these venues if I would sing at the Los Angeles Music Festival that would be held at one of these churches the first part of the year. I took the booking in January, 1991.

After my concert, a man named Tom Jackson approached me and told me he was signing new Christian artists to represent World Vision, the hunger relief organization, as "Artist Associates." Tom is renowned for his "On Stage Success" seminars and has staged and worked with well-known Christian and secular artists through the years. He asked if I would be interested in becoming an artist associate, sponsoring children through this organization during my concerts. I was thrilled at the possibility of this, considering that at fourteen years of age the Lord had placed the love of these third-world children in my heart. This started a long-term relationship with Tom from that day until the present. His daughter, Izzy, went through IGNITE, our Mission Training School, and now works for our ministry in Whitefish, Montana. He is a great friend, as well as his brother, John, who actually lives in Whitefish.

When I came home from this exciting time of meeting Tom, I conveyed to Michael what had been offered to me, but he wasn't in the least bit excited or interested in pursuing it further. My hopes had been dashed, and I was beginning to question if I had even heard from God about being involved with third world children. I started to pray and, once again, trusting in my heavenly Father who is true to His promises. He would fulfill this desire that He had placed in my heart one day to help these children. But it would be in His timing.

I was still struggling with the "old" me becoming "new." I didn't feel quite right in my skin, but I didn't actually know what I was supposed to feel like. The Potter was making me into someone new, but sometimes it was so hard I couldn't even drag myself out of bed because it was so difficult to face a stripped down version of myself. I knew that I had to go to total death in this area of my life before I could wholly be used to my full potential with the Lord. But this kind of dying takes perseverance, courage, and a resolve to stay the course through the layers of artifice to get back to the "real" me that God had intended. It was daunting. I hoped that I had the steadfastness to stick it out.

During my quiet time and prayer one morning, I felt compelled to start writing songs about the potter and the clay. This had not happened until this particular morning. I had written songs about my marriage, praise songs to the Lord, and songs inspired by the scriptures, but not about the potter and the clay. So I set out to do so, and contacted my friend, Claire Cloninger, the multi-Dove Award-winning lyricist, to help. We started writing together, and two titles came into focus: "Center My Spirit On You," about being centered on the wheel, and "On The Potter's Wheel."

Center My Spirit On You

Written by Pam Rozell & Claire Cloninger

When my life is pulled in all directions
When I fall so far from Your perfection
When my mind is filled with all the worries of my days
When the road I'm walking seems to be a twisted maze

CHORUS
Center my spirit on You
Be at the center of all that I do
Teach me to dwell on what's worthy and what's true
(REPEAT)
Lord, center my spirit on You

Lord, I know that I'm Your own creation
Restore to me the joy of my salvation
I know my only hope of glory, is Your life within
That is why I turn to You and lift this prayer again

BRIDGE
In Your hands I can rest, knowing You hold my life
In Your hands I can trust, You're making me, more like Christ

On The Potter's Wheel

Written by Pam Rozell & Claire Cloninger

Resting in Your hands yielded and still
Mold me Lord and make me what You will
Shape this heart of mine to Your desire
As You make me ready for the fire

CHORUS
On the potter's wheel, mold my life with loving hands
On the potter's wheel, fit my future to Your plans
As You turn my life I find
You imprint Your life on mine
I'm remade to Your design
On the potter's wheel

Would I dare to question what You do
Knowing that You're making me like You
In Your hands I choose to simply trust
As You shape my life with every touch

BRIDGE
And I will not fear the fire
And I will not pull away
And I will not fear tomorrow
I will trust You Lord today

About two days later, I received a phone call from our pastor's wife, Diane, asking me if I would write a couple of songs about the potter and the clay and if Michael would bring down his potter's wheel and do a demonstration and teach at the Women's Retreat.

The theme scripture for the retreat that year was Ephesians 2:10 – *"For we are His workmanship, created in Christ Jesus for good works, which God prepared beforehand that we should walk in them"* (NKJV). I had never thought about combining our two gifts for the glory of the Lord! A potter and a singer sounded kind of cheesy, but I

I knew the Holy Spirit was in this place and we were standing on holy ground.

figured I'd definitely give it a go; it could be interesting. I told her that I would ask Michael if he wanted to do it when he got home. When I told him about Diane's request for us to be a part of the Women's Retreat, he said he would definitely do it.

Over the next month or so, as the time for the retreat was coming around, I would periodically ask Michael if he had thought about what he was going to teach while "throwing clay." He'd slough me off with, "Yeah, yeah, I've thought about it, and I've got it down." I knew in my heart he hadn't even thought about it. But I was trusting that God was in this, and knew that He would take care of the situation.

The retreat was held on June 20, 1992, up north in West Palm Beach. They had gotten us a lovely room at a really nice hotel where the retreat was being held. I got there on Friday evening, but Michael had to work that night at The Down Under restaurant and would be joining me really late after his shift. I waited up for him and he arrived a little after 1 a.m. We went to bed and I asked him once again if he had prepared anything to say in the morning. We were going on at 8:30 a.m. He told me to go to sleep and to not worry about it. So I fell asleep, and around 4 a.m. I woke up and saw that Michael wasn't in bed. I heard talking coming from the bathroom, so I went in and Michael was on his knees praying. I said, "Tell me you have something prepared to say tomorrow." He looked at me with a worried look on his face and I exclaimed, "Oh no! You haven't!" I got down on my knees right beside him and we both started fervently praying for God to show up during our presentation in the morning.

Michael and I hadn't even talked about what this "thing" was going to look like – him making a pot and me singing original songs. So right before we went on we were still praying under our breath, and he looked at me and said, "You just start singing and I'll throw a pot." I replied, "Okay!" We went up and I started singing, and as the wheel began to turn, Michael began forming a piece of clay into a masterpiece. I began to see a thick white cloud hovering over the two hundred fifty ladies in attendance. I knew the Holy Spirit was in this place and we were standing on holy ground. I had chills all over me, and the Spirit of God began to speak to my heart. Something special was taking place, and God was working in the hearts of the ladies watching, and you could hear a pin drop. When my husband began to speak, I couldn't believe what I was hearing! Oh my! He was comfortable, knowledgeable, a natural speaker, and funny, too! He was speaking the words God gave him so eloquently that I couldn't believe my ears! Was this the reason I had endured such demonic attacks on me and on our marriage? Was this why the relentless assaults kept coming on us from the enemy trying to tear apart the very fabric of our being and our union? Had this all had happened to us because the very forces of Hell itself had tried to come against this actual moment I was now witnessing? Beyond a shadow of a doubt we were in the midst of a divine hour, and a ministry was being birthed.

What happened next shook me to the core. The Lord spoke these words resoundingly to my soul: "THIS is what I've created and prepared you two to do before the foundations of the earth!"

I knew it to be true! I couldn't have disobeyed that voice even if I had wanted to – it was that clear to me in a foundational part of my being. We were to walk in this call.

However, we weren't out of the woods yet...

Chapter 16

LEAP OF FAITH

All I knew at this point was that we would be in complete disobedience to the Lord if we forsook this call that He had placed on our lives! But convincing a man that had a particular view of what work should be and what it looked like was a whole other puppy. The Holy Spirit would have to show Michael that this is what we were created to do together. God is so creative and knows what will speak to the hearts of His people. How could we know that our ministry would be called Potter's Field Ministries, and that it would end up being a timeless, audio/visual experience for His people, "For A Time Such As This," that would endure over twenty-five years – and however much longer that He wants to use it?

For A Time Such As This
Written by Pam Rozell & Walt Harrah

A smell of desperation
It's in the air we breathe
This hopeless generation
O how they've been deceived

Unmoved – taking it all in stride
Tell me – shouldn't these eyes have cried?

CHORUS

For a time such as this
Could I shrink from the challenge?
There's a harvest that's ready to reap
I surrender my will
Marching forward with courage
For a time such as this

Though truth has been abandoned
And stumbled in the street
I'll go where You've commanded
Refusing all retreat
Send me – light to a darkened land
I'll be – part of the master plan

BRIDGE

SCRIPTURE READING:

Jesus went through all the towns and villages, teaching in their synagogues, preaching the good news of the kingdom, and healing every disease and sickness. When He saw the crowds, He had compassion on them, because they were harassed and helpless, like sheep without a shepherd. Then He said to His disciples, "The harvest is plentiful, but the workers are few. Ask the Lord of the harvest, therefore, to send out workers into His harvest field."

— Matthew 9:35-38

I will never forget a couple that we met one year at Calvary Chapel Costa Mesa after we had done PFM at their New Year's Eve service. They came up to us and proceeded to tell us their names were Mike and Pam! He was a professional potter, and she was a singer on the worship team for Joyful Life for Kay Smith. They were crying after our service and came up onstage to share something with us. They told us that the Lord had laid it on their hearts years before to do what they had just witnessed onstage – and they didn't heed the Lord's call! They were so broken over the missed opportunity and what God could have done with their lives. They had chosen the "safe route" for themselves and their family. There is one thing for sure, if you aren't obedient to what God has called you to do, He will certainly find someone else to do it!

We started doing little venues locally, with me doing concerts and Michael throwing pots in the middle section of the concert while I sang, and the impact was tremendous! As I would witness people staring at him making a pot on the wheel while I was singing, I was beginning to realize that the visual along with the audio had a greater impact than just one or the other onstage. I was no longer the one commanding center stage and holding the audience's attention – and I wasn't used to that – but I knew that two were better than one. The Bible even tells us that. The Lord was starting to build us into a team. It was also a great example of what a marriage working in tandem should look like, each complimenting the other like a well-choreographed dance. It wasn't easy for me because I was used to being the front person, but I was willing to die to that part of myself for the greater good. If I did this, I knew deep down that the message of Christ would be much more impactful.

It took yet another level of dying to my preconceived notions of what I had previously planned for my life. I would vacillate in the years to come over this decision, and have to fight my ego on a regular basis. I would struggle over wanting to go back into show business time and again, until I would totally surrender this part of myself on the altar and sacrifice it once and for all.

Our two devoted aunties who lived in Tustin, California, were faithful prayer warriors for us ever since we got married in 1987! Aunt Vernette Swanson is still faithfully praying for us, as was Aunt Lucy Higgins until she just recently went to be with the Lord. Aunt Lucy always prayed and had dreams for us that one day we would be able to do churches like Pastor Mike MacIntosh's church in San Diego. When Michael and I started touring, we would sit in parking lots listening endlessly to Pastor Mike's messages. We would be so inspired, and hoped we could at least meet him one day. We ended up doing Potter's Field at his church for many years, and I taught Christmas Teas for his wife, Sandy. We actually became friends with them and also have vacationed together! We were so glad that Aunt Lucy knew all of this before she passed away, and that her prayers were answered.

"So you are a Christian. If you actually walked out what the Bible said and stood on some convictions, then maybe I would actually take a look at your religion."

Michael had been threatening to take his old job back with the Wall Street firm that wanted him to take more territory. He had set up another job interview right after we did Potter's Field for the very first time. I knew that I had to act fast, so I called the Aunt's to start praying and to put us on their prayer chain. I also called everyone I knew to pray that he wouldn't take the job.

This was another time that the Holy Spirit spoke through me – it wasn't my nature to say something like this, and I remember thinking that I was being used as a conduit to speak to my husband. It actually felt like someone else had taken over my mouth, and the words were freely flowing off of my tongue – but they weren't my words. I found myself saying, "I love you more as a broke potter than I ever did as a regional marketing director working for a Wall Street firm." Michael lamented, "Oh Pam, don't say that!" I could tell it pierced his soul.

> *The preparations of the heart belong to man, but the answer of the tongue from the Lord.*
>
> — Proverbs 16:1 NKJV

He met with his old boss about a week later. He was serious about his walk with the Lord now, and he said he could now go into this workplace and lead these people to the Lord. He could make a boatload of money and give it away, and do it all better this time around. I knew that this was a recipe for disaster for him spiritually. And I knew we were supposed to do Potter's Field together. I also knew it would be just a matter of time before he would be pulled back into the old patterns of trying to please his boss.

When he was on calls, invariably the men he would be hanging out with would end up going to places that they shouldn't. One time Michael found himself in south Florida in a strip club with all the men he was working with, and he was so convicted that he called me that night and told me. I was really disappointed that he had made this choice, but I could hear in his voice he really didn't want to be there. I asked why he decided to go, because I had seen him growing in Christ, but he said he felt pressured to go and be a part of the group. He told his boss on the phone that Monday that he couldn't do this job because he was a Christian, and he couldn't find himself in places like this. His boss, who was an atheist said, "Is this part of your job description?" Michael answered, "No." He replied, "So you are a Christian, and the other guy you travel with is a Mormon. If you two actually walked out what the Bible said and stood on some convictions, then maybe I would actually take a look at your religion." Michael was so convicted after this happened that he started getting even more serious about his relationship with Jesus, walking the walk and not just talking the talk. Michael was a really quick study and could apply the scriptures and sermons to his life better than most godly people I'd ever known.

When he said that he could go back this time and be a witness, I had my doubts for even the strongest of believers. I was praying hard that he wouldn't take this job, that he would obey and take the risk, believing that God indeed had a call on our lives as He had so clearly shown us. I prayed that he would put the Bible to the test and take that leap of faith.

> But without faith it is impossible to please Him, for he who comes to God must believe that He is, and that He is a rewarder of those who diligently seek Him.
> — Hebrews 11:6 NKJV

When the day came for him to let his former boss know whether or not he was going to take the job, I asked him what he was going to do. He told me, "I don't even know why I'm doing this, but I'm not going to take my old job back." I was thrilled that the fervent prayers of many had been answered! *"...The effectual fervent prayer of a righteous man availeth much"* (James 5:16 KJV). Michael showed up to give his old boss his answer – in purple pants, his hair in a ponytail, and white boat shoes. His boss said, "Well I guess you've made your decision." Michael told with trepidation, "Yes, I have." His boss inquired, "Well what have you decided to do?" Michael said, "I may be crazy, but my wife and I are going to try this pottery thing while she sings. I don't even know what it looks like." He wished him luck.

He was going to need it.

Chapter 17

HUMBLE BEGINNINGS
Be Faithful in the Small Things

My friend Claire Cloninger had called me to sing her songs again while she was teaching a Women's Retreat at a large Baptist Church in Satsuma, Alabama. She also wanted Michael and me to do this new ministry that I had told her about, and she was really intrigued. We would be presenting Potter's Field after her teaching. While she was teaching, she would use her songs to illustrate and emphasize the stories she would tell. It was a very effective way to teach. This would be our next "official" service as a ministry apart from our own home church at the ladies retreat. We had three thousand dollars in unpaid bills as we were embarking on this journey, and Michael had no idea how we were going to pay for them. We both had abandoned our previous jobs, and we were going for broke.

We loaded up my Honda Civic with boxes full of cassettes and small pots in the trunk and we strapped and stacked his larger pots with bungie cords to the roof of the car. About twenty miles up the road, we heard a crash, boom, bang, and looking in the rear view mirror we saw the pots flying off the top of the car and disintegrating into dust on the freeway! We started laughing so hard, and it looked really cool seeing them just disappear into powder on the roadway. Well, at least we had some small pots and my music to sell for the upcoming weekend. We presented Potter's Field, and the Holy Spirit fell heavily on the women at Satsuma Baptist. At the conclusion of the service, women were crying and repenting on the altar. We were astounded. The pastor's wife, Carol, said, "You guys are staying to do all three of my husband's services tomorrow!" Michael asked, "Don't you have to ask him first?" She said, "No, I'm just telling him he has to have you guys!"

We met Pastor Wes and stayed to do all three services the next morning. It was so anointed, and there was a mighty move of the Holy Ghost. Afterwards, at the back table where we set up our pots and cassettes, we ended up selling everything that we brought! Michael was in awe. It was the very thing that he needed to see so he could know that the Lord was capable of providing for our needs – if we would just trust Him! He provided all the money we needed to pay our bills that month and some left over to get home and buy groceries!

The Lord showed us when we decided to do PFM that we wouldn't do our ministry the way the world, or the Christian "Industry," did things. We wouldn't get an agent, because God is the best agent there is, and we wouldn't let a record company take all of our profits, or have Christian bookstores eat up the profitable revenue on Michael's pottery. We had already done it the way the world did – me with agents and Michael a marketing wizard. The Lord wanted us to forsake the way of the world. And we also believed, "Where God Guides, God Provides" (see Matthew 10:7-10). Most Calvary Chapels believed that way and would just put "agape boxes" in the back of the sanctuary, not taking up a formal offering. Not all embraced this philosophy, but we believed it and wanted to see the Lord move in our midst with our finances. We were exhorted early on in our ministry by a pastor in Nevada not to set a fee for what we did, and to just trust God and allow Him to lay on the hearts of those we would minister to what to give us. Or sometimes, we would take up a "love offering" in the denominations where that might apply. We took his advice, and we are so glad we did. We have watched the Lord's hand of provision in such supernatural ways, and we still tour and do our ministry this way. The Lord has blown our minds in all aspects which we surrendered to him, and we would've sold ourselves short! And what we've been able to do is nothing short of miraculous because we did it this way!!

Of course there are some churches that have taken advantage of us through the years. Two in particular come to mind. One was a church that took up a love offering and told the congregation to "dig deep" into their pockets; that every dime was going to go to the Rozells. It was a large church, so we knew that the check we received from

> I had to ask the Lord to not let my heart become hard and my attitude bitter. I was witnessing in the church what happened in the world – and it was disheartening.

them wasn't a true accounting. Michael confronted one of the pastors about it, and when they called for us to come back in the next few years, we opted out. Another one was a Calvary Chapel who basically did the same thing, and they had about five hundred people in attendance. As we were leaving, he handed us a check for fifty dollars! Even if everyone had just given one dollar it would've been five hundred dollars. Michael confronted this pastor and he stated, "Well we needed to pay the nursery workers and others…" Michael challenged him, reminding him that's not what he told the congregation. We never were asked back, and we have since found out that this church folded. I had to ask the Lord to not let my heart become hard and my attitude bitter. I was witnessing in the church what happened in the world – and it was disheartening.

We decided early on, along with our Board of Directors, that the Ministry would own all our products for the life of the ministry, and instead we would be provided with a set salary. A lot of Christian artists don't do that. They live off the proceeds of the sales of their products, like CD's, pottery, t-shirts, and such. That way, we would live above reproach, and we could use all the resources God provided to pour back into our ministry, enabling us to do more ministry in the years to come, providing Potter's Field with longevity. Michael was also smart enough to know that our products would have a "shelf life." Since we revisited churches every other year, they would already have the most recent CD or vase that we offered. Michael wasn't emotionally tied to his art like most of us are, so he had a clearer business mind than most, and he could see through the haze of trying to gain fame from whatever gift God had given us. This was invaluable for me to watch and walk through, although hard, because I only knew of one way to do things – that was from a worldly viewpoint. Michael has taught me through the years to think outside of the box and how to be a better businesswoman, and a better steward of God's money. If more artists could do this, they would have longer careers without tying their egos to what they do. This is easier said than done, however.

We sold our little Toyota truck and bought a white Dodge Caravan so we could tour. This was the most we had ever spent on a vehicle in our married life together. Looking back, we should've gotten counsel on what type of vehicle we needed to pull little trailers without taxing our transmission.

Through a connection with a friend at church, Michael met Lisa Berberian and her father, Rudy, and they were doing "mold pottery" for different chain furniture stores such as Ethan Allen. They hired Michael to make pottery for them. This was wonderful on many levels. It provided Michael with much needed income after he turned down his old job. Plus, this was a great apprenticeship for Michael to learn how to mass-produce the pottery that he made so we could sell numerous pieces at our church events. Michael gained so much knowledge about how to throw his own pieces, and then send them off to a mold maker in California who could make as many molds as he wanted, pouring liquid slip clay into them so he could make hundreds of pieces a week. This education was invaluable for the future; we would need a high volume of pottery for our touring ministry that was to come. It was also fun to go to an Ethan Allen chain furniture store and see Michael's creations being sold in the secular sector. The Lord was preparing us for what was coming. Calvary Chapel Fort Lauderdale moved into a new church facility which had formerly been a warehouse, and they gave Michael a space to have a pottery studio to make pots for tour. They also loaned us the money for my second CD, which was quickly paid back after we did the PFM presentation at the church.

After our appearance in Alabama at Satsuma Baptist, Michael was approached by Assistant Pastor Gennarino DeStefano at our church. He challenged Michael, asking him if he had tithed on the money we made over the weekend. Gennarino asked, "You probably made some good money over the weekend, huh?" Michael told him, "Yes, and we made enough for our first van payment." That's when he asked the question about tithing. Michael skirted around the answer and implied that we needed the money to make our first van payment. He asked Michael, "Do you expect the Lord to bless PFM?" He said, "Yes, of course I do." Gennarino replied, "Don't. How can He trust you with this money if you can't give your firstfruits to Him?" Michael was so convicted that he went home, wrote the tithe check, and put it in the agape box in the back – knowing we couldn't pay our first van payment. I had booked a women's event to sing in Palm Beach, Florida, and I went and faithfully sang to about thirty-five women that week. At the end of the event, I literally walked out of that place selling six hundred fifty dollars worth of my CD's, and they blessed me with a generous love offering as well. We not only paid our first van payment but a lot of our other bills as well. The Lord was teaching us the basics about tithing where the Lord says to test Him in this area:

> *"Will a man rob God? Yet you have robbed Me! But you say, 'In what way have we robbed You?' In tithes and offerings. You are cursed with a curse, for you have robbed Me, even this whole nation. Bring all the tithes into the storehouse, that there may be food in My house, and try Me now in this," says the Lord of hosts, "If I will not open for you the windows of heaven and pour out for you such blessing that there will not be room enough to receive it...."*
>
> — Malachi 3:8-10 NKJV

When I arrived home, the answering machine had three churches that had booked us just through word of mouth! God had blessed our socks off because Michael was obedient to tithe to Him the firstfruits! He has never missed another opportunity to tithe, and we've never been able to out-give God for twenty-five years!

A Jewish believer named Pam Graf went to our church and she worked at a local bar. She used this job to evangelize people, knowing she had their undivided attention, wanting to give them hope in knowing that there was much more to life than drowning their sorrows. She would always invite them to church. She met a talented artist, a world-famous linear expressionist named Jean-Claude Gaugy, and he was intrigued with this Jesus she would always talk about. Pam knew that we were presenting Potter's Field at the church on an upcoming weekend, so she asked him to come and see another artist at her church, a potter, and his wife, a singer. After the presentation he was blown away, and so moved that he bought all of my CD's – and he wanted to meet Michael. They made plans to spend time together the next day and meet at Michael's studio at the church. When they met, he told Michael that he had stayed up all night listening to my music and creating and art piece of the two of us, and wanted to show it to us. Michael ministered to Gaugy for hours and led him to the Lord right then and there.

We became quick friends. Gaugy was in church every time there was a service, and he sat in the front row with us and drank in God's Word. We went to see the painting that he did of us and it was amazing! It was Michael pouring the "red blood" food coloring over a vase and me singing with a microphone in front of me, and a Bible opened with the Holy Spirit dove in between us. It hangs in a place of prominence in our home today. We had beautiful posters and t-shirts made with the image on them too, and we sold those for a season along with our other wares. Gaugy blessed us over the years with many of his beautiful masterpieces, which we still have, and he also created the magnificent mural of Jesus that we unveil behind us at the close of every Potter's Field presentation.

It was a tremendous blessing that God used Gaugy to help heal and reach my dad. I attribute his boldness in explaining the true forgiveness of Christ to my father in a way only another soldier could understand and convey. My husband had explained it first to Gaugy through a great word picture the Lord gave him right before leading him to the Lord. Gaugy had a lot of guilt regarding the killing he had to do during wartime, which is why he could relate to my dad. Gaugy didn't think the Lord could forgive him of all he had done in the war. The Lord gave Michael a question to ask Gaugy. "Did you kill ten thousand people during the war, Gaugy?" He exclaimed, "No! I didn't kill ten thousand!" Michael said, "Well it says in the Bible that Paul had the blood of at least ten thousand Christians on his hands before his conversion. And he ended up writing half of the New Testament!" Gaugy asked, "So I'm forgiven? I'm really forgiven?" Michael said, "Yes! Truly forgiven, and your sins forgotten. The Bible says as far as the east is from west!" It finally dawned on Gaugy – the far-reaching love and forgiveness of our Heavenly Father. The Lord in turn used Gaugy to minister to my dad about his wartime and war stories. My dad would never talk about his experiences while in the Korean War or World War II. He had received a purple heart and commendations during his Marine Corps days, so we knew that he had seen atrocities that were never spoken of, and was in dire need to vent to someone who understood. After Gaugy used the word picture with my father that Michael had used, he truly understood God's grace and forgiveness in a deep place for the very first time. It wasn't long after that conversation took place that my dad was standing at the altar during that Christmas Eve service I've mentioned in a previous chapter, rededicating his life to Jesus and serving Him until his death in 2003.

> No one had ever seen anything like what we were doing to share the gospel.

I booked our first tour for us in North and South Carolina in some churches where I used to do my own concerts before becoming "Potter's Field Ministries." The Lord was moving in these little country churches, and also some very large Baptist venues. No one had ever seen anything like what we were doing to share the gospel. Word was spreading from pastor to pastor that they needed to book this "different ministry" that wasn't the typical concert ministry so popular in the eighties and nineties. We actually had a true audio/visual message, and people were getting saved!

We met some characters along the way. We met a "vocational pastor" that pastored two separate churches within two miles of each other. He told us about the good "gig" he had. He had a large antebellum parsonage where he and his wife lived. He would do two services on Sunday morning; one service at one church, and then he would drive over to the other church and do the other one. Michael asked him why didn't he just combine the two services into one and just meet in one venue. The pastor told us, "Oh there was a church split years ago, and some of the people bought a building down the street and started meeting there. They don't like each other, so I do two services every Sunday." Michael wondered, "What are they going to do when they get to Heaven?"

It was amazing to see God work through this new ministry, and people at our church were getting excited about how God was using us too. We had a couple loan us their makeshift open trailer – made out of a cut-off truck bed – which we could tow. We knew that eventually we needed a legitimate, enclosed trailer that could be locked to haul the mural, potter's wheel, pots, and CD's in, so we started praying for one.

One time, our pastor asked us if we would do Potter's Field at someone's house where he did a weekly Bible study one week because he couldn't make it. We were kind of intrigued, because doing our ministry could be quite messy because of the clay. He assured us that they would cover all of the furniture. We loaded up everything and went to a lovely home on the intercoastal waterway. When we drove up, Michael said, "Oh my gosh, there's Matt Nokes, there's Randy Velarde…and Steve Howe!" I didn't know who any of these people were except Steve. I wasn't much of a sports buff. Michael was telling me that we had been asked to do a Bible study for the New York Yankees! They were all there with their wives because spring training was held in Fort Lauderdale.

We set up everything just like we did at churches, and they had a sound system already set up – so we did Potter's Field in a large living room. The Spirit fell on this place, and at the end, Michael felt the Lord leading him to give an altar call. He told me that he was fighting doing it all night because it felt weird in such a small setting…and they were the New York Yankees! He was obedient, however, and gave the call, and everyone came forward and they were on their knees crying! Some even gave their lives to the Lord that night! We were amazed! Before we left, after doing a lot of one-on-one ministering, one of the guys came up with a folded check and thanked us for coming. We got in the car, and on our way home I opened the check – and it was for three thousand dollars. This was the exact price for a new trailer to pull behind our van. We bought it the next week! This was the beginning of a move of God in this ball club over the next few years, and we were blessed to be a part of it. We were flown up to New York each year during home games to do Potter's Field for the next three years. It was truly a blessing to minister to these guys and their wives during the beginning of the growth of our ministry.

Once when we were ministering at a small Baptist Church while on tour in Proctorville, Ohio, we dropped our transmission on the way to the event. The minivan was not designed to pull the kind of weight we were pulling in that little trailer. It was really just a passenger van with no capacity for towing. We didn't realize its limitations, and it wasn't an issue at the time we bought it because we weren't towing anything then. It was going to cost a lot of money to fix it, and these were the days when we were trusting God like never before. We took "give us this day our daily bread" literally. We didn't have any extra money to have the transmission fixed, and the Lord did not release Michael to let this congregation know what had happened. We prayed, and the pastor picked us up for the service that evening.

After the service, a woman came to the back table to purchase a mug and a cassette and told me that she had never been as blessed as she had been tonight at our service. She said she would never be the same again after witnessing our ministry, and she handed me a folded check, asking me not to look at it until she left. When she departed I opened up the check and it was for two thousand dollars! I started crying, and knew our Lord had heard our cries, and we didn't need to tell our needs to anyone but Him. He is indeed our Jehovah Jireh: "Our Lord and Provider!" It paid for the entire replacing of the transmission and got us to our next church destination.

Back when we were on the side of the road, Michael had called his pastor to let him know that we had dropped our transmission. He said, "I'm sorry Michael. We are praying for you brother." Michael was so mad that our church didn't care about us stranded out on the side of the road. But after this lady had handed us a check, he called him back with the praise report. He told Michael, "I wasn't worried Michael. We know that the Lord is in your ministry, He just wants you to know that He is in your ministry!"

Not too long after this, and after losing another transmission in the minivan, we knew we needed a new vehicle that could handle towing a lot more weight. These are things we learned as we went. Michael wanted to look for a large Ford 350 fifteen-passenger van. He had done some research and we found a beautiful two-tone, dark green van that we wanted to purchase. Once again, we started praying. We were able to buy this van after a church in Michigan took up a love offering. The pastor told his congregation to dig deep like they never have before, that this couple had blessed their church so much that they now needed to be a blessing to them. They proceeded to take up a love offering that took care of the sixteen thousand dollar purchase!

Not too long after we got the white trailer that held the PFM contents, a famous airbrush painter came up and introduced himself to us at our home church and offered to do a mural on each side of it to match our new green, fifteen-passenger van. Michael had heard of this guy, and he painted both sides that truly depicted what God had put together. It was a beautiful work of art. We were starting to look like an actual, viable ministry.

We had a few assistants in the beginning that tried to do their best, but sometimes we would be out on the road doing a church in one area in the Midwest, and when we would pull out our instructions to reach our next destination for the evening service we would discover we had a drive of over one hundred fifty miles. When we would question the reasoning for this, the assistant would innocently say, "It was only an inch on the map!"

It took a while to work out the kinks of traveling and touring, and motels that would have roaches in them because it was all we could afford. We would also sometimes stay with host families. These are usually the people in churches that have the gift of hospitality who would offer you a room in their home – and didn't care if you brought your dog too. Once we stayed at a home in Colorado where the mattress was so broken down that we would both sink deep down into the middle of it; it was so uncomfortable that we couldn't sleep. Laying in the crevasse of the bed, Michael looked at me and said, "I feel like a loser." I assured him he wasn't. But I knew how he felt. We were both used to five-star hotels, caviar and champagne, and now we were staying in basements or in the kids' room in a racecar bed with plastic still on it. (I told him once that at least he got the Ferrari he dreamed of!)

This season didn't last too long, and it got harder to stay with people because I needed privacy. I rejuvenate away from people, but Michael is the exact opposite! We would usually get to the homes late at night after driving all day long, and the sweet people would want to talk and know our story. I got to where I would politely excuse myself and go to bed, and I would have Michael take over in the talking department. Many of the couples we stayed with are still friends today. One couple in particular, Pastor Steve and Jan Miller, and their daughter, Rheanna Miller Taylor, who used to live in Chicago, now live here and work for our ministry! Another couple we still keep in touch with is Pastor Steve and Kathryn Jones, who now have a ministry to kids in Africa. But these humble beginnings are what keep us grounded today in what the Lord is doing globally. We never lose sight of the awe and wonder of what God has done, and is doing, to this very day.

Once we were traveling on Highway 70 near Aspen, Colorado. The mountain passes are steep and go on winding around the majestic Rocky Mountains for miles, and there aren't a lot of gas stations around. I would always try to get Michael to gas up our van when it got below the halfway mark because that is what my dad taught me to do as a teenager. It would always frighten me when Michael would push the envelope and not fill up when we got low on gasoline. I would say to him, "We are going to get stranded out on one of these highways one night, and I will be alone in the car with the dog while you find a station." It was one of my biggest fears. Sure enough, when we were ministering in the Aspen area one night, I had the discussion before we left and I was met with resistance. I started praying because I knew that we would use more gas going up and down the hills. So when the needle was on empty I was panicked, and there was no gas station advertised for miles. Michael started getting nervous as well. It was winter and freezing, and we could literally be stranded on the highway overnight. I was praying out loud that a station would be around the corner. We actually drove for fifty miles completely on empty! I had heard stories such as this over the years, but we are eyewitness testimonies that we drove on the wings of eagles – because it certainly wasn't on gas! Right before we lost all hope, there was one gas station with one light on! Just as we pulled in, that light went off as they closed for the night. Michael ran to the window and pleaded for him to reopen so we could get to where we were staying. The nice man opened up and we filled up our tank. Needless to say, Michael never let the gas get low again during our entire ministry life.

The spiritual warfare was tangible! We ended up having three blowouts in one day!

We were traveling in scorching heat during the summer near Richfield, Utah, and at this time we had purchased a thirty-four-foot Jayco travel trailer to tow behind our vehicle, and we had graduated to a Ford 350 truck to tow it. All of a sudden we had a blow out on our back left tire on the Jayco. This was the second flat tire of the day. The spiritual warfare was tangible! We ended up having three blowouts in one day! Neither Michael nor I are really good with cars, but he did know how to change a tire. He got the jack out to lift the trailer, and the asphalt was so hot that the jack sunk a foot down into it! We didn't know if we were going to be able to change the tire. We both would get so anxiety ridden when anything went wrong with our vehicles. So to keep my eyes on Jesus in an almost impossible situation, I started singing the chorus of a song by Twila Paris that would comfort me in times of trouble. I was walking around the trailer on the side of the road, while cars and semi trucks were whizzing by, and I sang:

You can see my heart,
You can read my mind
And You got to know I would rather die
Than to lose my faith in the One I love
Do I trust You, Lord?
Do I trust You?

As I circled back around, I met Michael halfway and I heard him humming a song, and he was singing the exact same words of the chorus, at the very same time we were singing together:

I will trust You, Lord, when I don't know why
I will trust You, Lord, till the day I die
I will trust You Lord, when I'm blind with pain
You were God before and You'll never change
I will trust You, I will trust You…

We were going to trust the Lord, but at times it would be a very hard journey.

It was a blessing, and sometimes amusing, to watch my husband while he was preaching to be full of passion, exhorting people in the Word, running on the prayer benches in the front of the church where the vestries in Methodist churches were kept, and I knew they'd never seen anyone like him – or allowed anyone like him to share in their sanctuaries ever before. And he was sporting a ponytail while doing it to boot! I watched as he would give an invitation at the end of the service while every head was bowed, and there were times when he asked for people to raise their hands if it was the first time they had accepted Christ – and we would see the Pastor's hand go up!

We went to a church once where I felt resistance the minute we drove onto the property. An assistant pastor met us at the front, and when Michael got out of the car, his hair tied back in a ponytail, I could feel the consternation pouring from this guy. He said they were supposed to have a potter teaching there tonight, along with his wife. Michael told him he was the guy. The man's face said it all. He said, "Wait right here." He went and got the senior pastor. No one helped us to unload, set up the back table, or the stage. It was just Michael and me. It was often that way for the first few years of our ministry. I think we were such an anomaly when we started that we confounded most churches and their pastors. When Michael talked to the senior pastor for a while, he decided we were "okay folks" and allowed us to share with his congregation that evening. When he introduced us, he made some joke about Michael's hair and him being barefoot in the pulpit, and for the congregants to accept us. As we began to share, the Spirit started doing His work in the hearts of the people that were in attendance, and the altar call was beyond anything they had ever experienced in this church! As we started packing up everything to go, we had so much help that we did it in record time. They had been so convicted that they judged us as soon as we pulled up, they were over the top as we departed. They called soon after to book us for the next year. When we arrived the next year to minister, we were all met with something that was so funny. When we pulled into the church, there was a team of men ready and waiting to help us – and each one of them was wearing a baseball cap with a long ponytail attached to it! I had to break the bad news that Michael had cut his hair. They were so disappointed.

We had a visiting speaker at our church, Gayle Erwin, who is a storyteller and unique in his teaching style. It was the first time that Michael knew God could use "different" types of people to teach His Word. He's a jovial, heavier-set older man who wears suspenders and makes the Bible come alive. We got to know him and his lovely wife, Ada. God used Gayle to challenge Michael. He said, "So the Lord has you guys teaching in a lot of denominational churches?" Michael said proudly, "Yes!" He asked, "What do they think about your hair?" Michael replied, "Well at first, they don't like it." Gayle retorted, "Why would you keep it if it would make one person not listen to God's Word? The Bible says to be all things to all people. So if you're in an area where you know they are stumbled by such things, why not cut your hair?" Michael thought about what Gayle had said for a few days, then one day he came into the house with a cut ponytail in his hand – he was clean cut with short hair once again. I actually kept his ponytail because he has such beautiful hair – even today he has the best head of "man hair" I've ever seen! He was so honored that Gayle took an interest in him and our ministry that he climbed up on the high shelves in his studio to retrieve a pot to give him, then lost his footing and fell backwards onto his ankle and broke it! Gayle was mortified, but loved the vase. So when you see the first poster that Gaugy has made of the painting he did of Michael and me, he drew his foot three times larger than it really was.

We were meeting pastors all over that wondered what Michael's theological background was, and we discussed that it would be great for him to have more schooling. We also thought it would also be great if he could work towards becoming an ordained pastor. When we returned home from this particular tour, he met with our pastor and asked how he could get ordained, since it would help pave the way to open unending doors in the denominational churches. God was flinging doors open for Potter's Field Ministries, and if ordination would help open even more doors, we wanted all God had to offer us. Unknown to us, the pastor had already gone to his pastoral staff to take a vote to ordain Michael. Some of the guys were hesitant to move in this direction with him, but our pastor told them that he was teaching more than they were in pulpits every week across America with his wife. He was going to leave the room, and when he returned, he wanted them to have made the right decision. He felt confidence from the Lord that Michael would indeed rise to the calling that ordination brought.

Michael was ordained in 1993, and he has indeed risen to the call and beyond. As a pastoral staff, a plan was put together to take Michael through Bible College studies and to be held accountable to go through Chuck Smith's *Five Thousand* series. He was growing in leaps and bounds, and I was scrambling to keep up with him.

The promise the Lord had given me earlier in our marriage while in the midst of our hardest struggles was now coming to pass.

Pam and Leona.

Pam and her first pony – "Spring."

Michael (on the left) in the galley on
the private airline Regent Air.

"Marathon Mike" throwing twenty-eight hours
for Hudson Adult School.

Michael hot-dogging on skis.

42nd Street Cast.

Miss Georgia 1977-78.

Competing in the Miss America Pageant.

Official Miss Georgia Headshot –
18 years old.

Granddaddy and Grandmother Bennett
("Slim" and Ida Pearl).

42nd Street Brochure – Pam in front bottom left on dime.

"The Girlfriends" at Cristal's and
Jimmy Z's in Monte-Carlo.

Pam as 42nd Street Lead as "Dorothy Brock."

Our Wedding Night – Dinner at Bally's Las Vegas.

Michael making pots at "The Clay Pen"
in Santa Monica, California.

The Aunties – Lucille Higgins and Esther Vernette Swanson, and Michael's mom Roberta.

9/28 11:15 pm

GOD LOVES YOU! AND SO DO I! —

HAPPY BIRTHDAY! MRS ROZELL 😊
___

P.S. I GOT SAVED TONIGHT.

Michael's letter to me on the day he got saved – two days after eloping.

Our formal wedding day photo in Thomasville, GA – one year after eloping.

Below: Wedding Party: Cayla Miller, Melinda Phelps, Patricia Souders, Deborah Balfour; Steven Rozell, Kevin Hanks, Greg Souders, Teresa Lee. (niece – Christa Souders: flower girl).

Bottom Left: Pam's Daddy walking her down the aisle as Tom Faircloth and Fred Allen look on.

Bottom Right: Pam's Christian Concert Poster.

PAM ROZELL
In Concert

JOIN US FOR AN INSPIRATIONAL EVENING OF CHRISTIAN MUSIC AND WORSHIP

DATE:
TIME:
LOCATION:

First time ever presenting "Potter's Field Ministries" at the
Calvary Chapel Fort Lauderdale's Women's Retreat – June 1992.

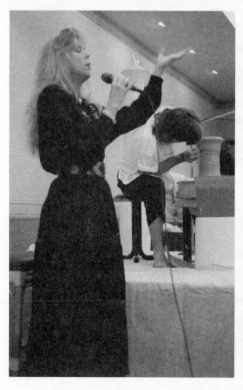

Michael and Pam – photo taken on Pam's last "world cruise."

Michael at an outdoor event – early years.

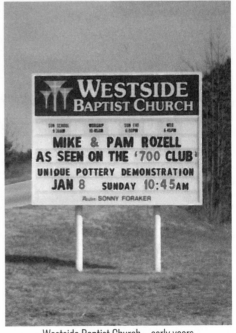

Westside Baptist Church – early years.

One of our first God Pots.

Gaugy painting of Michael and Pam.

Michael teaching how God can make us into another vessel seeming better to Him.

Pam walking with precious girls -
"Lazarus" is over Pam's left shoulder.

Michael and Pam's first mission trip to Honduras –
island where they exiled the sick.

Pam's brother and sister-in-law, Greg and
Patricia Souders (with Pam's niece, Alyssa).

Steve and Betty Looney with Michael and Pam.

Our friends: Steve and Cindy Howe with Chelsi and Brian. (Photos used by permission.)

OPPOSITE PAGE

Top: Calvary Chapel Fort Lauderdale, Florida.

Center: Calvary Chapel Melbourne, Florida.

Botton Left: Calvary Chapel High Desert, California.

Botton Right: Calvary Chapel Vista, California.

THIS PAGE

Top: Calvary Chapel Melbourne, Florida.

Center: Saddleback Church, California.

Bottom: Calvary Chapel Tallahassee, Florida.

THIS PAGE

Top: Michael teaching at Calvary Chapel Delaware County in Pennsylvania.

Center: Calvary Chapel Miami Beach, Florida.

Bottom: Water of Life, Fontana, California.

OPPOSITE PAGE

Top: The Rock Church, San Diego, California.

Center: Outdoor event at Calvary Chapel Delaware County, Pennsylvania.

Bottom Left: Our loyal assistant, Joanna Chung.

Bottom Right: Mark Smith and Joanna signing up sponsors for Potter's Field Kids Programs.

Top: Michael and Pam with Pastor Chuck Smith after PFM presentation at Calvary Chapel Costa Mesa.

Right: Pam and her pastor, Pastor Chuck Smith, singing "O Holy Night" at CCCM.

Bottom: Pam with mentor Kay Smith.

Above Left: Our first teaching facility in Olney, MT – Potter's Field Ranch. **Above Right:** Our first two ordained pastors that went through IGNITE and now full-time staff; Austin Hiatt and Jordan Cole. **Lower Left:** Our church: Selah Fellowship in Whitefish, MT. **Lower Right:** Don McClure teaching our IGNITE students at our PFM Mission Training School.

Above Left: Headquarters in Antigua, Guatemala. **Above Right:** IGNITE students taking patients from the hospital for a walk. **Lower Left:** Potter's Field Center in Guatemala. **Lower Right:** Our PFK children on our soccer field at the Center.

Potter's Field Kids Programs in Uganda, Kenya, Costa Rica, El Salvador, Guatemala, and Blackfeet Reservation in Browning, Montana.

Potter's Field Kids Programs in Guatemala, Cambodia, Uganda, and Democratic Republic of Congo.

Top Left: Construction on MudMan in Columbia Falls, Montana, was completed (former A & W).

Top Right: Our fresh fries were voted the Best in the Valley too!

Right: Drive-through kiosk in Whitefish, MT: first location.

Bottom Right: Some of our stellar staff that also serves at MudMan.

MudMan was voter #1 Burger in the Flathead Valley for 2017! (Burger photo by Marianne Wiest.)

Our MudMan Food Truck is a big hit everywhere it goes!

THE BEST OF FOOD AND DRINK

Best burger

MudMan

MUDMAN IN Columbia Falls has claimed the coveted prize for Best Locally Made Burger in the Flathead. MudMan also won first for Best Locally Made French Fries. The restaurant is staffed by interns at Potter's Field Ministries, based in Whitefish. MudMan began with a coffee kiosk that operates in Happy Valley. Proceeds from burger and coffee sales are used to fund mission work both internationally and on the Blackfeet Reservation in Browning. (Brenda Ahearn/Daily Inter Lake)

The Pam Rozell record collection (available on iTunes and Apple Music).

Chapter 18

THE 700 CLUB

It is such a stress reliever to leave the outcome of what happens in your life in the hands of an omniscient God. When I was in show business, I was always auditioning for jobs and working hard at staying in shape, taking dance, voice, and acting classes, and always looking the part. It was exhausting and time consuming. What a joy it is not having that pressure anymore.

This was God's ministry, and we always said from the beginning that no man's fingerprints were going to be on it – especially our own! We never wanted the taint of "the world" on this ministry. The Lord let me get all of that showy feeding-the-flesh stuff out of the way early on in my life. Now I can discern the difference between the real and the counterfeit. The counterfeit takes too much time, energy, and money to maintain. When God is directing things, you don't have to strive. You just get to strap in and go along for the rollercoaster ride and enjoy the journey when God is in control.

The Word of God is alive and still as powerful today as ever. We love simply teaching the Word and sharing our testimony and allowing the Word to "cut like a double-edged sword, separating bone and marrow."

For the word of God is alive and active. Sharper than any double-edged sword, it penetrates even to dividing soul and spirit, joints and marrow; it judges the thoughts and attitudes of the heart.

— Hebrews 4:12

Over the years, I've had to navigate through separating my idol – being the center of attention while performing on the stage in shows and productions – with presenting our ministry on stages across the country. God uses anything and everything, as evidenced by our unique ministry. I've had to really dive into "dying to self" in this area of my life, especially early on in the ministry. When you read chapter twenty-five, "Slaying My Isaac," I will walk you through what I had to endure, which eventually led to victory in dying to my flesh.

Michael tells me that he can never own a Porsche again, because as soon as he starts revving up one of these high-performance machines, all the sights, sounds, and smells of a mid-engine 911 Targa come back all at once, and he's transported back to his "heathen" days. We always chuckle that for him: Pastor and Porsche – "Ne'er the twain shall meet." I can totally relate to that. When we go to some of our favorite megachurches, they have beautiful stages. I'm in a "sanctuary" that seats three thousand people, and the dry ice starts to blow smoke (which I'm allergic to) and the "robotic" intelligent laser lights start to flash patterns on the backdrop, and I look up and see my face on a gigantic screen with my nostrils as big as my head, and I am suddenly transported back to the day where the Broadway stage fed my flesh. It's not the church's fault – it's the way some people do church, and some of our favorite churches use these – the real problem was my flesh, and it stumbled me early on. And the Lord had to eradicate that part of myself.

We are believers in accountability. It is so easy to get even just a little off course without it. We are all made of the same thing – clay – so we all have the capability of being self-deceived. Far too often we have witnessed ministries which, having started out humbly, begin to change as they start to experience growth. Something alters the vision or mindset, and next thing you know they are preaching like a televangelist with the timbre, swell, and cadence of a snake-charming Southern preacher, revving up emotions to a fever pitch for the claptrap of applause that will come. These how-to's of audience manipulation are things I learned through show business while performing on the cruise lines. These are the things I walked away from when I came back to the Lord.

In a similar fashion, there is a fine line with using social media. It is useful for promoting our events, what God is doing, and our resources – but it becomes a snare when it all turns into self-promotion. At Potter's Field, we are ever mindful of maintaining that "happy medium" when it comes to social media and maintaining accountability. Our media department watches trends to measure when it is "just too much." We don't want to be among those who shamelessly and blatantly plug merchandise, or "merch," or tout their latest and greatest book, whose true goal seems to be to make a name for themselves. We know the greatest book is the Bible! As Christians, we have to be so careful not to start looking like the world. We are to be in the world, but not of this world.

> *If the world hates you, you know that it hated Me before it hated you. If you were of the world, the world would love its own. Yet because you are not of the world, but I chose you out of the world, therefore the world hates you.*
> — John 15:18-19 NKJV

And do not be conformed to this world, but be transformed by the renewing of your mind, that you may prove what is that good and acceptable and perfect will of God.
— Romans 12:2 NKJV

In Hebrews 13:8, the Bible says that Jesus is the same yesterday, today, and forever. We just need to proclaim His Word and allow the Holy Spirit to do the job that He was left here on earth to do. I have to be careful here, because I do think that social media is a great way to get anointed books and sermons into the hands of the people that God wants to touch. I'm not saying that we shouldn't use the tools of the day to get the gospel out to more people. I'm all for that. And social media can be a great tool in today's world. What I'm saying is this: We, as Christians, need to be mindful not to emulate the world. The world seeks to promote itself. We must seek to promote Jesus. And when He does something amazing through us, the glory belongs to Him! When the Potter makes a beautiful vessel, who deserves the praise – the vessel, or the Potter who made it? It is extremely seductive, and it's something that I struggled with for the first half of my ministry life. I was constantly being tugged at, pulled away, and sometimes swayed by the enemy with the lure of the world always knocking at my back door. It almost derailed me at times. I have actually wanted to leave the ministry on numerous occasions and go back into the

What are the odds of finding a half-torn brochure in the parking lot of *The 700 Club* and having the producer book us over the phone right then and there?

secular world and do another show. I wanted to feed my flesh. This ministry "thing" didn't give me the "zing" that a standing ovation did. The battle is real. Idols are subtle. We are to proclaim Jesus' fame and not our own. We are to worship Him alone. We are tools in the Potter's hands to lead others to a real and living God who has a purpose and a plan for their lives.

I admired Pastor Chuck Smith's constancy, steadfastness, and commitment to the purity, reverence, and holiness of God's Word. I love it so much that he didn't change with the fads or trends of this world and just taught the Bible, sticking to verse-by-verse, chapter-by-chapter expository teaching all through the years, right up until his death in 2013. And the fruit he left behind is undeniable!

God was Potter's Field Ministries agent! We weren't going to let the "Christian agencies" or record companies make a buck off of us to get us booked. God could do it better than any of them – and He did! I must admit, it was on Michael's bidding that we didn't sign with a large recording label for my music. I knew of only one way to get my product out there, and that was through a company with a large distribution and marketing arm. We signed my music temporarily with Calvary Music (which is no longer in business). Michael is a savvy business man first, and an artist second. And I, being an artist and performer since the age of eighteen, kicked against the goad thinking my husband was holding me back. In reality, he was protecting me, our product, our rights to my songs, and his pottery, and we were the ones able to receive the profits from our non-profit work, which went right back into our ministry to pay our salary and fund the continued work of Potter's Field. I attribute the longevity of our ministry and the acquisitions of properties and assets – which further what God has called us to do – to Michael. He has been a good steward of God's resources, obedient and vigilant to hold fast to his convictions in order to keep our ministry sacred without the stain of the world, or anyone but God Himself getting the glory.

One time, we got a call from our assistant telling us that the producer of *The 700 Club* had contacted us and wanted to book us on the show. We started laughing, thinking she was trying to pull our leg. She assured us that she wasn't kidding. Jay Edgerton, an award winning producer and director who did three thirty-minute specials a year, had called and wanted us to be the third featured special for the year. So we called him back. He told us that he was walking to his car after work one rainy day and saw a crumpled up, black-and-white, partially-torn brochure in the parking lot which we had just had printed about our ministry. From what was left of it that he could read, he said it sounded really intriguing, and that a potter and a singer would make for great television. He proceeded to ask the particulars about what we did, and if he could book a date for us to come to Virginia Beach, Virginia, to film a special of Potter's Field for *The 700 Club*. We couldn't believe our ears! God did this! What are the odds of finding a half-torn brochure in the parking lot of *The 700 Club* and having the producer book us over the phone right then and there?

We drove to Virginia Beach and pulled into the complex where we saw a beautiful hotel, The Founders Inn, where we would be staying over the next few days. The day before we were supposed to film the special, the "God Pot," which we unveil at the end of our presentation, broke into numerous pieces – and we didn't have another one to replace it! Michael was mortified. He went to the store and bought Elmer's Glue, and started putting back together this large, white vase that we traveled with back then, piece by piece. It took hours to do it, and he wasn't even sure if it would hold together. The enemy was all over us trying to keep us from doing this special.

Michael was always so nervous doing any television or radio spots. I reassured him that God was going to use this mightily, and he could do this. He wasn't used to "hitting his mark" so a camera angle got the best shot. We had to do quite a few takes, and Michael was getting increasingly frustrated having to be in a small space and virtually choreographed, him being such a free spirit. We finally got the show in the can, and it turned out surprisingly well! When we unveiled the "God Pot" you couldn't even tell that it had been broken at all! They did close-ups of it from top to bottom; miraculously, you couldn't see a crack.

When the special aired, it was one of their highest-viewed shows to date. They decided to show it again at Christmas. They showed it again the next year, and later that same year it was translated into twenty languages and aired in countries around the world! We were told that twenty-eight million people had seen it! They put on the screen how people could contact our ministry to book us at their churches. The phone started ringing and we were off and running, doing every denomination across the board. God, our cosmic agent, was leading and guiding us where He wanted us to go.

We were invited two more times to be on *The 700 Club*. The co-host, Terry Meeuwsen, was crowned Miss America 1973, so she and I had a lot in common. She interviewed us on the show and went in-depth about our ministry, and she and I talked on air about being in the Miss America Pageant. She's a delightful woman who loves the Lord with all her heart. Every time we were on the show they would allow Michael to throw a pot and me to sing. And of course, they would put all of our booking information out there for God to do with it as He saw fit.

The next time, we were asked to be a part of their Operation Blessing program which feeds the poor in America. We were on the bill with Mr. T, a former, retired wrestler known for his roles in the film *Rocky III* and the 1980s television show *The A-Team*. He wears gaudy gold jewelry around his neck and on his wrists, inspired by a picture of an African warrior from when he was younger. He sports a Mohawk, and coined the catch phrase, "I pity the fool." We were also with Billy "White Shoes" Johnson, who played for the Houston Oilers, Atlanta Falcons, and the Washington Redskins.

The 700 Club took us around to different Junior and Senior High Schools. Mr. T would bring his suitcase full of jewelry, and putting it on right before his appearance, then get into character. When he would enter the school gym where hundreds of kids would be surprised and elated by his appearance, their deafening screams could probably be heard into the next county. He talked to these kids, demanding respect, and spoke to them about Jesus. He teased Michael and me the entire trip about being lovebirds, and he and Michael loved eating ice cream together before every meal we ate. We went to areas that needed food, and cameras were rolling the whole time we were there. It definitely opened up Michael's eyes to the needs of the hungry and poor.

This was a stone in his walk with the Lord that started shaping the things to come.

Chapter 19

THE LOONEYS

World Vision approached us again. We received a call from Tom Jackson, who headed up the Artist Associate Program with World Vision; he had not given up on me to sponsor children. It had been a couple of years, and a lot had transpired in our ministry since we last spoke. I told him what God had done in Michael and me, combining our gifts and building a ministry together as a team. I asked if he would be interested in signing Potter's Field Ministries to sponsor kids. Michael spoke with him, and Tom booked a flight to come and see our presentation at our next venue.

Tom loved what God did through us. He'd never seen anything like it. By the tears in his eyes he was obviously moved. He said it was powerful, and he wouldn't change a thing because God's hand was all over it. To this day, Tom is still one of our biggest fans. We decided to sign as Artists with World Vision to start helping children in third world countries. A stone that was erected in my heart at fourteen years old was coming to pass. When Tom first approached me in 1990 at the LA Music Festival and Michael put a damper on ever doing it, I thought that desire would never resurrect. I just had to wait for God's perfect timing for this promise of working with children to evolve.

We had some churches to visit up in the Ohio area, and we decided to visit my brother, Greg, and his family that lived in South Point, Ohio. He was a youth pastor at an Independent Baptist Church. (Today he's a senior pastor at a church in Thomasville and a critical-care paramedic.) Churches in this area tend to be "religious," and some quite legalistic. We drove up to his church and Greg was playing basketball with some of the youths wearing a dress shirt with a tie, and wing-tipped shoes. Confused by his attire, Michael inquired how he could be relatable with this generation, playing basketball dressed like he was. Greg agreed, explaining that his pastor had rules and regulations that he had to adhere to. This was the first time Michael had ever experienced anything like this at a church. I had grown up seeing it in different pockets down in the South. He also told us that he was really sorry, that he tried to get us booked at his church but the pastor wouldn't allow us in the pulpit with him barefoot and with a ponytail, and the tracks for my songs had drums, which weren't allowed. Michael said, "No problem, that's not why we came. We came to visit you, Patricia, and the kids. And we already have a couple of churches to do near you."

Some of the congregation members that attended Greg's church came to see our ministry, and were captivated by it. They were determined to get us at South Point Baptist. A couple of them were elders of the church, and they confronted the pastor, telling him it was a viable, anointed ministry. Reluctantly, he allowed us to do it

> I was sitting there thinking to myself that these guys were such hypocrites. They were the type of religious leaders that Jesus always got mad at.

upstairs in the fellowship hall. The people could choose to come, or not. We had a pretty packed upper room that evening, and the people were even more determined than ever to get the pastor to relent and allow us a Sunday evening service. Though averse, he again agreed to let us do Potter's Field at his church. There was a mighty move of the Holy Spirit, and word spread among many of the pastors in the region.

South Point is in a unique area called the "Tri-State." It's where Ohio, Kentucky, and West Virginia all connect. Greg received a number of calls from pastors that wanted to have lunch with him and Michael. It was decided that they would eat at Giovanni's, a local hangout where pastors would get together weekly and wax the wise with each other. Michael told me to come along. I knew that these men looked down on women in general, and certainly believed women had no business being in a pulpit with their husbands. Michael loved rocking the boat. We walked in together, and you could see the men looking sideways at each other when I entered the room. I loved every minute of this. The boat had started to rock!

We sat down, and the heavier set, senior honcho of the group began by saying, "I know that God is using your ministry, Michael, but we just don't think our people would receive it from someone who has long hair. I don't think we could book you guys at our churches." You could tell that they already had a discussion going about us before we arrived. Michael responded, "First of all, I just came to lunch. I didn't come to this area to get booked in your churches."

I was sitting there thinking to myself that these guys were such hypocrites. They were the type of religious leaders that Jesus always got mad at. Inside, I was like a cat wanting to pounce on each and every one of them, to bring to their attention to the fact that they were overweight. Most of them would have been considered morbidly obese by doctor's standards. And they wanted to talk about my husband's hair? Michael excitedly shared, "It's interesting that you brought up my hair. I'm sitting here thinking that you probably don't know that gluttony is a sin. Pull the plank out of your own eye!" I was cheering my husband on in silence, with my eyes getting bigger by the moment. I was so proud of Michael's boldness in sharing truth with these men in a way no one had probably had the courage to previously. "We come from a church in south Florida that is one of the fastest growing churches in America. How many people did you guys baptize last year?" Not one of them had baptized over five people the entire year. "We have any where from fifty to two hundred people a week coming to know the Lord! We had baptisms last week down at the beach in Fort Lauderdale, and we baptized over three hundred fifty in the ocean. And their hair is longer than mine! Now who's church would you want to go to?" It was an unforgettable lunch.

We went back to Greg's house, and he was thrilled that Michael had confronted these men. Starting that evening, my brother started receiving phone calls, and over the next two days he got calls from every man who was at that lunch. Behind each other's backs, they all booked Potter's Field Ministries.

This was the beginning of God testing our hearts. Were we truly in this ministry to go where He would send us? Would we have the stick-to-it-iveness when people's hearts were cold, calloused, and undemonstrative? Would we till the hard soil in this area when you couldn't see the fruit right away? Would we love Him even if this was all we ever had?

The refining pot is for silver and the furnace for gold, but the Lord tests the hearts.

— Proverbs 17:3 NKJV

These were what I call our hungry years. We literally saw God provide and move miraculously on a daily basis, no matter how small or large. Our "walking by faith and not by sight" was being strengthened daily. After doing some of the churches from the pastor's lunch at Giovanni's, revival broke out in this region. We saw God moving in a supernatural way.

We felt led to stay in this area for a while to see what God wanted to do. It was decided that my brother would handle our bookings, and he could make ten percent of whatever we did and make a little extra money on the side. We moved into their quaint but really small, cramped house, where they had just had their fourth child (they have five grown children today). We had Katie, our dog. So there were four adults and four children getting ready on a Sunday morning, with one bathroom in the house. Although it was really sweet of them to offer us a place to stay, I needed my own space. And though we didn't know it at the time, we would need to get ready for the one hundred fourteen churches that were going to book us over the next year in this Tri-State area!

The people in this area had never seen anyone like Michael. He was evangelizing with power from above and shaking this region!

I got a newspaper and started looking to see if there were any homes in the area for rent. I was at a phone booth (they don't have those anymore) calling on ads I thought might fit our needs. One ad in particular stood out to me. It read, "Detached mother-in-law house for rent. Three hundred dollars a month on Looney Mountain in Catlettsburg, Kentucky." I promptly called the number and a laid back man answered, wanting to know our story and who we were. I told him about our ministry and that my husband was a pastor. After talking for a few minutes, he made an appointment for Michael and me to come and meet them. He gave me directions and ended the conversation with, "I'm the only Looney up on the hill." I figured this was going to be really interesting.

Catlettsburg is a home rule-class city in Boyd County, Kentucky, with kindhearted country folk that look out for and police their own. In 2010, it had a population of fewer than two thousand people, so back in 1994, I'm sure it was considerably less. We drove around winding hills with lush green pastureland, with black and white cows grazing by the dozens. On their necks and heads and hind ends they were black and in the middle they were white. Michael jokingly told his mom when she visited that they were called "Oreo cows" because they were white in the middle.

We arrived at the address and saw the mailbox which read, "The Looneys." We drove down the long driveway to their house and there was a trampoline in the front. We knocked on the door and no one came out, so Michael started jumping on the trampoline. I saw someone peering out of the window while pulling back the curtain just a bit. We were being spied on! They finally answered the door and a tall, jovial, salt-and-pepper-haired man named Steve Looney answered the door along with his wife, Betty, who was a strikingly cute, petite brunette. He extended his hand to shake ours and I saw that he had a huge Looney Tunes belt buckle, and they had matching Looney Tunes t-shirts on as well. They definitely had a great sense of humor. We later found out that Betty was the one checking us out. She was thinking, "What kind of pastor has long hair?" We secured the house and moved in with Katie for what turned out to be a little over one year.

The people in this area had never seen anyone like Michael. He was evangelizing with power from above and shaking this region!

There was an outpouring of the Holy Spirit in this area like they hadn't seen in years. We were indeed living out the prayer I had uttered years before, that God would give us a ministry of fire like Keith Green!

With all the fruit of our ministry, and all the souls coming into the Kingdom, I knew that Satan would soon be on the prowl to continue to try to sever our marriage. If he could break us up, then this ministry would be stopped. We went to Solida Missionary Baptist Church one Sunday morning and I could feel the darkness looming around us. I figured that God wanted to move in a mighty way at this particular church. I prayed for protection as I normally did, but this morning felt particularly foreboding. I looked into Michael's eyes and I had seen that look before – when his rage was ramping up.

We had a fight, and he started yelling and swearing at me in the parking lot of the church. We were already running behind and hadn't set up yet, and he was escalating. He looked at me and said, "Take a long hard look at yourself in this rearview mirror before you tell me what's wrong with me!" He twisted the mirror off and kicked in the front glass of our truck, breaking the windshield! I was so scared. I was praying out loud and rebuking Satan in the name of Jesus and the power of His blood. He realized what he had done after the windshield broke and started repenting and asking me for forgiveness. We grabbed each other's hands and

> I knew that we were in the midst of an awakening in this region, and with it, a mighty spiritual battle. It was time to get more callouses on my knees through prayer.

prayed sorrowfully that God would grant us grace to go in and minister to these people. From the front of the church, Michael shared that we had gotten into a fight before coming inside. The altar call was nothing short of amazing. One hundred people were literally crawling to the altar, crying and wailing unlike anything we'd seen up until this point.

I knew that we were in the midst of an awakening in this region, and with it, a mighty spiritual battle. And the battle would be intense. It was time to get more calluses on my knees through prayer. Michael mistakenly took his outburst to be okay with God because of the way in which He still blessed the service, despite what had happened – in his heart and to our windshield. He would soon learn that it was not okay with God to behave in this manner.

Michael's rage escalated beyond anything I'd experienced while ministering in this Tri-State area. If you've ever read the best-selling novel *This Present Darkness*, an amazing story depicting how demonic forces move in to take over a Midwestern region of the country to oppress and destroy lives – I felt that way here.

One day we were driving around, looking at the countryside in Kentucky, not very close to home. I said something that triggered such a deep rage within Michael that he couldn't contain himself. He was yelling at me at decibels that I'm sure anyone half a mile away could hear. The Lord wanted this part of Michael to die and be gone for good! We were still ministering in the midst of his sin. He was filled with rage and hadn't found victory. For how long would He allow this to go on? He was yelling and braking, sliding to a stop on the side of the road, then going again, then stopping. Then he actually told me to get out of the car! In fear of what would come next, I got out. We were miles from where we were living, on a pretty desolate country road in the middle of nowhere, with only a few houses in sight. Michael sped away. My heart was beating so fast in fear, and my body was trembling. I was scared and my mouth was dry. Mind you, this was before cell phones.

I walked for a while and was praying profusely. I came across a farmhouse, and the Lord told me to go and tell the woman who lived there what had happened. I did, and told her I was staying at the Looney's. Fortunately she knew them, and she called Steve to come and get me. By this time, Michael had found me, and he was yelling for me to get back in the car. The woman told me to go inside and wait until Steve arrived. When he got there, he quieted Michael down, then he put me in his truck and took me back home.

Steve ministered to Michael over the next couple of days. He told Michael the story of his son-in-law and his daughter Melissa. They had lived in the house we were now living in. He was actually physically abusing her one night when Steve overheard. He walked across and onto the porch with a loaded pistol, and put it to his chin. He said, "I love my daughter more than anything. And if I ever catch you doing this to my daughter again, I will put this gun under your chin and blow your head off. And then I will preach in prison for the rest of my life." I remember one night when my dad was over for dinner, I asked him, "If Michael ever touched me to hurt me, you'd kill him right?" Dad replied, "Yes, I would!" I wanted Michael to know that if he ever crossed a line with me, there would be dire consequences. He never did, but the verbal abuse was so damaging to my soul and my heart.

My dad and Steve Looney were great father figures for my husband. I will always appreciate the time we spent on Looney Mountain, waking up on the weekends to the strains of bluegrass music on loud speakers in the trees on their compound. And the easy going family life that was exemplified to us while living there.

And the love and counsel that was given to help heal my husband's wounded heart.

I loved that my mom and dad visited often, along with my brother and Patricia and my nieces and nephews and Michael's mom, Roberta. We all spent Thanksgiving together there that year. Roberta told Steve that she saw the Oreo cows, and knowing those were Michael's antics we all started laughing. It was just another prank that Michael played on his Mom – he still gets her today. The Looneys forever became a part of our extended family. A Christmas doesn't go by without a phone call from the Looneys to touch base, even to this day. By the end of my daddy's life, Michael had won him over. My father loved Michael and called him his son. Michael finally had a father.

> Their huts and makeshift shanties, made out of sticks and anything else they could find to prop them up, wouldn't withstand any storm; though they were so proud of them they would even sweep the dirt floors.

World Vision wanted to take us with them to Honduras on our first mission trip. They knew it would change our lives, and set a fire underneath us to sponsor more children during our concerts. What we saw forever changed our lives. I had never seen such poverty on such a wide scale. The children would have to walk for miles just to retrieve water for that day. Most of them didn't wear clothes. Their huts and makeshift shanties, made out of sticks and anything else they could find to prop them up, wouldn't withstand any storm; though they were so proud of them they would even sweep the dirt floors. They were hungry, dirty, and sick. And my heart broke. I cried the majority of the trip. We took a canoe to an island that people that had the AIDS virus had been exiled to. Most of them were children and orphaned.

The only lighthearted moment came one day when the six of us artists got into the van to go to the next village. Michael had purchased a Baby Ruth candy bar. He nudged me saying, "Watch this!" He ate a piece of the chocolate bar with peanuts in it and partially chewed it. He took it out of his mouth and smeared it on the bottom of his shoe. He started sniffing and saying, "Oh gross, do you smell that? I smell poop!" Taking off his shoe he exclaimed, "Oh it's here on the bottom of my shoe!" He scraped it off and started waving it in the air. By this time everyone was screaming and shouting, "NO!" With all the shock and awe possible, he put the whole gooey mess in his mouth! One of the artists almost vomited, the others howling in laughter. I was laughing so hard I couldn't catch my breath, and he finally let everyone in on the joke. He's such a comic, and by this time we needed a little comic relief.

Later in the trip, one of the guys, Steve Darmondy, suddenly started running a really high fever – over one hundred two degrees. He needed a doctor. They didn't know a lot about the AIDS virus back then, and the hospitals were questionable there, so he asked us to make sure they didn't stick him with a needle. They didn't have actual rooms, only beds enclosed with curtains. After being seen by the doctor, Michael rallied the troops and asked everyone to gather around to pray for Steve's healing. Steve confessed, "I don't believe the gifts are for today, and I don't believe I can be healed. I'm a Seventh Day Adventist, and we don't believe like this." Michael rallied, "Well I do, and we will all believe for you!"

We all laid hands on him and prayed for his healing, and then we were asked to leave him alone with the doctor.

Ten minutes later, the doctor came back in. We overheard Steve saying, "I feel one hundred percent better! No, really, I do! Take my temperature again. I don't believe I have a fever anymore!" The doctor took his temperature and it was completely normal! There in the hospital he started proclaiming at the top of his lungs, "I'm healed, I'm healed!" He jumped off the gurney and we all followed him outside, and he started singing in his beautiful operatic voice, "Our God Is an Awesome God!" We followed behind him, singing with him as loud as we could. We started calling him "Lazarus." We stayed in touch for a few years after this trip, and he would always sign his letters at the end with: "Love, Lazarus."

Another stone had been erected. These children needed our help. Our ministry would take on a global viewpoint from here on, and we would forever be changed.

Chapter 20

THE RAGE EXPOSED

We were back at our home church and Michael would have accountability again. After the year at Looney Mountain, we returned to Fort Lauderdale, our "home base," where we had kept our apartment at Coco Parc in Pompano Beach less than three miles from our church. We were getting fed the Word on a regular basis and I didn't feel isolated, with no safety net, like I had felt while we were ministering out on tour. I was trying to navigate through ministering while Michael still didn't have victory over his rage.

I never knew what would set him off. I lived with Michael, walking on eggshells, never being able to let my guard down. Life would seem to be moving along nicely without any major incidents or my doing or saying anything to set him off, but it seemed the minute I would relax, another rage fit would ensue. I think I can imagine how soldiers who have gone through battle must feel when episodes of PTSD are triggered. The battle was just of a different sort, with the aftermath just as destructive, emotionally devastating, your soul as the casualty lying on a barren and bloodied battlefield, wondering if life will ever get back to some form of normal.

I was exercising on the elliptical machine and Michael was walking in and out of the living room from the bedroom. He was very talkative, shooting questions at me and being all-around inquisitive while I was exercising. His energy level was more heightened than it had been all week. I could feel an agitation beginning to rise in him.

The apartment in Florida was so small that I had the exercise equipment in the living room, and the grand piano that Michael had bought me as a wedding gift was in the small dining room which was attached to the minuscule kitchen. It was a little over nine hundred square feet. All I knew was that it was hard to concentrate and talk while doing cardio, and I was slightly annoyed at having to carry on a conversation while breathless. I could feel the levels of his intense energy levels rising. I was beginning to see a pattern in his behavior. Today, I understand that this was the precursor to the serotonin levels in his brain getting out of whack to where he would finally explode into what I called a "manic episode." Back then, I was simply bracing myself for what I knew was inevitably coming.

> Before I knew it, he was standing directly in front of me, screaming and yelling at such levels that any neighbor could hear him.

I don't even know what I said to him – but it sent him flying into a rage. I thought I had just answered a question in the same way I would answer anyone else. Before I knew it, he was standing directly in front of me, screaming and yelling at such levels that any neighbor, or even someone in the parking lot, could hear him. I was trying to placate him by answering him with soft answers, because the Bible says that a gentle answer turns away wrath, but then the vitriol and horrible things he started verbally hurling at me made my own anger start to rise within me, and I wanted to defend myself. Michael would always use the secret things that I shared with him in my heart, my fears, and my family against me as a sword in these rage attacks. It was so hurtful that I thought my insides would explode with pain. How incensed it made me that he didn't know how to fight fairly. You don't speak or act toward someone you love the way he did. The fear I felt was consuming every molecule of my body. I never knew where these fights would end up.

I was continuing my workout on the elliptical hoping this would just stop or he would just go away. As I was answering him, inquiring why he was so mad, I was trying to stay as calm as possible while every fiber of my being was bristling like a dog raising its hackles who feels it's in danger. Every hair was standing up on my neck and down my backbone too. My mouth was dry as a cotton ball, and I felt the panic and fear threatening to consume me, even though I would stand toe-to-toe with this out-of-control human being.

I had been taught by my Marine dad to stand up for myself ever since I was a small child. But this was beyond anger and rage that I was dealing with – it was "other worldly." Michael continued to escalate irrationally, the veins in his neck popping out and the saliva spewing towards me with each cutting, vitriolic word he could never take back. I felt a power, beyond myself, taking over from within. I knew it was the Holy Spirit taking control with every prayer I was saying under my breath. The Lord would always show up mightily at times such as this to comfort me, reassuring me that I had a diamond in the rough, and that He would give me the power to endure. I would hold on to the scriptures that He had given me – to hold fast to the promises for our future. I had no choice but to hold onto Jesus.

Holding On To Jesus

Lyrics by Pam Rozell, Walt Harrah & Kenn Hayes
Music by Walt Harrah

When I place my hands upon you
In your peaceful slumbering
My silent cry to Heaven
Is what will the morning bring
I stayed right here beside you
I want God's will to be done
But with every morning sunrise
I'd dread the day that's just begun
It's not that I don't love you
I know we both must count the cost
But each day without an answer
A piece of me is lost

CHORUS
Holding on to Jesus
Looking through my tears
I can trust His promise
We'll overcome each fear
Saying "no" to any faithless compromise
He showed me how to love you...
To see you through His eyes

Love that's from the Father
Now fills this darkened room
Those thoughts that held me captive
Well they no longer loom
Here's proof that God has changed me

This truth can't be denied
God's forgiveness stirs within me
Those thoughts of vengeance now subside
His healing truth discloses
Our hearts' most secret place
Now each time I behold you
I see Him in your face

I had become and a prayer warrior for this man on a daily basis, even laying hands on him at night, pleading for the Lord to take away this horrible anger that I had to endure. I truly had to trust God on such a deep level to believe beyond what I could see before my eyes. This was walking by faith and not by sight within a relationship which I didn't know whether we would really make it or not.

This was one of those times that the Holy Spirit spoke through me, beyond what my logical mind wanted to say. He had control of my tongue, and I found myself saying, "You can kick me, spit on me – say horrible things to me all you want Michael – I am NOT going anywhere!"

He was stopped in his tracks! The Holy Spirit, through me, had just spoken to Michael's deep abandonment issues! Not only was I not going to leave him – although subconsciously that's what he was trying to get me to do – but God was not going to leave Michael either! This was the second time I saw that the Holy Spirit was getting through to Michael. It was as if a cold glass of water was being thrown into his face. There was a connection in Michael's heart. I wasn't going to leave him, no matter what, and neither was the Lord.

All of a sudden, from the only other room in the tiny apartment, our personal assistant, Sheri Kaufman, walked out with a look of disbelief and fear on her face. "What is going on in here?" she said alarmingly. I proceeded to tell her that I had been putting up with this kind of behavior from Michael ever since our marriage began, and even in the ministry for the past three years. I also told her that I couldn't take it anymore, and she calmly said, "Well, today it stops. Let's go over and let the elders and pastors know this has been going on so it stops!"

I decided right then and there on that Wednesday night I was going to stop being the recipient of this kind of verbal abuse. I knew there would be ramifications – that our livelihood was connected with our ministry and we both had decided to quit our former professions and trust the Lord. This would be another level to trust our Savior. I was willing to take whatever would come our way, or lose whatever we needed to, so we could get our marriage right and have our ministry be a pure and holy representation of our Father in Heaven. We were once again walking into uncharted territory. I knew the Lord would honor this decision. If we were to have a godly ministry, the hypocrisy in our marriage needed to be pruned. I couldn't live with this compromise or deception anymore. The phoniness in our marriage was going to be revealed on this day!

At that moment, the Lord reassured my heart and infused me with His confidence and strength that we were doing the right thing.

Michael became contrite, and started trying to negotiate, promising Sheri and me that he would never let this behavior happen again. I knew in my heart that he didn't have the tools to stop his behavior, and we needed help from people in the church who we trusted, who did have the tools to come alongside and walk us into a healthy relationship. I got dressed, and all the way up to our leaving the apartment Michael tried to get us to change our minds. He was using the same persuasive manner he had always been successful with in the past to get me to relent, perpetually promising that he could stop his scary, ungodly behavior.

When he saw that I wasn't listening, he tried to speak to my fear that we wouldn't be able to minister ever again and would lose our way to make a living. I could tell he knew that I meant business this time. I heard a frantic tone in his voice and his mouth was extremely dry. I felt the fear – mixed with anger – starting to escalate in Michael.

At that moment, the Lord reassured my heart and infused me with His confidence and strength that we were doing the right thing. And I knew that Michael and I could always make a living. I could always go back to the cruise ships as a headline entertainer if push came to shove. I could always call my agent. I could always teach voice lessons again. The Lord would take care of us. Always.

As we left the house, I looked Michael in the eye, reassuring him that I loved him. Sheri and I walked out of the door together, not even looking back once. We were on the way to the church to tell on him…

Chapter 21

NO MORE COVER UP

W hen Michael completely surrendered to Jesus Christ in 1991, his addictions to alcohol and cocaine were miraculously taken away that day. It doesn't always happen this way, but in his case I praise God that it did. However, his rage lingered.

Now I was hoping that the exposure of Michael's rage issues would be the beginning of having this area of his life being put under the control of Christ.

I was tired of the phoniness and hypocrisy in our marriage. I couldn't go on ministering with him knowing that his rage was still bubbling under the surface and could explode at any time and any place. It would leave me so deflated, trying to minister from a deficit when his episodes would occur. It took me a long time to recover after his verbal rants would slash open already-gaping wounds. This was the first time that I felt empowered and hopeful that someone could help us, and that something might be done to help remedy his volatile mood swings.

Sheri and I went to the elders that Wednesday and told on him, and some pastors took him aside and ministered to him for quite a long time after the Wednesday night service. He did his regular song and dance about how sorry he was, saying it wouldn't happen again. I was incensed, thinking that he basically got off with a slap on the hand from the good ole boys club. The next day, I went into the office at the church to talk to my friend, Margaret DeStefano, who was the senior pastor's personal assistant. I told her everything that had been going on in our marriage from the beginning and that Michael's rage was intensifying, and it was happening while we were out on tour as well. I left nothing out. She told me to go home and tell Michael that our marriage was in jeopardy. Margaret knew this would set Michael in a tailspin, causing his anger to come to the surface. She was really good at counseling because she had several divorces, and some of the men were abusive to her. She had worked through many of her issues, and she was good at helping others walk through theirs, too; she is a no-nonsense kind of gal. She shoots from the hip just like Michael.

I went home after my meeting, and I must've been wearing my heart on my sleeve. Michael asked me, "What is wrong?" "Nothing," I said in response. He said, "Something is wrong." I told him that I was really mad that the elders didn't discipline him or hold him accountable like I thought they would. I told him that I had gone to talk to Margaret – he was furious! I quickly added, "She told me to tell you that our marriage was in jeopardy!" His anger exploded! He couldn't believe that I had gone and told her. "You've put us and our livelihood in jeopardy!" Couldn't he see that is exactly what HE was doing every time he chose to rage? I didn't care. I just wanted these episodes gone, once and for all.

He got in his car and drove down to the church and marched himself into Margaret's office and snapped. "Who do you think you are? And where do you get off telling my wife that our marriage is in jeopardy?" he yelled. He continued to escalate to a point where the pastor walked out of his adjoining office and said, "This sounds like a closed-door meeting." Michael snapped, "It is." So the pastor proceeded to close the door with himself and Michael inside her office. Margaret told him about the rage in our marriage, and that it had been happening from the beginning – even while on tour. He commented, "I knew it was something. I just couldn't put my finger on what it was – I just knew something wasn't right." He told Michael he was going to be removed from ministry for a season. He also told him that if he heard that he raged on me again, they would move me in with him and his wife until things changed. Michael didn't know what we were going to do because we already had some upcoming churches booked.

Michael knew that he needed to take what was coming to him, submit under authority for the very first time, and have accountability – the Lord would take care of the rest. Pastor Bob told him he would be shadowing his Assistant Pastor, Gennarino, who was Margaret's husband, and he would be giving his marching orders. He also told him that he would be in counseling with Pastor John Chinnelly, our missions pastor. He would be meeting alone with him once a week, then he would have another session with me. Michael had no idea how long he wouldn't be able to minister. It's a good thing that he never asked, "How long will it be?" because Pastor Bob later said that he would've doubled the time if he had, knowing that Michael didn't have the right heart and wasn't ready to change.

Michael had to be at the church every day, as if he was on staff, even though officially he wasn't. The first day after this happened he met with Gennarino, who handed him a broom and put him in the custodial department. On the first Wednesday night service after his discipline had begun, he told him to sweep the front entrance as people were entering the sanctuary. Michael was humiliated. Gennarino told him, "Michael, you are going to feel like this is the biggest demotion of your life, but if you learn the lessons God wants you to, this will be the biggest promotion of your entire life!"

As people were entering the sanctuary, they were greeting Michael, wondering why he was in the front with a broom. One man in particular who loved our ministry, Tom Duquette, said, "Hi Pastor Mike, what are you doing out here sweeping?" Michael was always told by his mentors at Calvary: "When asked, tell the truth." He told Tom what had happened, not as a touring evangelist pastor, but as a lowly servant, humbled by the Lord in the process of restoration. Tom and his wife, Donna, had seen Potter's Field and loved what we did. We had gotten to know Tom pretty well because he had been praying for his wife to come to church with him for a long time. She had been an alcoholic for years, and Tom wanted her to be set free. So did their precious daughter, Jessica. We had all prayed for her. Tom so appreciated Michael's humility in telling him what had happened to him. And over the next year or so, Donna did start to come to church, and eventually gave her heart to the Lord! Sadly, she passed away a few years later, but Tom had the satisfaction and hope of knowing he would see her again in Heaven. We just found out recently that Tom had passed as well. They are now enjoying Jesus' presence together in glory.

Michael started meeting with Pastor John, who had such patience with him and knew how to give him word pictures which Michael could understand quickly. Michael gives word pictures to illustrate his points so well, and God knew that John would be the man that would help him more than anyone. John and his wife, Connie, had weathered some really difficult struggles in their marriage while on the mission field, but God got hold of John's heart and changed him from the inside out. He and his wife have counseled and helped save so many doomed marriages through the years. Connie is a master in teaching women how to forgive their husbands. Together, they are a dynamo team for the Lord. They are still at Calvary Fort Lauderdale helping others.

John explained to Michael, "Spiritually, it's like Pam has had a head on collision. She's has a broken leg and broken arm, with casts on both. She also has a halo on. You have a few scratches with some Band Aids. You say your usual 'I'm sorry and you have to forgive me' and you both go forward. You and she go along for a while, and Pam starts to heal and the halo comes off. Then a cast gets ready to come off, and you have another head on collision! She's reinjured all over again. You are doing this to her every three to five weeks! You've had dozens of them. You have to be consistent in your behavior and stop having wrecks, spiritually speaking, if there's ever going to be complete healing in your marriage!" Michael was beginning to get it. He was a sponge and learned quickly. That is one of the many thing I love about him.

"You both need to have grace for each other, so let's move forward knowing God can heal you both, and wants to heal and use this marriage for His glory."

John told me, "Pam, it's like you are living with a wild tiger. He lives in a cage and doesn't know anything about being in domesticated life. But you're expecting this wild animal to know already how to live in a house without mauling you. You need to stop expecting Michael to know how to be a husband, because he doesn't know anything about how to be one. He didn't grow up having a man in his life, or having a healthy marriage modeled for him. Give him a season of grace during this time. I promise you, I will teach him over time, to the best of my ability, what it means to be a husband."

Then to the two of us, he added, "You both need to have grace for each other, so let's move forward knowing God can heal you both, and wants to heal and use this marriage for His glory."

Little did I know to what extent the Lord would be able to use the testimony of this marriage through our ministry in the coming years. It's mind boggling to think of where we were then, and where we are today. God is truly a God of the impossible!

All of this happened in February 1995. For three weeks after Michael had been sat down for discipline, all of the pastors and the counselor had watched his life and his consistency at being at church. They saw him eagerly wanting to learn how to be a good husband and a servant leader. He was learning to love others, and to be accountable under godly authority. He took every correction, rebuke, and exhortation, and saturated himself with the Word of God, listening to Pastor Chuck's Five Thousand series every day. He was growing leaps and bounds.

They released him to go back on tour. We went back on tour with churches close by without missing a single booking that we had on the calendar. God was good.

Fast forward eight months to October of that same year. Our pastor asked Michael for us to present Potter's Field at all three morning services at Calvary Fort Lauderdale, and he wanted him to share about his rage and what had been happening in our marriage. Michael said, "We'll present Potter's Field, but I don't want to share about my rage." Pastor Bob responded, "If you don't share about it, then you won't be doing Potter's Field." He decided he would share about his embarrassing shortcomings. The pastor asked,

"How has your marriage been doing over the last eight months?" Michael answered, "Pretty well I think."

We actually had been doing quite well, with no major incidents. I was beginning to trust him again. I was willing to take the risk to love him again and trust him with my heart. I'm usually a skeptic by nature, and secretly I was just waiting for the other shoe to drop.

I went to a baby shower for the pastor's wife and took her home afterwards. She asked how our marriage was doing, and I told her it was going surprisingly well, and he had no major outbursts. She had shared what I had said with her husband, who shared it with Michael.

Michael asked, "If she's saying that we are doing so well, then why haven't we been more intimate?" The pastor answered, "Is that why you're doing all of

> "Well that's your whole problem, right there. You need to love without ever expecting anything in return! To love her like Christ loves the church."

this? If it is, she can smell it a mile away, and she's testing to see if you are really sincere in changing. What if she never does Michael?" Michael lamented, "Don't even say that!" He said, "Well that's your whole problem, right there. You need to love without ever expecting anything in return! To love her like Christ loves the church. He laid His life down for others – a sacrificial love. You have the wrong motives for doing it, and God won't honor it!"

During all of this upheaval in our marriage, the Lord had given me a conviction not to forsake our "marriage bed," even though I no longer had emotional feelings for this man I married. As a matter of fact, I despised him at times, and even felt borderline hatred. But I knew that intimacy was designed by God to be the glue that would keep us "one" despite my feelings, and that when God decided to heal our marriage this would be one area of our life that we hadn't neglected, keeping us from being tempted to stray, even during our most tumultuous times. Through the years, I've been able to minister to so many women in this area of their lives. Satan will use a lack of intimacy to get into a marriage if you allow him to. More marriages break up over sex and finances than any other struggle. Don't give the devil a foothold!

That weekend, as Michael and I presented Potter's Field at our church and shared about his rage, the Holy Spirit moved so mightily that hundreds of people came forward to rededicate their marriages and their lives to the Lord, and there were many first-time conversions, as well. We were blown away by God's faithfulness and grace that was lavished on us. We couldn't believe He chose to use us despite the cracks in our lives. Instead, He chose to shine His light through the cracks, imperfections, weaknesses, and vulnerabilities of these broken lives.

The next day, the phones started ringing off the hook at the church with marriages that had problems just like ours, and others with different problems altogether, and they needed counseling. They were booked out for weeks. Satan had been defeated, and other marriages were going to get healed and walk in victory. The phoniness was unmasked! We knew that we would have an even larger target on our backs. We needed to gird up and keep our armor on, and not give the enemy a crack to put his toe in. There could've been no real Potter's Field Ministries until everything was put into the light, where Satan couldn't wreak havoc with us, as a couple or our ministry. I was willing to lose our livelihood – and whatever else it took – to get our marriage, and us individually, right before our Lord! I knew the Lord would take care of us even if we lost everything and had to find something else to do to make a living. I just couldn't live in the phoniness anymore! If more people were willing to do this today, I think we would have more powerful ministries, marriages, and lives that were actually viable in the world today. But we must risk being real, raw, uncovered, and usable in the Master Potter's hands.

Michael and I had made plans to travel to Whitefish to see our friends, the Howe's, and to attend a marriage seminar with them. We were still going to counseling with John. He thought it was a good idea to get away and spend some time together. We needed to let everything that had happened to us during this year sink in and take hold. We flew to Montana never imagining what the Lord had in store for us next.

It's amazing how you open up the flow of God's blessings when you're obedient to do the hard things...

Chapter 22

THE HEALING OF THE RAGE
In the Home We Now Own

We were attending a marriage seminar in Whitefish, Montana. We were staying with our friends, Steve Howe, the New York Yankees pitcher, and his wife, Cindy. Every time we would travel to see the Howe's, Steve would try to get us to buy a home there. I would get alone with Michael and tell him, "I'm never going to move to Whitefish. He can look all he wants and show you condos and homes when we visit, but I'm a city girl, and there's nothing there!" Never say "never" to the Lord!

The marriage seminar was informative, but a little too Pentecostal for Michael and me. During one exercise, we had to break all soul ties with people we had been intimate with in our past. We had never heard of doing something like this and thought it was a little strange, but we were here, so we went along with it: We had to write down all the names of the people we'd been with, or something that reminded us of them; then we would pray, and destroy the paper. We weren't supposed to sign our names on the paper, but Michael forgot he wasn't supposed to, and we were all frantically looking for his paper in the conference room where we all were meeting. We all were laughing so hard as Michael was looking under chairs, in the trash, and anywhere this paper could've ended up. We always had a great time with the Howe's, and for the season we were all together there are really good memories.

The next morning, Michael took Steve into town and dropped him off. He borrowed his truck and drove up to Big Mountain to the village where the ski runs were, and sitting in the parking lot and spending time with the Lord, contemplating things we were learning from John and Connie through our counseling with them. Michael was always drawn to John 5, the healing at the pool of Bethesda where disabled people would lie – the blind, the lame, and the paralyzed. There was a man who had been lying there for thirty-eight years, unable to walk. When Jesus saw this man who had been in this condition for such a long time, he asked him, "Do you want to be healed?" The man told him that he had no one to help him into the pool when the water was stirred so that he might be healed, and someone else would always go down ahead of him. Then Jesus said to him, "Get up! Pick up your mat and walk." At once the man was cured; he picked up his mat and walked.

The Holy Spirit pierced his armor, and Michael started trembling, and as if a dam broke, he started crying from the top of his head to the bottom of his toes.

Michael was always fascinated and moved by this story in scripture. Then the Lord, speaking to his heart, asked him, "Michael, do you want to be healed?"

He came back to the house, and I was sitting in the living room. No one was there except me. Michael came in and we sat down on the floor together. He started sharing with me how the Lord was speaking to him up on the mountain that morning. He told me that he was like the man on the mat. That when the Lord asked if he wanted to be healed, he wouldn't answer the question – he just told Him his story. And the Lord said to him, "I know your story, Michael. I know that your parents weren't at your little league games and didn't make you meals, or nurture you or take care of you the way they should have. I'm just asking today, do you want to be healed?" Looking straight into his eyes, I asked him that very same question, with certitude mixed with resoluteness, "Well do you want to be healed?" While his eyes were transfixed and fastened on mine, he confessed, "Yes!"

The Holy Spirit pierced his armor, and Michael started trembling, and as if a dam broke, he started crying from the top of his head to the bottom of his toes. It was an excruciatingly heart-rending cry that I'd never heard come out of him. It went on for what seemed unending minutes while I held his head in my lap, rocking him back and forth, comforting him in his moments of healing where he was being made whole by the touch of the Potter's hands. I went into the kitchen and got some olive oil and came back and anointed his head while I prayed for him. I knew we were experiencing a "holy moment," and that God had decided on that day in 1995 to heal the secret places of Michael's heart. He would not be plagued by the nagging, recurrent throes of rage that had haunted him in years past any longer. On this day, Michael was healed, picked up his mat, and walked.

I always wondered if Michael could actually cry. I had only seen him cry once when his Gram died in 1988. He so loved his grandmother, and he cried true tears of sorrow for her when she passed. For these eight years we had been married, his heart was so hardened that once I actually had our friend, Dr. Bill Otto, who went to church with us while in Boca Raton, check his tear ducts to see if they were working. They were functioning perfectly. He just couldn't connect his emotions with his tears until this moment.

While we lived in Florida, we tried to buy several condos and put offers on homes, but the Lord closed the doors on all of them. Michael asked our pastor one afternoon while sitting by the pool at his beautiful home, "Will we ever own a home?" He would assure Michael that we would, and that he was looking at many years of ministry and of God's provision and blessings. We were just starting out; we needed to be patient and trust.

I had started feeling the tug of the Holy Spirit to move out of South Florida. It was so far south, and we were doing churches all over America now and needed another base of operation. It took so long to drive back home from anywhere after touring. When we came home, it was getting stressful to be the ones called to minister to marriages that needed help at our home church. We were also trying to juggle our personal lives while balancing being involved at church. In addition, Michael was making and replenishing his pottery in between tours. After the rigors of touring, we really needed to just recover, regroup, and get fed the Word. Then we would be ready to go back out and pour ourselves out in ministry once again. But that wasn't happening. To top it off, I also began seeing some squirrelly things starting to happen in the leadership at our church that I was questioning my husband about. I've always had the gift of discernment, and while I couldn't quite put my finger on it, I knew it was time to quietly move on.

Two years after I had voiced my concerns, we decided to leave South Florida. It took Michael a little longer to embrace change than it did me. The Howe's were building a large home on Whitefish

Lake, so Steve offered to sell us his existing home in Whitefish at missionary prices. The home was beautiful, but not over the top; it was in the forest on a mountain, very quiet, and it was the only thing that was going to peak my interest enough to even consider moving to Montana. It was peaceful, and wildlife would even come up into the backyard. This could be a place where we could physically and spiritually replenish ourselves before going back out to minister.

> # The Lord answered Michael's prayer for a home far and above anything we could've hoped for or imagined.

We decided to buy the house, and we moved to Whitefish in May 1997. The minute my feet hit the driveway, I knew I was home. I couldn't explain how God had changed my heart. This is where I was going to be buried. It didn't happen that quickly for Michael, but eventually it became his home and his refuge. He'd always wanted to live in the Rocky Mountains, and God had now provided him a home there. We can't think of any other place we'd rather live, and the Lord knew that. It's why He never opened the door for us to buy in South Florida. I can't believe we have been in our home twenty years!

In the early years, our home served as the Potter's Field office, though we have since moved downtown. With the ministry board's approval, we turned the large garage on the property into Michael's pottery studio where he could mass-produce his wares which we sell at the back table. As we got busier with PFM, his first cousin, Kevin Hanks, would take over the helm and manage the pottery production, and he has in turn taught some of our interns how to clean, glaze and fire pottery. As our ministry has changed through the years, Kevin and his wife, Renee, have faithfully served the ministry wherever they are needed.

Before we actually moved in, Michael was out on the back deck talking to Cindy. He had never seen the house in the springtime. We had always come up during winter to go skiing, so it had always been under a few feet of snow. As he looked around the landscape, he had a flashback to 1987 when he and I were watching *The 700 Club* in our Santa Monica apartment, and he recognized this scene! This is when he and I vowed to pray for Steve, an athlete who I'd never even heard of, but who Michael had a burden for. He asked, "Cindy, is this the home you owned when you and Steve were interviewed years ago on *The 700 Club*?" She told him, "Yes, it is." Then he wondered, "Was it here in this backyard where Steve and Chelsi were playing catch during the interview segment?" She told him, "Yes, it is." He was so humbled and in awe of our God. "Can you believe that, ten years ago when Pam and I started praying for you guys, God knew we would be friends, and that one day we would own the very home that was featured on *The 700 Club* interview that motivated us to pray for you guys?" God is so good! He is the ultimate connector of the dots! He sees and knows and cares.

Sadly, Steve was killed in a car accident en route from Arizona to California in April 2006. We know he loved the Lord, and he had a heart of gold. We miss him, and Cindy has since happily remarried.

God had been so good to us! The Lord answered Michael's prayer for a home far and above anything we could've hoped for or imagined.

But God knew...even when we began praying for this family twenty years earlier...

Chapter 23

SIGNS AND WONDERS

We were on the front lines of ministry now. We had a larger target on our backs for the enemy to try to take us down. We needed to be prayed up, studied up, and ready for battle. We weren't always successful, but God is merciful and full of forgiveness if you will repent and keep marching onward. We were witnessing healings, salvations by the thousands, supernatural provision, and marriages getting strengthened and salvaged from divorce court. It's no wonder the evil one wanted to tear our union to shreds, rendering us ineffective for the Kingdom of God.

A pastor and a friend, Denny Martinez, was a tool in the Potter's hands at just the right moment to keep Michael from walking out on the ministry that God had entrusted to us. We had done PFM at his church, a Calvary Chapel in Washington, and he had put us up at a lovely hotel. Michael and I had a fight; he snapped on me because he was feeling the pressures of traveling, walking by faith for provision, and we were both exhausted. The enemy wanted to sift us like wheat, and at a vulnerable moment during our heated argument, Michael quit the ministry, packed his bags, and got in the car and drove away, leaving me at the hotel. Luckily, I had Denny and Lynette's number. I called him and he was over in a flash. He started calling Michael, asking him to come back, and after much coaxing, they spent the afternoon together. He exhorted Michael and me to grow up, wanting us to look at how we each contributed to our problems and own them – rather than blaming one another or becoming the victim. He was divinely appointed in that place and time to reclaim and redeem our ministry. Denny's son Zach has gone through our school, IGNITE, and now works with us in Whitefish.

> As we all grabbed hands, a thick cloud descended on the people.

After I unveiled the Gaugy mural of the crucifixion during a service in Alabama, I looked at it in a new way, and the Lord said audibly to me in my head, "I want you to write a song called 'Soften My Heart.'" Usually when He gives me marching orders such as this, or a song in a dream – which has happened about five times over the ten CDs I've recorded – I knew it was a message for me to keep my hands on the plow in my marriage and ministry. This song has been sung in numerous languages all over the world. I knew He wanted me to keep my heart soft towards Him, Michael, and our ministry. Even though that song has blessed many, I know I wrote it that the message would pierce my own heart.

Soften My Heart

Lyrics & Music by Pam Rozell & Walt Harrah

I heard Your voice today
Then turned and walked away
My heart is now a hardened piece of clay

Just like a broken shard
This pride has made me hard

Let this cup
Pass from me

CHORUS
Soften my heart, Lord
Soften my heart
Tear down the walls
That keep us apart
Soften my heart
Lord Jesus
I give my everything
Soften my heart

Look deep within and see
Refine impurity
Create in me a sensitivity
And with Your gentle words
A voice inside me heard

Quietly
Work in me

BRIDGE
Chisel away at this heart of stone
I'm yielded and still
Make it pure like Your very own
I want Your perfect will

In Alamogordo, New Mexico, we had another big argument, and this time we both wanted to quit. Our fights were usually over stupid things that would escalate into full-blown sin on both our parts. We were beginning to notice a pattern of the enemy, and were learning how to combat him. We figured out that if God was going to do mighty things in the church where we were sent, Satan was going to attack us in our most vulnerable state. We started recognizing his tactics, and we would grasp hands and get on our knees before the Lord and actively pray against the forces that were coming against us. We told the pastor that evening what had happened and we all three lay prostrate on the altar and asked for forgiveness, for the Lord to cleanse us, and for us to be used that evening. An older, frail woman came into the church that night, dragging an oxygen tank. At the end of the service, she asked if we would all lay hands on her and pray for her healing. Michael, the pastor, and I prayed for her. We went back to this church a year later and an attractive, tanned, middle-aged woman walked by me, staring at me. She said, "You don't recognize me do you?" I said, "I'm sorry, I don't." She replied, "I was here last year and you all prayed for me. I had an oxygen tank, and the Lord completely healed me!" I couldn't believe my eyes! She looked healthy, fifteen years younger, and vibrant. She told me that she had brought her priest to see our ministry this night because she wants him to know this Jesus that she's been talking about!

We were in Indiana doing a service and there was a pre-teen boy on the front pew. He was in obvious pain during the entire presentation. I was praying for him because I knew he didn't feel well; he was bald, so I assumed he was getting chemo for some sort of cancer. His mom motioned for him to leave midway through the service and he adamantly said no to her. He was determined to stay until the end. We found out that God had told him specifically to come and have us lay hands on him and pray. After the altar call, the pastor got up and asked if we could join hands across the congregation, and for Michael and I to come and lay hands on young Josh and pray for his healing. As we all grabbed hands, a thick cloud descended on the people. You could've cut the cloud with a knife as the Holy Spirit came down. The pastor and Michael prayed a beautiful prayer, imploring the Lord to spare this young man's life. I had such a heart of compassion for him as my hand lay gently upon his gaunt shoulder. When we left, Michael and I knew that something special had happened in this place. We went back exactly one year later to this church, and a young teen came bounding up to me. He was filled out, healthy, and had dirty blonde hair. He gushed, "Hi Pam, I'm Josh! The Lord healed my brain tumor!" I was amazed and called Michael over to witness the miracle that God had performed in this sweet boy's life.

Then the disciples went out and preached everywhere, and the Lord worked with them and confirmed his word by the signs that accompanied it.

— Mark 16:20

A man named Bill came to a service in Vista, California, to see us. The Lord told him to find out where we were and to fly anywhere in the United States so we could lay hands on him and pray for him. His body was covered in cancer. We prayed for him at all three services. A lady came over to me with her precious three year old. She said that two years before the child was born, I had prayed for her to get pregnant. She said, "Meet the answer to your prayer!" A gal in the front row came up to me in excruciating pain, knowing that even walking over to me would hurt. I prayed for her healing right there, before our service that evening, and she later told me that as the evening progressed the Lord had healed her back and leg and took away her pain – it was completely gone! We recently received this email:

> Mike and Pam recently gave the Potter's Field presentation to our congregation. At the altar call for the night service, Jaylee went up for healing prayer. She was recently diagnosed with Stage 4 cancer, and when she went in today for a diagnosis, it came back negative! Praise the Lord for His healing hands, which not only forgive all our sins but also heal all our diseases (Psalm 103:3). God is doing amazing things through your ministry. Be encouraged ☺.

Michael recently had a herniated disc, confirmed by an MRI scan, and was looking at surgery, and not being able to tour until he healed. This would've put a strain on our ministry and staff. He was at a pastor's conference at our Central American Headquarters in Antigua, Guatemala, and was in so much pain that he decided to come home two days early. Before he left the property to board the plane, a Guatemalan pastor who was attending the conference told him the Lord wanted him to lay hands on Michael and pray for a healing. The entire conference had already done this the night before, but Michael acquiesced. So the pastor and his wife prayed over him in Spanish; Michael said later it was like being prayed over in tongues. He thanked them, and as he was leaving the grounds with Pastor Danny Hodges, the pain suddenly went away. He started doing deep squats, telling Danny, "I'm healed! No really, I think I'm healed. I have no pain whatsoever!" When he got back to the States he went and got another MRI scan and it confirmed that the herniated disc was gone! Holding both scans side by side, he used it to minister to all the doctors involved here in the Flathead Valley.

About twice a year I get laryngitis. It always scares me because I think my voice is never going to come back. Just this year I got the worst case I've ever had, complete with a bad cough, and it lasted about three weeks. We were passing it all around the office to each other, and at church as well. When I would speak, absolutely nothing would come out of my mouth. We had churches booked – I had to go, but I trusted that the Lord would come through. I can count on one hand the times I've had to lip sync with my records. So I went onstage, not being able to utter a word, and when it came time to share my testimony and sing, I opened my mouth and the purest sound came out – I knew it was from God. It was as if I wasn't sick at all! When I had finished the entire service and went backstage, I couldn't speak once again. This has happened several times during the last twenty-five years. His wonders never cease to amaze me.

The Lord has always provided for us in miraculous ways. A woman came up to me at a Potter's Field service in Las Cruces, New Mexico. She didn't go to this church, but the Lord told her to attend that evening. She really enjoyed the service and inquired if we had a place to stay for the evening. I told her that we didn't, but that we really didn't want to stay in another host home because we needed some alone time. She smiled brightly saying, "Now I know why I'm here. I own a motel on the edge of town. If you both come in an hour I will have a room ready for you." I was so happy and relieved. As we drove to the outskirts of town, we rounded the corner to a large motel sign. The marquis read, "The Lord God is Sovereign!"

Another time, Michael and I were completely broke. We wouldn't be paid until the next church service, and didn't have money for lunch. We put our hands in the crack of the car seat and found ninety-nine cents, just enough for us to split a Subway sandwich.

Coming back to Florida during one of our earliest tours, we came through the toll plaza and we didn't have the money to pay for the toll. I told Michael not to worry, that I would go back the next day and pay for it. He said, "No, where God guides, God provides, and since He's not providing, I'm going to take back my old job." I started praying, and when we got to the tollbooth the lady leaned down and told us, "The car in front of you just paid your toll!" We were blown away! I said, "I guess we will still be in the ministry, huh?" That has never happened again in twenty-five years, and Michael and I have driven together over one million miles.

In the early years of our ministry, we came home from a tour and Michael was stressed because we didn't have enough money left over for groceries that week. He remembered that the year before, some friends had given him a letter and told him to put it away until we were down to our last six dollars – well the time had come! He had put the envelope in the back pouch of our Dodge Caravan. When he came back inside, he was almost in tears, his head low and humbled. The note read, "This is to bless you when you get down to your last six dollars." It was a crisp one hundred dollar bill! That same weekend, we went to do our ministry for a homeless shelter, knowing they couldn't pay us anything. At the end of the service, they walked us over to a large garage and rolled the doors up. It was completely stocked with food, from the ground to the ceiling, left over from donations from Hurricane Andrew – and they told us to go shopping. The Lord will provide!

He has provided three-ply specialty trailer tires for us in the middle of nowhere when we had a flat. Money has randomly arrived in the mail from people that our ministry has blessed through the years, just at the right times to pay the bills. The zeros have changed through the years, but His provision has been consistent. The Lord has financially blessed our ministry, above and beyond anything we could've dreamed, and His principles do not change. He is the same yesterday, today and forever!

We had a man see our ministry one morning in Brea, California, and he was moved to tears. He found out where we were going to be that evening and asked his pastor if he could get a ride to meet us there. That night, in Diamond Bar, California, he stood there with the pastor, holding a zippered pouch. He told Michael that it was the last twenty dollars he had in this world but he wanted us to have it. It was twenty dollars worth of nickels. We have kept this "widow's mite" in its original zippered pouch to remind us of the heart behind sacrificial gifts and to never forget how much these gifts mean to our Lord.

There are so many stories related to sponsoring our Potter's Field Kids. A man, covered in tattoos, wanted to sponsor our work, but didn't have the twenty dollars a month it took to do so. He started thinking that, before he got saved and did drugs, he used to sell plasma for twenty dollars a month. So he went down to the blood bank, and when he asked if they still paid for plasma, they said they did. So, he decided, since Jesus gave His blood on a cross to save me, then I could sell my plasma for twenty dollars and send it to a child in need. "And they give me some orange juice and a cookie!" he said.

Recently at Calvary Chapel Philadelphia, Michael shared that before he met me, he had paid for three abortions. One woman became so emotional over this that she couldn't speak. Finding us the next Sunday at an affiliate church, she decided to sponsor the work, choosing three PFK prayer children in Costa Rica, one for each of the three abortions that she had in the past, and she wants to go down and meet them some day!

At Calvary Fort Lauderdale, a former drug dealer came bounding up to Michael. He said, "Dude, my girlfriend got saved a week-and-a-half ago and cut me off. Everything you said up there was me! Here take this!" He pushed a roll of hundred dollar bills into Michael's hand. "This is the last of the drug money, and I'm flushing all the drugs tonight!" Michael said, "I can't take it man." The man insisted he take it, so Michael said he'd give it to missions. He said, "Okay man." He left with his starter Bible, promising he would be in the New Believers class on Tuesday, and his life was forever transformed. Michael gave the wad of cash to our loyal assistant, Joanna Chung, who has been with us over twelve years, and she told us the gift came to four thousand six hundred dollars!

In Southern California, a woman approached me and handed me a ten thousand dollar check! I was amazed. She said, "I've always wanted to go to Uganda and couldn't, but I can send money to take care of the children in your program over there!"

A woman in North Carolina came with a change purse that she had been hanging onto since her mom died two years prior. After hearing about our Potter's Field Kids Program, she knew that this was where her mother would've wanted to give her money. This is when Michael "coined" the phrase – "Change for Change."

An older man sponsored a little girl at the back table and left, but then came back with his seven-year-old adopted son. He had gotten in the car and introduced him to his new "sister." When they looked at the picture and information more closely, they learned that his new "sister" had the exact same birthday as the son – same date, same year! This has happened so many times through the years, and it always blesses me.

From San Diego, one woman wrote, "I came to you and you prayed over me for my financial situation. I mentioned I wanted to sponsor, but couldn't afford to. By sponsoring we get one free CD. And instead, you gave me five CDs, even without a sponsorship. I just want to say 'Thank you' for your kind gesture. I pray God will bless you and your ministry all the more. Love in Christ, Erlinda." You can never out give God.

It amazes me to no end how the Lord has used Michael's pottery and my music through the years to bless his people. I love going into people's homes and churches seeing my husband's pottery in places of prominence. I love the stories I've heard through the years of how my music has blessed others. They play my CDs as people come into this world and as people depart from it. Kids fall asleep listening to it, or sing along daily with it. A third grader told his mom, "Aw, you always drop me off at school when the good songs come on." It was a song off of one of my albums. It blesses me to hear a man in Boston, who had a really hard life and gets extremely depressed, telling me with tears in his eyes that my music has gotten him through some really hard times. A lady told me that something broke in her that particular day when she heard, "Soften My Heart." As she was shaking and crying, she told me that she had been holding on to bitterness; she fought it in her heart for years, but that day she had been set free!

> It has always been a blessing to hear my songs on Christian radio stations, and since God was our agent, sometimes we wouldn't know how certain radio stations would get hold of my music.

Or the Jamaican Rasta who said, "First of all you have a 'sic' (good) voice. Tonight while you were singing the hair on my body stood up. I told the guy sitting beside me that I was having an encounter with the Holy Spirit! It wasn't until you offered that we fill out the envelope and put in twenty dollars for a free CD that I understood what God was asking me to do. He wanted me to tithe the first-fruits of the new business I just started – not just my personal tithe – and then He would bless my business. I didn't bring my checkbook or credit card tonight, but when I put my hand in my pocket and found two ten dollar bills, I gave it to your kids!"

It has always been a blessing to hear my songs on Christian radio stations as we would be driving down the freeways in different states, and since God was our agent, sometimes we wouldn't know how certain radio stations would get hold of my music. And it was playing on good stations on regular rotation! I wrote and chose songs all about Heaven on a recent CD, and I wrote a couple songs for my dad after he passed away. One woman wrote:

> "I wanted to drop this email to you to congratulate you on such an amazing masterpiece! The *Love Lives On* CD is amazing. I have listened to it endlessly since receiving it last Sunday after attending a service that you and Mike did in Massachusetts. I especially love the song "Thy Will Be Done." Having lost my father five years ago when he was sixty-two, the words were healing and perfect. In fact, I turned around and shared this song with some of my other girlfriends that have lost their dads! What a wonderfully moving piece! It brings me both tears and joy. You are so gifted! Thanks so much for sharing your gift of music, and thank you so much for the gift of your ministry! Keep up the great work! — Regina

Thy Will Be Done

Lyrics & Music by Pam Rozell & Walt Harrah

Semper Fi
A pair of purple hearts
Faithful as the day is long
That's my Dad
Chipped beef on toast
Glenn Miller tunes
My Daddy was the best a daughter ever had

He treated me
So tenderly
He'd say to me,
"Widget you're the apple of my eye."
He taught me right from wrong
If I hurt him, he'd never let on
Whenever I would sing
It never failed to make him cry

But on Memorial Day,
Two thousand two
The Lord said papa's days were
Down to just a precious few
Doctor's called us in to break the news
Now who would walk in my Daddy's shoes?

Outside his door
I overheard him pray
He said, "You know me Lord,
How much I'd dearly love to stay.

My kids and wife,
Can't believe how You've blessed my life
All I ask of You, to take this dread disease away."

Then I heard the words that linger still
That echoed Jesus yielding to the Father's will
A vic'try there was finally won
When he prayed, "Let Thy will be done."
Thy will be done

Now there's a hole in my heart
I've cried a bucket of tears
They keep floodin' back
The memory of those years
We're apart for now
But very soon we'll be
Reunited where there's no more night,
And no more tears.

So as I come to terms, and face the grief
I find that resignation brings me sweet relief
When I pray the prayer my Daddy prayed,
"Father let Thy will be done."

Then the peace of God consoles my loss
As I think about the Savior up there on that cross
In all the trials of life that are sure to come
Help me say, "Thy will be done."

Thy will be done (Repeat)

There are so many stories to tell through the years, they could fill the pages of this book ten times over. I will just close this chapter out with a few more.

A couple in Ramona, California, left during the invitation at Calvary because they weren't ready yet to accept the Lord. On the way home, they almost had a head-on collision with another car with a child in tow. Immediately they turned around and came back to the church, and Michael and Pastor Rob led them to the Lord.

I had ministered to two ladies the last time I was in Melbourne, Florida, and counseled them not to leave their husbands. When I came back two years later, one introduced me to her husband whom she had stayed with, and the other gal told me that she and her husband were doing great in their marriage.

There was a man in Howe, Indiana, that waited for Michael after the service. He told him that he had gotten out of prison

> Halfway into the song, I opened my eyes and nearly the entire church had come forward – at least five hundred people were repenting, and there was no more room left on the floor.

and didn't know how he got out; he was in for a life sentence for murder. Michael asked him if he did it, and he said "yes." He had killed the wife of his best friend. She had kept telling him, "I'm a Christian, you can't kill me." He told her, "Watch me." He was crying while telling Michael that he understood what she meant now. She would never die because she has eternal life in Christ. He gave his life to Jesus!

We've had countless couples tear up their divorce papers and stayed together throughout the years. We've had a couple that filed for divorce and it was still pending. One of them ended up at the main campus of a church in Florida, and the other one at a satellite campus. While watching PFM, at the end of the service they both went forward, not knowing the other was attending that day. Subsequently, they came back together and decided not to divorce each other.

People have told us throughout our ministry that they've been Christians all their lives and they've never seen anything as powerful or life changing as Potter's Field Ministries. I particularly like to hear that when they are elderly and have been walking with Jesus for fifty years or more. We've known this has been God's ministry from the very beginning, and we will continue to give glory and honor to Him as He continues to use it as He sees fit.

In 1996, we started doing churches in Southern California. And through word of mouth, our ministry spread like wildfire throughout the Calvary Chapels, all the way from Sacramento to San Diego – and everywhere in between. We were at Calvary Chapel Chino Valley and the church was packed. The movement of the Holy Spirit was manifest and palpable that day. When it came time for the altar call, Michael began his plea and I began to sing with my eyes closed. All of a sudden, halfway into the song, I opened my eyes and nearly the entire church had come forward – at least five hundred people were repenting, and there was no more room left on the floor. They descended upon the stage, and I had people packed in so tightly that they were up underneath my armpits! I was crying, the people were crying, people were on their knees repenting…it was an ungraspable, phenomenal moment that we will never forget.

The Spirit was on the move! We were up and running…

Then I heard the voice of the Lord, saying, "Whom shall I send? And who will go for us?" And I said, "Here am I. Send me!"

— Isaiah 6:8 NKJV

The Spirit of the Lord God is upon me, because the Lord has anointed Me to preach good tidings to the poor; He has sent Me to heal the brokenhearted, to proclaim liberty to the captives, and the opening of the prison to those who are bound...

— Isaiah 61:1 NKJV

Chapter 24

A SEASON OF FAITHFULNESS

Michael was healed. The anger, the rage, and the fear – conquered. In victory, we were set free to genuinely walk in step with the Lord, and in unity with each other. These next few years became a time of creativity and high energy. Michael produced thousands of pieces of pottery, and I began writing songs that would help fill another eight music CDs. We were doing two hundred services a year. We continued to experience supernatural provision, and together we walked in faithfulness as God opened many doors.

In 1996, the Lord told me during my devotional quiet time that I was going to record an album entitled *Living Water*. When it came time came for its release, I found out that Pastor Chuck Smith was releasing a book that same year, also called *Living Water*. I was astonished. I knew that this was a confirmation; not only was God going to use this CD, but it was also what was going on in the Father's heart – His timely message to His people during this period. We have sold countless thousands of this CD through the years.

We got to know Pastor Chuck quite well during the next few years. I had always loved him, from that first weekend when he told me that Michael was going to be my ministry. I'm sure his heart was warmed by the fact that God had healed our marriage and given us a ministry together. It's not a well-known fact, but Chuck and Kay got married after three weeks, too – just like Michael and me – they were strong Christians at the time, however.

I got to know Kay Smith quite well through Jean McClure, who is still one of my dearest friends today, and many other godly women at Kay's Joyful Life Bible Study. Jean and her husband, Don – one of the original pastors that Pastor Chuck sent out – run their ministry called Calvary Way Ministries. They have pastored and planted several Calvary Chapels through the years, and Pastor Don is the Chairman of Calvary Chapel Association (CCA), which heads up eighteen hundred Calvary Chapels worldwide.

We were growing spiritually like never before. Michael was being challenged by our Board of Directors, pastors, and godly men. He was becoming a good steward of the money entrusted to our ministry by the Lord. I was so impressed with his growth, knowledge of the Word, and his ability to evangelize that my respect and admiration for him was growing exponentially. God was strengthening us as individuals and in our marriage.

In 1999, Pastor Chuck lent his speaking voice on the title cut for my recording, *For A Time Such As This*, which was a blessing. This and many other songs of mine were played for years on KWVE – the Calvary Chapel radio station based in Costa Mesa whose far-reaching broadcasts aired from Southern to Northern California. Kay asked me to sing special music at her Christmas Tea; it was a large event and I was so excited! The next year she asked, "If Chuck says yes, would you sing a duet with him?" "Of course I would!" I exclaimed. I didn't know that Pastor Chuck had some operatic training. She suggested that we sing "O Holy Night" – and together we brought the house down. It was the most fun, and it started a tradition...Pastor Chuck and I sang "O Holy Night" together for the next ten years. The next year, Kay asked if I would teach the Christmas Tea, so not only would I sing, but teach as well. I was thrilled, but also intimidated; I'd never taught that many women at one time. I ended up teaching the Christmas Tea two more times, and singing every year as well.

I had always wanted to record a Christmas album. Envisioning fully-orchestrated songs, lush with strings, I was aware it would cost over a hundred thousand dollars. I knew this would NEVER happen. So I started praying that the Lord would provide a way for me to have the excellence I wanted, but without the cost. I had sung "Light of a Million Mornings," one of Claire Cloninger's songs which she had written for a musical, and had the kind of orchestration I had dreamed of. I asked Claire what it would cost to lease that track from Word Music. She hooked me up with Phyllis Addison at Word, Inc., and three days later I was provided with the fully-orchestrated track, complete with strings, originally sung by Sandi Patty – with permission to use the recorded track free of charge! God is simply amazing!

Recording my Christmas CD was the first time I actually produced my own record. I worked with Walt Harrah, who arranged these songs beautifully. This turned out to be one of my favorite records, and one of my best sellers. Pastor Chuck and I recorded "O Holy Night" as the last cut. We offered the CD at Calvary Costa Mesa in 2000. After Pastor Chuck and I sang, we sold out in less than an hour, selling over a thousand units. God blessed our ministry that day with record pottery and CD sales beyond any other event to date. I am so thrilled I have his sweet voice on a recording.

Kay took me under her wing. She asked me to share my testimony at her Women's Retreat, and I would be going on before

Elizabeth Elliot. Thank the Lord I didn't have to follow her! At dinner, after I had shared, Kay prophesied that the Lord was going to use our ministry mightily. She went on to say that as time went on, the biggest thing that I would have to fight is that I wouldn't want to go – and she was right. You are so full of zeal at the beginning, and as time presses on it gets harder and harder to want to go out.

Once while we were still in Kentucky, Michael received a prophecy from a woman who told him, "Your brother, Steven, will not die from AIDS, and you will have an eleventh hour with him." This woman didn't know anything about Michael. As a young man, Michael's brother had married, and he and his wife got saved at Calvary Costa Mesa in the early years. Steven and his wife had two girls – our nieces, Jade and Tara. He walked strongly with the Lord for quite a while, and it was in Steven that Michael first saw a changed life and the light of the Lord. Even back then, Michael was strangely drawn to it, though he was still in the height of his sinful lifestyle. Eventually, however, Steven left his wife for another man. He lived a life of debauchery until he was diagnosed with the AIDS virus, and towards the end of his life, liver cancer.

It was seventeen years later that Steven called Michael on New Year's Eve to break the news he was in hospice care. So Michael indeed had an eleventh hour with his brother; spending Steven's last six weeks together. He would fly to San Francisco every week to see him. They had a much-needed time of healing, reminiscing about their childhoods and reliving stories from their past. Michael had the privilege of leading his brother back to Jesus at the end. As a confirmation of this woman's prophetic words, the official cause of his death was recorded as liver cancer, not AIDS.

Roberta, their mom, was able to spend time with him, too. On one February weekend, Michael had a strong sense from the Lord that his mom needed to go and see Steven. She wasn't supposed to fly in until that Monday, but Michael paid the change-of-ticket fee for her to arrive sooner. She's so glad that she did because that weekend, on February 19, 2011, Steven died in her arms. She had cradled Steven as she welcomed him into the world, and she embraced her son as he exited, releasing him into the arms of Jesus.

If you call our Potter's Field Ministries phone today, you will hear a sweet voice saying, "Hello, this is Potter's Field Ministries, Roberta speaking, how may I help you?" Michael's mom is our receptionist now, and the Lord has healed and restored the years the enemy tried to destroy. She has a tremendous prayer ministry that is helping change lives, reaching out to our sponsors on a weekly basis, providing prayer. She is eighty years old – it's never too late to be used by the Potter.

> I knew God had never let us down; I didn't know how He was going to provide, but I knew somehow He would.

As God kept opening doors for us, we continued doing more churches and events. We did an outdoor venue at Acacia Park in Colorado Springs. Michael was preaching and sharing Potter's Field with passion, and there were a lot of non-believers in the crowd. We would hear people yelling, "Shut up!" or "Be quiet!" but a lot of people were listening as well. He and I have ministered all over the world together, and it's a sad testimony that only in America have we been told to "shut up" when sharing the Gospel. This particular day was for one man. Michael was sharing about his old days as a wholesaler on Wall Street, and how he got saved. He also said, "Perhaps you're here today, and you've even thought about killing yourself." Right at that moment, a man on a bicycle was riding through the park and thought he heard his named called, and he stopped to listened to this portion of Michael's sermon. He threw his bike down onto the ground and got on his knees, crying. Afterwards, Michael went over, and the man shared that he was on his way to go home to kill himself. He had a job like what Michael used to have, and he was hopeless. It was truly a divine appointment from God, and Michael led this young man to Jesus.

After a particularly spirit-filled service at a church in Northern California, Michael and I were driving out of a long, dirt parking lot to get onto the main road. A man approached Michael on the driver's side, so he rolled down his window. He told Michael to get out of the car, so Michael put the car in park and told me to stay inside. When he got out, the man put a gun to his head! I was in a panic, to say the least, and I started praying fervently.

Gesturing for me to lock the doors and stay in the car, Michael spoke with this man for what seemed an endless amount of time until the man finally put the gun down and started crying. This guy wanted to kill Michael, and next thing I know, Michael is leading this guy to the Lord. I learned later that this man had found a small, dried hard ball of clay on the windshield wiper of his car, which he saw as he was getting ready to leave the service. He thought that Michael had put it there and was trying to tell him something. Michael was trying to talk this guy off a ledge, telling him that he didn't do it, but apparently the Holy Spirit was trying to get his attention, so he should pay attention.

After receiving Christ, Michael told him to come to the church the next morning. Michael went back in and told the pastor what had happened, and that hopefully this guy would show up. He called the next day and found he had not only come, but was willing to do whatever the pastor asked him. So he was given a broom, and that started the beginning of his serving in the ministry there, where he began to grow in the Lord.

I know that something like this would deter most people from going any further. But Michael and I knew this was God's ministry, and He has His hand of protection upon it. Often during a Potter's Field presentation, while I was sitting and Michael was sharing, the Lord would show me the people in the audience that He wanted me to pray for. Sometimes He would even let me know what was going on in their lives, and I would approach them afterwards, telling them what the Lord had showed me about them. Other times I would just pray and hope that He would touch them and that they would obey His voice, and perhaps come forward for prayer or do whatever else the Lord would ask of them.

We were doing a Crusade in El Cajon, California; it was a large, four-night event. Before we went on the last night, Michael informed me that we were fourteen thousand dollars short to pay our bills for the ministry that month. I knew God had never let us down; I didn't know how He was going to provide, but I knew somehow He would. Michael just laughed. He knew we could come up with fifteen hundred dollars pretty easily in back table sales, but fourteen thousand in a couple of days…he knew it would have to be God. After the presentation that evening, we sold a lot of product and they took up a healthy love offering for us. While I was at the back table, a man came up and handed me a folded check. I thanked him, then simply put it in my pocket, since we were so busy at the moment. After Michael and I helped pack everything up and we got to the van, I told him that I had forgotten that someone had handed me a check. He said, "Well let's look at it." I was standing outside the van, getting ready to hop in, and I unfolded the check. I started crying and slumped over on the seat. Michael asked, more intrigued than anything, "What's wrong? How much is it?" I flipped it over – and it was for ten thousand dollars! So with the love offering, product sold, and the check we received, we had all we needed to get us through to the next month to continue sharing the good news of the Gospel!

God has always been so faithful in supplying vehicles when we needed them. After four years of staying in host homes and inexpensive motels, we really wanted to price out travel trailers.

> "If you had left Michael so many years ago, when you so desperately wanted out of your marriage, you wouldn't have waited long enough to see all the Lord could do!"

In Anaheim, California, we found a thirty-four foot Jayco trailer, with a slide out that made the living space larger. The sticker price was thirty-two thousand dollars. Michael and I prayed, we didn't want to pay over twenty-four thousand, five hundred dollars. We agreed that if it was a dollar over the price we agreed upon, we wouldn't buy it. Well that's the exact price that the salesman came back with, and we qualified for it with no money down.

Early on in our ministry we had seen a beautiful American Coach; it was our heart's desire to have one of those beautiful buses one day. However, the price of a high-end Class A Coach was the equivalent of a house mortgage, so we knew that if the Lord ever wanted us to have one, He would make it possible. Four years later, in 2000, we began shopping for one. We went to an RV store in Southern California and found the one we wanted – it was over two hundred thousand dollars! This one, however, they would negotiate on, because it was a coach that the company had used for road trips, so they couldn't sell it full price. We kept going back, time and time again, praying. We didn't know how we would pay for it, but if the Lord was in it, He would provide. The man that was working with us was really kind. We found out that his dad used to be a traveling evangelist, so he understood how hard it was traveling around and having to stay in host homes or motels, and how stressful it was hauling things behind another vehicle. He had empathy for us. He went to the company and got the coach reduced to one hundred seventy-three thousand dollars. We knew if we could get it for this price, it would be a steal, even so, we waited so long that they almost put it back on the lot. By faith, we decided to buy the American Tradition coach. We couldn't believe that we could actually drive our house around!

This would give us longevity in the ministry, especially for me. Women love to nest, and in my entire married life I had never been given the chance to nest and make a home for us. Granted it would be a home on wheels, but nonetheless, it was a palace to me! The scenery would change, and the states and cities would change, but the inside of this blessed RV would be our home for the next fourteen years. One year into buying the coach, someone wrote us a check to pay off the entire amount for this beautiful RV. God is so faithful! We still have it, and it was a home for some of our Resident Assistants recently for one of our Kid's Program locations in Browning, Montana, on the Blackfeet Indian Reservation. Now it sits behind our little church where it serves as a guesthouse for visiting pastors and their wives, or guests who come to visit our ministry.

Years before, Connie Chinelly, during one of the first times she saw us do Potter's Field, had turned to her husband, John, and said, "He's an angry man, we need to pray for the two of them." After this season of obedience, growth, and faithfulness, she saw us again at a Women's Aglow. I will never forget when she came up to me and said, "Just think, Pam…if you had left Michael so many years ago, when you so desperately wanted out of your marriage, you wouldn't have waited long enough to see all the Lord could do! That He was going to give you a ministry. That it was going to be called Potter's Field Ministries. And that one day He would be able to use that ministry all over the world – to bind up the broken-hearted, to set the captives free, and to make you into instruments of healing for broken marriages…For such a time as this…"

Yet another stone to erect in honor of our mighty God!

Chapter 25

SLAYING MY ISAAC

With any spiritual mountaintop experience, you expect to be bombarded by the enemy. You will be hit with doubt, fear, discouragement, and discontentment. I was being blindsided by Satan himself, with a nagging desire to go back to Broadway to do a show where I would feel useful, and where I could use all my gifts. This was an incredible lie from the enemy, and my thoughts were tormenting and assaulting me on a regular basis to the extent I was actually looking into the possibilities of going back to New York to start auditioning again for a show. Time kept on ticking; I was getting older and I wanted one last hurrah on the stage. The self-centeredness of ego was rearing its ugly head once again.

I felt invisible doing Potter's Field Ministries. The enemy whispered in my ear that I was just singing on a stool, with no speaking voice, like a ventriloquist dummy. "Michael doesn't really need you, and you won't be missed if you leave," rang the devilish voice in the battleground of my mind. The struggle, the battle, was evident and irrefutable. I couldn't hide my restlessness. I wore my heart on my sleeve. And I truly didn't make it bearable for Michael. Looking back, he had so much patience with me, and he even gave me the go ahead to leave, stating however, it would ruin our ministry, our marriage, and our livelihood. He was finally so worried about me that he flew up a pastor's wife he knew I would listen to so she could speak some sense into my life. She and I sat on my bed in our house. When she heard me out, stated, "If you go back into the world now, you will die this time. And I mean literally!" I heard her, but my flesh was winning this dispute.

Little children, keep yourselves from idols.

— 1 John 5:21 NKJV

This verse sums up everything in the book of 1 John. We must keep ourselves away from anything that would distract our hearts from God. We must make right choices. Before I came back to God, I had made my career an idol in my life. This desire to be in the limelight was once again rekindling in my heart. It was an idol that wasn't dead yet, and He knew it. God wanted to know: Would I sacrifice this "idol" once and for all and make the right choice?

Just at the moment where it looked as though I was going to quit PFM and go back into the world, God sent a stranger with a prophecy, at just the right time. We were doing PFM at a church in Las Vegas, Nevada, and I was particularly conflicted that morning, and weary with this warfare going on day after day. A lady was visiting the church that day from Tifton, Georgia, which is only fifty-five miles from my hometown in Thomasville. I didn't know her, and I found it odd that someone that close to home would be at a church in Las Vegas. She approached me the minute I came into the sanctuary and informed me that she had been sent by God, to this church, just for me. She had a word from the Lord for me.

I'd had a few strange experiences with people like this through the years, but fortunately my friend, Peg Goldring, had been assigned to me that day as my bodyguard. The woman suggested that she would rather say what needed to be said in private. I looked at Peg with fear, who suggested that we go and sit in a corner near the offices, away from the crowd, instead of going behind closed doors. The lady agreed. She told me that I had to take off my shoes and sit with my bare feet flat on the floor. This was getting stranger by the moment, but I relented.

She knelt before my feet, looked straight into my eyes, and proceeded to say, "The Lord says, 'My daughter, I love your humility and your willingness to obey what I've asked you to do, so don't be discouraged and keep your eyes on Me. I will lift up your ministry in due time, be patient and press on. Keep walking in humility, for it pleases Me like none other. I've heard your cries. I love you My daughter…'"

By this time I was dissolved in tears, and could barely see through them to watch what she was going to do next. She took one foot in her hands and kissed the top of my foot,

> **This desire to be in the limelight was once again rekindling in my heart. It was an idol that wasn't dead yet, and He knew it.**

and then repeated the same with the other foot. I was dumbfounded, bowled over, and encouraged beyond belief that my God would know what was going on in my heart and care enough about me to send a stranger like this woman to lift me up!

At a church in Montana, not too long after this, I had another woman come up to me after the service. She told me that when I unveiled the God Pot at the end of the service, the Lord told her to come and tell me, "You are a trophy of God's grace!" God was asking me to hold on because He was getting ready to do something in my life.

As I was walking in this season of malcontent, wanting to sow to my flesh to get accolades for my gifts, I suppose I was looking for some sort of personal payoff. The Lord needed to crucify this part of me. I was fighting tooth and nail having to die to this. I never knew anything differently. I'd never worked so hard in my life. I was tired, weary, and wanted to do something else. I wanted to go back to Egypt, to the land I knew…

> *Then he said, "Take now your only son Isaac, whom you love, and go to the land of Moriah, and offer him there as a burnt offering on one of the mountains of which I shall tell you."*
>
> — Genesis 22:2 NKJV

> *Then they came to the place of which God had told him. And Abraham built an altar there and placed the wood in order; and he bound Isaac, his son, and laid him on the altar, upon the wood. And Abraham stretched out his hand and took the knife to slay his son. But the Angel of the Lord called to him from heaven and said, "Abraham, Abraham!" So he said, "Here I am."*

> *And He said, "Do not lay your hand on the lad, or do anything to him; for now I know that you fear God, since you have not withheld your son, your only son from me."*
>
> — Verses 9-12

> *"…By Myself I have sworn," says the Lord, "because you have done this thing and have not withheld your son, your only son – blessing I will bless you, and multiplying I will multiply…"*
>
> — Verses 16-17

It was the late afternoon and I was alone in the Jayco trailer. Michael wasn't there; he was running errands. I was talking to God out loud and asking Him to help me have an undivided heart. All of a sudden, I fell under such great conviction that I fell to my knees and started confessing my sin. I was truly sorry from the depths of my heart for being ungrateful, for forgetting what the Lord had done in my marriage and ministry. We had come so far! I felt like the Israelites, grumbling and complaining in the midst of God's blessings and provision. I bitterly wept tears of repentance, and knew right there on my knees in that trailer, crying out to God, that I had finally surrendered any chances of going back into the world. This time was different – I knew that this desire had died within me. It no longer had a hold on me like a vice grip. Jesus was all I wanted, and He was all I needed. I finally felt free of that gnawing yearning to feed my flesh. I had slayed my Isaac.

> He had passed the point of no return – so he let his ships burn!

Michael had a similar experience one evening while he was driving to where we would be doing a few churches. I was sound asleep with the dogs. He was listening to Steven Curtis Chapman's song, "Burn the Ships:"

In the spring of 1519 a Spanish fleet set sail
Cortez told his sailors this mission must not fail
On the eastern shore of Mexico they landed with great dreams
But the hardships of the new world make them restless and weak

Quietly they whispered, "Let's sail back to the life we knew"
But the one who led them there was saying

Chorus
"Burn the ships we're here to stay
There's no way we could go back
Now that we've come this far by faith
Burn the ships we've passed the point of no return
Our life is here so let the ships burn and burn"

In the spring of new beginnings a searching heart set sail
Looking for a new life and a love that would not fail
On the shores of grace and mercy we landed with great joy
But an enemy was waiting to steal, kill, and destroy

Quietly he whispers. "Go back to the life you knew"
But the one who led us here is saying

"Burn the ships we're here to stay
There's no way we could go back
Now that we've come this far by faith
Burn the ships we've passed the point of no return
Our life is here so let the ships burn and burn"

Nobody said it would be easy
But the one who brought us here
Is never gonna leave us alone

Michael knew that he could never go back into finance or that old life again. He'd burned his ships by making a decision to let his license lapse, and he wouldn't be able to work in finance without it. He had passed the point of no return – so he let his ships burn! That was his Isaac. He laid his career down and knew that he wouldn't even want to go back to retake exams or put people in investments they shouldn't be in. Neither one of us were ever going to turn back! Our hands were on the plow! We weren't going to look to the right or left, we were just going to do what was set before us. We were ALL in!

Literally the day after I did this, I got a call from Calvary Chapel Costa Mesa. They were putting together their first Women's Conference at the Anaheim Convention Center. I was one of two singers chosen to do special music at the CCCM Women's Conference in 1998. It was going to be Jamie Owens-Collins and me. I was on the same program as Chuck Smith, Greg Laurie, Elizabeth Dole, Gigi Tchjvidjian, Kay Smith, and Becky Tirabassi, with Harvest Praise Band doing worship and playing two of my songs. They chose "Soften My Heart" and "Make My Life A Miracle" for me to sing. Harvest's worship leader, Hanz Ives, would sing the part that Terry Clark did on my original recording. I only brought my *Living Water* CD to sell – and I sold out that afternoon! It was crazy! There were thousands of ladies in attendance.

I started getting booked all over the United States, teaching Women's Retreats, Spring Teas, Christmas Teas, Women's Conferences, and was invited to sing special music at the Irvine Meadows Amphitheatre for Calvary Chapel Costa Mesa for Good Friday and Easter services in 1999, 2000, and 2007. We were also doing a full schedule of Potter's Field – two hundred dates a year. PFM took off with so many bookings and churches scheduled that we'd never get to all of them! I had been holding back the move and the flow of the Holy Spirit because of a divided heart. He wanted my undivided devotion to Him…and Him alone.

He wanted to bless us our ministry all along, but I was the one standing in His way.

Chapter 26

CROSSING THE JORDAN ON DRY GROUND

I am so thrilled that I have a chronological record of events to archive the goodness, miracles, and faithfulness of our God. I will shout it to the next generation. I never want to forget what He's done for us through the years. I know how fickle I can become, and I need to refresh my memories from time to time. The heart of man is so prone to wander, and to forget the loving kindness of an omnipotent God.

The Israelites, when they were with Moses, got impatient and let their hearts wander and become hardened. They wanted new things and were discontent with the daily provision of the manna, and they made and set up idols in their lives. As a result, they were not permitted to see the Promised Land. They didn't die to their desires. They didn't wait on God. They took matters into their own hands. Therefore they wandered in the desert for forty years.

> *Do not harden your hearts, as in the rebellion, as in the day of trial in the wilderness, when your fathers tested Me; they tried Me, though they saw My work. For forty years I was grieved with that generation, and said, "It is a people who go astray in*

their hearts, and they do not know My ways." So I swore in My wrath, "They shall not enter My rest."

— Psalm 95:8-11

We must wait on our Commander in Chief for His timing, and not grow weary of waiting. Has He given you a promise that seems like it will never happen? I know that those years in which I waited for His promises that He was making a way in the desert and streams in the wasteland and that we would be ambassadors to the nations, it NEVER looked like they were going to come to pass. I had to wait and trust in the One who gave me these promises in the first place. I had to wait for Him to fulfill them in His own way and in His timing. I had to die to what I thought it should look like. I never would have put a singer and a potter together, but He did – and look at the fruit He produced in His time. We can't assume that God's plan is going to look like our plan. He will make beauty from ashes. He will take cracked and broken vessels and make a beautiful bowl that will hold more fruit, instead of a "showy" vase.

> We must die to our preconceived dreams and goals in order for the Lord to resurrect something beautiful out of our lives.

But in order to do this a death must occur first. That is truly the paradox of the Bible – Jesus had to die in order for us to have life. And so must you and I. This is evident not only in the death, burial, and resurrection of Jesus Christ…but take a look at nature as well. The winter of 2017 in Montana was one of the harshest ones that I've experienced in my twenty years of living here. I've grown to love the seasons, and I have my favorites: spring and summer. However, I think I've learned much more from my not-so-favorite seasons. Take fall for instance, although everything is dying, the colors have a beauty all their own, and it's the time my hobby of gardening never makes sense to me. It is pruning time. As all of the flowering bushes and plants die off right after the first freeze, I have to cut them all down to at least one foot above the ground if I want new, beautiful foliage in the spring. I'm always alarmed as I am cutting them down, thinking they will never return! I clean out the leaves from around them and cut away their former beauty, hoping for the best as winter approaches.

When the winter arrives and the plants are buried underneath two feet of resplendent frozen snow, which makes for a magical Winter Wonderland, I can't imagine how – after the spring slowly drags around – out of the gray, dead bushes of the former flowering plants and trees, the green will ever resurrect. And so it goes every year through the winter snow, after the spring melt, little green buds start to emerge everywhere, little by little, as life again begins to course through the vines and branches, much to my awe and amazement! Flowers bloom everywhere, and the fragrance of lilacs fills the air. Spring comes into full bloom, and it is miraculous and marvelous.

Isn't this the same process that our loving Father takes each one of us through in our Christian walk? Scripturally speaking, our sanctification process is seasonal in our own lives as well. If we will allow the excruciatingly painful process of pruning to take place in our own lives – the cutting away of the chaff, the useless, dead leaves to be raked away to allow for something new to begin; to forsake the comfortable, the routine, and believe that new growth will take place in His time – then our lives would reflect the beauty and new life that God wants for each of us as believers and followers in

Him! We must die to our preconceived dreams and goals in order for the Lord to resurrect something beautiful out of our lives.

I am the vine you are the branches. He who abides in Me, and I in him, bears much fruit; for without Me you can do nothing. If anyone does not abide in Me, he is cast out as a branch and is withered; and they gather them and throw them into the fire, and they are burned. If you abide in Me, and My words abide in you, you will ask what you desire, and it shall be done for you. By this My Father is glorified, that you bear much fruit; so you will be My disciples.

— John 15:5-8 NKJV

And those twelve stones which they took out of the Jordan, Joshua set up in Gilgal. Then he spoke to the children of Israel saying: "When your children ask their fathers in time to come, saying, 'What are these stones?' then you shall let your children know saying, 'Israel crossed over this Jordan on dry land;' for the Lord your God dried up the waters of the Jordan before you until you crossed over, as the Lord your God did to the Red Sea, which He dried up before us until we had crossed over, that all the peoples of the earth may know the hand of the Lord, that it is mighty, that you may fear the Lord your God forever."

— Joshua 4:20-24 NKJV

Thus, as in spring, there are new beginnings being symbolized by the stones of remembrance which were set up in Gilgal. The Israelites had crossed successfully into Canaan under Joshua's leadership. God had shown the miraculous once again by parting the Jordan River, and everyone successfully crossed over onto dry ground. God had transferred power to Joshua, and they feared him as much as they did Moses while he was alive. Joshua commanded them to set up memorial stones to commemorate that the power and the hand of God is mighty, and nothing is too hard for God to do. Not even nature itself can obstruct what God wants done. God had parted the Red Sea for Moses, but in spite of that, and because of their disobedience, His people wandered in the desert for forty years. God only wants our obedience, and He doesn't want to withhold His mercy from us when we obey. He allowed the next generation of Israelites to cross the Jordan River on dry ground, and this time they would make it into the Promised Land.

We must listen to the leading of God. We must sacrifice our flesh. It must cost us something to get to the Promised Land.

Joshua and the children of Israel had to trust God and cross over it. It was a sacrifice, and they put everything on the line in order to get God's best. They had to have faith and a belief that they were going into Canaan. And when they crossed, Joshua was asked to erect stones, lifted from the dry bed of the river, so they would always remember what He had done, and to draw strength from that, not only for them, but for future generations to come. If you read this passage in Joshua 4 – I had to reread it in order to see this – Joshua actually erected two separate memorials. The first one only Joshua could erect because he, like the priests, could approach the Ark of the Covenant (Numbers 27:18; Deuteronomy 34:9), and everyone else was told to keep their distance. These were built at the edge of the Jordan River, put there as a reminder of the miraculous crossing of the Jordan. This is the place where John the Baptist started baptizing, and it was a well-traveled trade route on the way to Jerusalem. So when the people went by, they would be reminded of God's greatness and His power. The Lord directed him to put a duplicate of the memorial stones in Gilgal, so that way it would prove that God indeed parted the Jordan so they could cross over into Canaan. If Joshua hadn't had divine direction from God to prepare the memorial stones, it would've seemed self-serving, as if Joshua were lifting up his own name instead of God's. But these memorials of stones served as a reminder that God indeed did take His people across the Jordan and onto dry ground.

We must listen to the leading of God. We must sacrifice our flesh. It must cost us something to get to the Promised Land. I needed to first die to my performance, then die to my flesh in wanting to go back to Broadway, and then die to who I think I am – in my marriage, my career, and my identity – then die and die and die again...

We must train for discomfort. It must have been really hard for the Israelites to trust that Joshua was hearing from God as they started across the Jordan. I start thinking about the livestock, goats, and horses, and all of their belongings they had to carry with them. Would God really see them through to the other side? Would He be true to His promises that there was a land of milk and honey on the other side?

Would God bring me this far to let me down? Would He be a cosmic killjoy and laugh at me in the midst of my troubles? The Lord was training me for adversity. The Lord had isolated me from having friends for a very long time during my ministry life. I have been lonelier in ministry than any other thing I've ever done. But I knew the Lord wanted His and my relationship to be as solid as those stones that were erected in days of old. And today, He alone is my "go to" person, even before my husband, because of it. I wouldn't have it any other way. But it was hard at the time.

While on tour, I felt isolated, forlorn, and reclusive. I would be left alone quite a bit, and I wasn't in a place long enough to make friends. Most times I was usually stranded in RV parks without a car while others were out running errands. I love what Elizabeth Elliot said, "Loneliness is a required course for leadership." I believe that unless you can stand alone for Jesus Christ, you can't be fully used. I love the old song, "I Have Decided To Follow Jesus." My favorite verse is, "Though none go with me, still I will follow...No turning back...No turning back..."

The stones of remembrance are in my life today as a reminder of God's faithfulness in times of trouble, that He is mighty and nothing is too hard for Him, that He is our true source of joy, and He is the God of the impossible! Theses stories are my proof that He has parted the Jordan for us so many times as we crossed over onto dry ground, and I can now harken back and see the memorial stones that have been erected in His honor.

I love that the priests waited, not moving until Joshua ordered them to come out of the riverbed onto dry land, only when God providentially told him to do so. Joshua listened to the voice of God, and they trusted that he was a vessel divinely appointed to hear from Him. I imagine there were moments they began to grow weary of the wait as they guarded the Ark of the Covenant, which was a symbol of God's presence. I know that I had grown weary, waiting to see if I would ever be able to share what I had gone through during our ministry presentation. I had to trust that my husband was hearing the voice of the Lord, even in the midst of our adversities, and that when the time came for me to speak, I would know and he would confirm it. It had been a long, five years of sitting on a stool and singing while I watched my husband grow into the man of God that I had been promised he would become.

I had wonderful parents. Since I was very young, they were my most supportive cheerleaders. They attended every dance and piano recital, school play, and function – everything that I did up until they both passed away. I was one of the fortunate ones. Michael, on the other hand, didn't have parents like mine. His father was self-absorbed and too busy with his work and being a stepdad to his other wives' kids to actually take care of his own sons. His mom was just trying to make ends meet day by day, working early morning until late in the evenings, so there was no extra time to be Michael's cheerleader.

The Lord told me early on in PFM that I was to sit back and just sing, to support my husband as he grew in his faith, for me to be his cheerleader, and that if I talked during the pre-sentation this early on I would intimidate him, since I was so comfortable on stage, and it would hinder his growth. And while most of the time Michael would take my advice on what to keep and what to discard, sometimes he would be defensive and intimidated and hurt over what I had to say. This was a foreign concept to me; I had prided myself in being capable and smart. And in today's world, we, as women, need to speak up, right? Would I be willing to die to this part of myself and to what I thought was a God-given right? At first it wasn't so difficult, but as time went on, and in

> The Lord knew I needed to hear this so many times because I'm hard headed, and the message of the potter and the clay needed to be seared into my soul.

church after church, I had to sit back and watch, listening over and over again to stories – some that would work and some that didn't – as Michael developed into the man of God that He wanted him to become. It became harder and harder to do.

Truth be told, the Lord knew I needed to hear this so many times because I'm hard headed, and the message of the potter and the clay needed to be seared into my soul. I was willing to die to self for God's greater good, but it doesn't come without a cost – it was going to take five years! But those agonizing years helped chisel away my rough edges. God was working on me, too.

It was at a PFM event at Calvary Chapel Downey where I felt that I was supposed to start sharing my testimony. I was apprehensive to tell Michael that the Lord had shown me that this would be the time. I had numerous confirmations up until this point from people that I trusted, one being our trustworthy assistant, Lorie Welch. Other people had begun asking him when I would be able to speak in the ministry, because it would be a good thing to hear what happened from a woman's point of view. The Lord was already preparing him for this moment. I hesitantly broached the subject, and asked, "Do you think I could share a little bit tonight?" After thinking about it for a while we decided to add it in, working out the logistics of where I would begin sharing. I told him that I felt the Lord leading me to share about his rage and how it affected me, what I learned from it, and how he had been set free. It was decided we would let the Lord lead as He saw fit.

After I had shared in the ministry that evening, Michael gave the altar call. Michael implored the men in the congregation that if they needed to have a touch from the Lord, to have a better marriage and become stronger, loving leaders in their households, to come forward. People started coming forward in droves. At the end there were at least three hundred souls at the altar, and the majority of them were men! This supernatural outpouring of the Holy Spirit was a confirmation that we were to present Potter's Field in this new way – a new beginning. And He would pour out His spirit in a way that He had not done up until this point in our ministry. We had become a husband and wife ministry "team" from this night forward. A marriage, working together in tandem, the way God sees it.

> *Two are better than one, because they have a good return for their labor: If either of them falls down, one can help the other up. But pity anyone who falls and has no one to help them up. Also, if two lie down together, they will keep warm. But how can one keep warm alone? Though one may be overpowered, two can defend themselves. A cord of three strands is not quickly broken.*
>
> — Ecclesiastes 4:9-12

I'm not writing this book to dwell upon what has been in the past. We as humans, just like the Israelites, tend to forget God's goodness towards us. It has been such a cathartic experience remembering these stones that God has erected throughout our lives. I pray that when I start to grumble and complain in the future that I will get this out and read it to remind me of who He is to me – All-Powerful, Mighty God, Everlasting Father, and Prince of Peace who is the same yesterday, today, and forever. I am looking onward, forward, and upward to what He has in store for the things to come. I know that we have and will be able to erect new stones of remembrance in His honor.

I know that a lot of these stories seem implausible to you, but each one has happened just as I have recounted them to you. His signs and wonders are as real today as they always have been. I pray that this will be a handbook of sorts for when you struggle with unbelief, that you will grab these pages and read what the Lord has done in the lives of two improbable candidates. He took two broken shards and put them back together again, He made something beautiful out of their lives in order to shine His light through their cracks. He chose two of the truly foolish and fallible people of this world to confound the wise. These "stones" aren't just for us – they are for anyone who would believe upon the name of Jesus Christ. His is the name above all names. I dare you to believe.

> I pray I am still singing His praises and proclaiming His goodness until my dying breath.

Michael and I have hundreds of thousands of cards, letters, emails, and mementos stored away in our home in boxes, and in storage units as well. Hopefully, one day when I'm really old, I will find the time to go back and read the miraculously wonderful things that God did for His people through this ministry. If not, then I pray I am still singing His praises and proclaiming His goodness until my dying breath, and we will leave these behind so others can see what God can do with two willing vessels.

They shall still bear fruit in old age; they shall be fresh and flourishing...

— Psalm 92:14 NKJV

Hopefully, this ministry will continue long after Michael and I are in the grave, and they will serve as stones of remembrances to them to continue steadfastly, standing on His promises and believing He still is the miracle-working God through the ages.

*I will sing of the LORD's great love forever; with my mouth I
will make your faithfulness known through all generations. I
will declare that your love stands firm forever, that you have
established your faithfulness in heaven itself.*

— Psalm 89:1-2

This is the verse I put on my first record in 1990.

It still rings true today.

I will close this chapter with a card I kept and found while
I was writing this book. It was sent to me anonymously, but it
blesses me as much today as when I received it.

My faithful Daughter,

Why do you carry burdens you should not carry? You have
served Me faithfully for many years! Do not look at the
obstacles around you with your eyes. Look at the ministry I have given you and your husband through My eyes...
Daughter come up to the mountain and seek My face...
Remember, if you look at the people like Moses you will
become angry and frustrated...So come up and I will make
your vision clear again. You want to see the people changed
just as I do daughter. I hear you when you cry out to Me!
Remember when My Son was asked by his mother to somehow supply more wine for the wedding feast! The wine had
run dry...Jesus cried out to the servant to bring pots that
would hold the new wine Jesus was about to produce...and
then what was said of the new wine? "Then He called to
the bridegroom and said, 'Everyone brings out the choice
wine first and then the cheaper wine last after the guest has
had much to drink; but you have saved the best for last!!'"
Daughter this is what I have <u>Reserved</u> for the ministry I have

given your husband and you!! "The best for last!" I am going to pour out the wine of the Holy Spirit upon your ministry in these last days! Though you will go through much…the people will be transformed from the inside out…out of the clay pots will flow the best of My Spirit!! Be encouraged daughter!!

The best is
    Yet to
        Come…
            (John 2:7-11)

Chapter 27

REFINER'S FIRE

There is no doubt when the Lord God does mighty things –
like parting the Red Sea or the Jordan River – it's an invin-
cible act of God. He continues to do mighty things today,
as evidenced in what I've written thus far. And I'm sure that you
have your stories, or "stones," as well. He reminds us of His insurmountable power and wants us to revere Him and fear Him (be in
awe of Him) all of our days!

> *I will bring the one-third through the fire, will refine them as*
> *silver is refined, and test them as gold is tested. They will call*
> *on My name, and I will answer them. I will say, "This is My*
> *people;" And each one will say, "The Lord is my God."*
> — Zechariah 13:9 NKJV

> *When you pass through the waters, I will be with you; and*
> *when you pass through the rivers, they will not sweep over you.*
> *When you walk through the fire, you will not be burned; the*
> *flames will not set you ablaze. For I am the Lord, your God,*
> *the Holy One of Israel, your Savior…*
> — Isaiah 43:2-3

Through the Fire
Written by Pam Rozell & Claire Cloninger

When we stand in the heat of the fire
It's so hard to keep faith and believe
When the flames leap around us, may your mercy surround us
And show us what only You can see

CHORUS
Through the fire, You see us finished
For You see beyond today to who we'll be
For You see our souls perfected
At the heart of Your desire
Lord, You see us finished, through the fire

So we'll stand in the heat of the fire
And we'll trust You in spite of the pain
For we know the One who holds us, who heals and consoles us
Whose eyes can see the glory and the gain

BRIDGE
You will never leave us or forsake us
You're closer than a brother or a friend
And when this age is finished, Lord, You'll meet us,
To walk with You forever through a world that never ends

These are the lyrics to a song that I co-wrote with Claire Cloninger that is on my *Living Water* CD. I also recorded a song that Walt Harrah wrote, "I Am the Lord Your God," based on Isaiah 43:2, on my *For A Time Such As This* CD, that I often listen to so I can be encouraged. He is with us through our trials, hardships, joys, victories, and pain.

The fire is for purification. I know this because I've been married to a potter for thirty years. It speaks to my heart every time I watch Michael take a worthless, formless lump of clay and put it on the potter's wheel. As the clay starts to spin, he begins to make a beautiful vessel that only he can see as he is throwing it. He has said many times, "I can already envision what I'm going to make before I ever put the clay on the wheel." I love that, because God always knows what He's going to do with us each and every time we are put back up on the wheel. He may decide to use a needle tool to cut away or prune something or someone out of our lives. He could use a "rib" tool – used to smooth off the rough edges. I love the name of this tool, because He took a rib out of Adam to make Eve – a bone next to Adam's heart. The Lord may also decide whether or not to put you back into the fire – the kiln – and crank up the heat once again to make you shine more brightly, or to put you through the fire of affliction to bring you closer to Himself again.

Isn't that the way God is with us? He wants the final outcome to be loveliness, holiness, and purity.

When unveiling Michael's six-foot God Pot at the end of every Potter's Field presentation, I never tire of seeing how beautiful and brilliant the colors are on that pot. He actually uses an expensive eighteen-karat gold glaze, in addition to a mother-of-pearl glaze. When he puts it on the pot, he either has to wear a mask or have adequate ventilation; the odor is so strong and toxic that there is a warning label on the container. I like to look at this as God putting us through the ringer, whether it be a difficult relationship, an illness, a horrible situation that one must endure, a loss of a job or a loved one, or whatever else you might fill in the blank with. Next, he places the pot into the kiln for literally hours on end, and sometimes days, as the heat is slowly taken up to well over eighteen hundred degrees. Michael always expresses what he thinks it would feel like, screaming really loudly, "Lord what are you doing to me in here?" We laugh, but that's how it really feels. Then, as the fire cools down over several days and he goes back in to see what the intense heat has accomplished, he opens the door to the kiln and starts jumping up and down, yelling with elation, "God Pot! God Pot!" He is so excited that it has made it through the fire, and it is lovely and exquisite, it's beyond description! Isn't that the way God is with us? He wants the final outcome to be loveliness, holiness, and purity. But we can't get there except through the fire.

I continually want to be a usable vessel in the Master Potter's hands. However, our glaze dulls over time. We get lazy, skip our devotions, or don't obey what God has told us to do or how to be. He has to put us back into the fire of affliction so we can shine brightly again for our Lord.

Michael has re-fired that God Pot no less than seven times! I am astounded that each time he does it, it comes out shining more brilliantly than it did before. The potter is always there making sure it can take the heat that he is putting it through. He takes his pillow into his studio, staying with it through the night watch, making sure that it doesn't crack during the night. Our Potter cares and sees, and He wants us to be standing at the end of our lives with His arms outstretched wide as we hear these words spoken, *"Well done, good and faithful servant; you have been faithful over a few things, I will make you ruler over many things. Enter into the joy of your Lord"* (Matthew 25:23 NKJV).

For nearly ten years, we had been doing over two hundred services each year. I was about to crack – or what I feel is about as close to a nervous breakdown that you can get. I shared this with a few people on our Board of Directors at the time. Michael was pushing hard. He is a true savant when it comes to math and numbers. So he would take what our averages were financially and how many services it took to pay our bills, then run the numbers. Then he would calculate what that equated to and determine how many services we would need to do that year to meet this goal. But I couldn't keep up with the schedule, and my mental health was suffering. This was a season that Michael would be put into the kiln and come out shining on the other side.

> God has truly made him into everything He promised me – and much more.

The Board of Directors challenged Michael to trust God that He would provide everything that we needed. They told him if he didn't change our schedule, he would be visiting me in the "funny farm." They stongly suggested that he cut our services in half for the next year – one hundred services as opposed to two hundred – and they actually suggested only ninety per year. I could see the fear, mixed with chagrin, starting to form in his eyes. Once again, I had told on him like I did back in Fort Lauderdale. I knew for both of our sakes we needed to get a balance in our lives. He was being tested and tried by God to see if he truly believed: "Where God guides, God provides." The Lord was also increasing his faith. He was again being re-fired in the kiln in this area of his life. He spoke boldly to the Board, "We just bankrupted this ministry! You'll see."

Needless to say, when we had our annual Board meeting the next year, when we did the overview of our financials, the Lord had increased our profits through love offerings, gifts, and sales up twenty-three percent! The Lord doesn't work on our math scales. No one knows this better than our Administrator and Finance Director, Christa Stoltzfus, who has been with us ten years. When you walk into her office you will see a sign that reads, "5 loaves + 2 fish = 5,000 fed." We still run on this principle to this day, knowing God will provide all our needs in Christ Jesus! Michael had learned an invaluable lesson, and today he will be the first one to bring God back into the equation when we all see the zeros that still need to be met at the end of each month. God honored his obedience to place himself under authority by men that hear from God. Michael is such a stunning example in learning lessons and applying them, and then putting them into action. He has grown tremendously and is one of the best money managers I've ever come across. God has truly made him into everything He promised me – and much more.

Every so often, I will receive in the mail a song someone has written, or an already recorded song, which they think would work well in our ministry. I've actually recorded a couple of them that have been sent through the years. I received one called "The Potter's House" one particular year, and I loved it. It was recorded by Tremaine Hawkins and written by Michael McKay. Here are the lyrics:

In case you have fallen by the wayside of life
Dreams and visions shattered, you're all broken inside
You don't have to stay in the shape that you're in
The Potter wants to put you back together again

In case your situation has turned upside down
And all that you've accomplished is now on the ground
You don't have to stay in the shape that you're in
The potter wants to put you back together again

Chorus

You who are broken stop by the potter's house
You who need mending, stop by the potter's house
Give Him the fragments of your broken life
My friend, the potter wants to put you back together again

I had no idea when or with whom I would ever get to sing this song, but I knew that the Lord had this one sent to me with a purpose. It was early 1999, and I was in a drought, spiritually speaking, and not hearing very loudly from the Lord, as I had in the past. I was hoping I wasn't sliding down the "old rabbit hole" that I'd grown accustomed to. I thought I'd been experiencing bouts of victory in the discontentment department, but old habits die hard. I was making the drive from Whitefish to Kalispell to go shopping, and I had the radio turned to a Christian FM station. I rarely do this because I usually take the time in the car to talk to God without distractions. Then I heard the announcer say, "Grammy and Dove Award nominee Morris Chapman will be giving a concert at The Christian Center" (it is now called Canvas church), along with the date and time. I couldn't believe my ears! Morris Chapman was my favorite worship leader. I loved his voice! When I got home I called Steve and Cindy and asked if they wanted to attend the concert with me. Steve said he had heard he was coming into town and that Morris was a friend of his! They had met at a Promise Keepers event where they both were on the program, and they had stayed in touch through the years. I told them that I really wanted to meet him, so they arranged a meeting after the concert that week.

The three of us arrived at the concert and sat near the front of the church. When Morris came on he acknowledged Steve and Cindy, and the concert was sublime. I was singing along to songs that I used to listen to as I would drive down the 10 Freeway to the 405 to go and meet Michael after his work so we could go to Calvary Costa Mesa together. I was flooded with memories of me raising my hands out of the window praising Jesus, singing at the top of my lungs – with this man that was standing and singing before me.

After the concert ended and everyone had departed, Morris stayed for an hour afterwards to talk to us. I was thrilled to meet this man who had unknowingly led me in worship for years. I was so glad that I got to share this with him. After he and Steve and Cindy exchanged pleasantries, he asked me to sit down on the piano bench. He had just written a song on his favorite verse – Jeremiah 29:11. I said, "No way! That is my life verse!" He started playing a beautiful melody, then he added his soulful, rich, resonating voice to the lyrics: *"I know the plans I have for you (I have for you) declares the Lord (Yeah...) Plans to prosper you, plans never to harm you, plans to give you a hope and a future... These are the plans, these are the plans, these are the plans...for you."* He offered, "Sing along with me, Pam!" I learned the melodic line easily, and there I was, harmonizing along with Morris Chapman! As we were singing together on that piano bench, the Lord tugged on my heart and said, "I'm answering that prayer that you whispered in my ear twelve years ago. You are singing with Morris Chapman!" I started quietly weeping. My Lord loves me more than I can fathom. He will

> As an artist, the hardest thing for Michael comes at the end of every service that we do – he throws his work of art into the trash can.

go to the utmost heights or deepest depths to show His love for you. In my spirit I knew that this was a prophetic song just for me. It was a kiss on the cheek from Jesus. Morris told us that we were the very first people that he had played this song for. I was honored. He ended up recording this in 2000, and it became a huge hit in the Christian world.

While I was sitting there listening to Morris, the Lord impressed upon my heart to ask him if he would pray about doing a duet with me on my next record. He returned, "I don't even need to. While you were sitting here, the Lord told me to do a duet with you!" I asked him if he had ever heard of the song, "The Potter's House?" He started singing, "The potter wants to put you back together again…oh the potter…." We sang it a cappella right there in the church together. It was meant to be. He told me that he'd be honored to sing a duet on my upcoming CD, *For A Time Such As This*.

We recorded the song a few months later. It is still one of my favorite songs to listen to. A few weeks after this he told us that he wanted to send us something, and he sent us a large, beautiful painting called *The Vessel*, signed by the artist, Thomas Blackshear. It's about four feet tall, and it hangs on our wall next to where all ten CDs that I've recorded are framed! It's a man in a robe, kneeling in front of a large pot, and there is the oil of anointing being poured from two large clay pots by two women, over his head and into the large pot in front of him, and overflowing the sides into two smaller vases. And underneath the title, it has Psalm 23:5 – *"You anoint my head with oil; my cup overflows."* It is magnificent. God can and will do the impossible, and make His sweetness towards you so personal. Michael sent him a God Pot in appreciation, and recently we saw a picture showing that God Pot sitting in a place of prominence in his home.

I looked up the word "refine" in the dictionary. I wanted to see if "refining" was always shed in a negative light. It means: "to purify, or bring to a pure state; to improve or to improve on one's previous work." The thesaurus then led me to an interesting verb, "clarify," which means: "to free from ambiguity; to free from confusion; to revive." I was revived and freed from confusion about any ambiguities I had towards God's Word being true, and how my Lord really felt about me after my divine appointment with Morris Chapman.

God's Word is always pure and true. Men's words might not be trustworthy, but our Lord's words are precious, true, and like refined silver with no impurity. We can always rely on the steadfast and indomitable power of God.

> *The words of the Lord are pure words: As silver tried in a furnace of earth, purified seven times. Thou shalt keep them, O Lord, Thou shalt preserve them from this generation for ever.*
> — Psalm 12:6-7 KJV

As an artist, the hardest thing for Michael comes at the end of every service that we do – he throws his work of art into the trash can. The Lord told him early on that He wanted him to toss them out because He didn't want the people to remember him as the potter. He wanted them to remember Him, the Lord God, as the Master Potter. He has had to wrestle with this for our entire ministry life. He knows that he could sell these vessels, and they would help support our ministry. He does sell his production pieces, but he would love to sell his hand-thrown pieces. They would garner more money. He actually has sold two of his six-foot God Pot vases which we unveil at each service at a rate befitting a master potter. After he was struggling over tossing out his pots one day in particular, I reassured him, saying, "Don't worry honey, when you get to Heaven all your pots will be finished by *the* Master Potter – your Father in Heaven."

The Bible says, "The heart of man is desperately wicked, and who can know it?" We should continually ask our Lord for a purified and cleansed heart, like the gold on his pot that passes through the fire. We need refining deep within that we may come out the way He wants us to be.

At the end of our services, after I unveil the God Pot, Michael says, "I know some of you are saying, 'Wow! That would look great in my house!'" As he closes, I love how he responds to that rhetorical comment:

"You would look great in my Father's House!"

> *In my Father's house are many mansions; if it were not so, I would have told you. I go to prepare a place for you... I will come again and receive you to Myself; that where I am, you may be also.*
>
> — John 14:2-3 NKJV

> *Jesus said to him, "I am the way, the truth, and the life. No one comes to the Father except through Me."*
>
> — John 14:6 NKJV

Chapter 28

POTTER'S FIELD KIDS

Our hearts have been anchored towards impoverished children ever since we took that first short-term mission trip to Honduras with World Vision. Their little bellies were distended, caused by worms, ingested from bad water or contracted by walking in the dirt with bare feet. They ran around with no clothes on because they couldn't afford them. Their heads were shaved because of ringworm, or they had blonde hair, having lost its natural color due to extreme malnutrition. They just wanted a meal because they were hungry, or some affection because their parents had died of AIDS. Our hearts indeed broke over what breaks the heart of God. It's a heart-rending experience to see such destitution on this earth.

Michael and I were Artist Associates for World Vision, the world hunger relief organization, for over thirteen years. The Lord had answered my prayers from when I was a teenager to work with these children. We became one of their top-sponsoring artists, sponsoring over twenty-two thousand children on every continent on the globe. World Vision did a study on Potter's Field Ministries which revealed that if someone sponsored a child through us, they would end up keeping that child an average of seven-and-a-half years.

When we first started out in PFM, a woman named Joanne Lockhart called me and gave us a prophesy about things to come regarding children. We hadn't yet done anything with children at the time she gave us this word from the Lord. She said to me, "I see God lifting up your ministry to heights you can't comprehend. I see you in the future with so many children...and they are following behind you like the 'pied piper.' And then I see more children, and then more...more than my eyes can see...I can't even tell you how much He is going to use you and Michael with children all over the world." I've lost touch with her through the years, but I certainly would like her know that her words rang true, far beyond what we probably even know.

"It was as though I was having a dream-while-I-was-wide-awake – a vision. Time stood still and I felt like I was in a tunnel."

Our dear friends, Joe and Cindy Gregory, took us to Israel in 2014. This trip changed the way that I read the Bible, and it opened my eyes to my Jesus on a whole new level. I love Israel, and I can't wait to go back one day. When I arrived there it just felt like home. We went to the Wailing Wall, where the men go to one side to pray, and the women to the other side. It felt so reverent and holy at this ancient wall; I wore a shawl so I could cover my head with it as I entered, and they gave the men yarmulkes to wear. I started to write a prayer, which I wanted to stick into the cracks of the Wall: "Dear Lord, please continue to bless our ministry and our marriage. Please give us a million children to take care of through Potter's Field Kids in the years to come. Amen." I folded the prayer into a small wad and stuck it into a crack in the wall on top of thousands of other prayers left there.

After we had all prayed for a time, we met at a gathering spot outside the Wall. Michael came up to me and said, "The weirdest thing just happened to me while I was over at the Wall. It was as though I was having a dream-while-I-was-wide-awake – a vision. I was praying, and all of a sudden I saw children, millions of children right before my very eyes. Time stood still and I felt like I was in a tunnel. I know that the Lord is going to give this to us. It might be after we are long gone, but He will fulfill this for PFM." I was astounded! At the very same time I was praying for one million children, he was seeing them in a vision! God is amazing! I told him what I had written and placed in the Wall. We both were flabbergasted. We so look forward to seeing how the Lord will continue to unfold this in the years to come.

In the spring of 2005, the direction of our ministry was radically changed through a conversation over lunch with Don and Jean McClure. We were on tour in Southern California and had shared PFM at Calvary Chapel Laguna where Don was pastoring. He asked Michael a pivotal question about the World Vision children we had sponsored: "Where do those twenty-two thousand children go to church?" I was curious to see how he was going to answer that question, because I knew that not all of them did. Michael said, "I don't know. I know some do, but not all." He then said something to us that resonated with Michael. "God never called us to go into all the world and take care of kids. He told us to go into all the world and make disciples and we do that at the local church level." Michael has always had a passion and a heart to disciple young people. He then challenged us with the thought about taking all the connections and relationships that we had built through the years with all the churches in the States, and connecting them

with Calvary Chapels or local church affiliates on the field internationally. And we could help raise resources through sponsorship
to co-labor with churches on the field by taking care of children.
When Pastor Don asked us if we would be interested in doing this,
of course our answer was a resounding "yes!"

A few months later, Pastor Don was teaching at our ministry
training school in Montana and he sat down and flipped up his
laptop to show us something. "Are you guys ready for your lives
to change?" He showed us all these children from El Salvador in
Central America. He asked Michael if he would be willing to go
and scout out the land to see what the Lord would do, and what
our involvement would be there. So on October 5, 2005, Michael
and Don traveled to Central America along with pastors from his
church and some of our Board members. The Lord did wonderful
things in Michael, stirring his heartstrings with a love and a longing to help these less fortunate children in any way that we could.
During our annual Board meeting, Michael was able to convey
what God did in his heart during his trip. By December, the Board
made a motion that we would start our own sponsorship program
called Potter's Field Kids. We would offer sponsorship at each PFM
presentation, and the resources would go down to the co-laboring
church that we worked with on the field, and they would set up
Kid's Clubs at each of our locations. We gave our resignation to
World Vision, finishing our contract by the end of 2006.

We were setting everything into motion to launch the Potter's
Field Kids sponsorship program in 2007. We had to update our
501(c) 3 non-profit status to include fund-raising for children's
programs, but this was harder than we thought. The Internal
Revenue Service is extremely meticulous about this process; there
is a high level of accountability and preparation. After much back
and forth, we were accepted as a non-profit sponsorship program,

and we presented our first PFK sponsorship opportunity in May 2007 at The Warehouse Church in Sacramento, California. Since then, we have offered sponsorships in thousands of services across America.

Our programs provide education, medical assistance, nutritional needs, discipleship, and scholarships to over fifteen thousand children around the world. We have Kid's Clubs that teach them about the love of Jesus, and we feed them a large meal. Sadly, for some, this is the only nutritious meal these children get during the week.

Religion that God our Father accepts as pure and faultless is this: to look after orphans and widows in their distress and to keep oneself from being polluted by the world.

— James 1:27

Defend the cause of the weak and fatherless; maintain the rights of the poor and oppressed. Rescue the weak and needy; Deliver them from the hand of the wicked.

— Psalm 82:3-4

Traveling to these third-world countries has had such an impact on me. We were not able to have biological children of our own, so the mere fact that the Lord allows us to take care of thousands of children all over the world has been such a blessing. I am honored that He is entrusting these little ones into our care as we continue to raise resources to do our part to make their lives a little better.

"Sing, barren woman, you who never bore a child; burst into song, shout for joy, you who were never in labor; because more

are the children of the desolate woman than of her who has a husband," says the Lord. "...You will forget the shame of your youth..."

— Isaiah 54:1, 4

We were visiting some of our boys in an orphanage we had in El Salvador and we had brought them toys and books in a suitcase. As we were leaving that afternoon, one of the little boys curled up in a ball and got into the suitcase. My heart broke. He wanted to come home with us. I wish we could take them all home with us, but with each country comes a set of laws. Most don't even allow adoptions unless you live in that country for anywhere from two to three years. These countries have so much red tape and make you jump through so many hoops to actually adopt.

One of the saddest things we have witnessed in these countries is the widespread corruption and greed that takes place on so many levels. For example, to get things out of customs that we've shipped overseas, they want special compensation. We love that Pastor Craig in Uganda refuses to pay this compensation for his things that are shipped over on a container, and he will wait for months, going back daily to request his property until the authorities eventually cave in and just release his belongings.

We have allowed the Lord to show us when it is time to move on from a village and know that our work there is done. He might move another organization into it to take it over, or sometimes or He moves us from a housing facility. We have learned to just trust in the Lord for His timing. Several times that we have been moved on, we have learned that dangerous gangs have moved into the country or into that area, and our safety would have been compromised. The Lord is in control and we just have to trust and rest in His sovereignty.

We also have witnessed a "class structure" of sorts that some of the children in our programs experience. It's unspoken, and we often don't even realize that it exists in certain cultures until something happens – like if a child has to go to the hospital. We thought they would automatically be taken into a good facility where they would receive good care, but instead they are taken to an inferior hospital, where the level of care isn't as good as it is for people who have the money and means to pay for better services. They treat these children as proletarian, not even worth dealing with. This broke our hearts and angered us. Unfortunately, this has even infiltrated the church in some locations. When we see this, we know that we aren't like-minded and move on, or we pass the location on to some other organization that wants to help.

> "When God wants to do an impossible task, He takes an impossible man, and He crushes him."

The Potter's Field Kid's Programs we were doing internationally were beginning to gain traction, and others started asking to come alongside to help. We started seeing the fruit of our sponsorship program through the resources that we were sending and through the mission teams that we were coming down from the States. We were building even stronger relationships with existing churches that we had co-labored with through the years, many who would send mission teams over to our facilities each year. They help with various building projects on existing properties and spend time with the children at the Kid's Clubs. We also take annual medical mission trips where doctors, nurses, and dentists from the States come down and see thousands of patients during the week, bringing thousands of dollars of donated medicines and supplies.

Michael and Pastor Don spent a lot of time together in those early years of Potter's Field Kids. Our lives were about to change further as Pastor Don took Michael to Entebbe, Uganda, in 2009. This became our next PFK location. He re-introduced us to Pastor Craig Linquist, a pastor who had been on his staff when he was senior pastor at Calvary Chapel San Jose where we had met him years prior while doing PFM there. Craig had grown up in Africa. His parents were missionaries there. He is also the grandson of Alan Redpath, the renowned British author and evangelist.

Alan had a great impact on Don and Jean early on in their ministry careers, studying with him at Capernwray Bible School in England where he was Pastoral Dean. He was awarded an honorary Doctor of Divinity by Houghton College. Towards the end of his life, he was a traveling missionary and international conference speaker. Here are some of his most notable quotes:

> When God wants to do an impossible task, He takes an impossible man, and He crushes him.

> The conversion of a soul is the miracle of a moment, but the manufacture of a saint is the task of a lifetime.

> The Christian life doesn't get easier as one gets older.

From the moment Michael landed in Uganda, he knew that we were going to be heavily involved at this location. We fell in love with Craig and his wife, Loren, and the work that they had been building since 2004. God was moving in their midst. They had already been working with hundreds of kids in this area, and we found that to be vital for us. They had established Calvary Chapel Entebbe, and it was thriving. They had established an amazing school which spanned what is the American equivalent of nursery, Pre-K, and kindergarten through seventh grade – ten years of classes for children aged three to twelve years old! We all know that education is a game changer in third world countries.

We have come to find out that the role of a good parachurch ministry is not to change the work that the pastor has established, but to come and hold his arms up in what he is already doing. Coming alongside Craig and Loren was very easy for us; we had like-minded philosophies, both in the direction of the church and in ministering to children.

The Lord had given Michael a verse before we went to Uganda.

> *...And if you spend yourselves in behalf of the hungry and satisfy the needs of the oppressed, then your light will rise in the darkness, and your night will become like the noonday. The Lord will guide you always; he will satisfy your needs in a sunscorched land and will strengthen your frame. You will be like a well-watered garden, like a spring whose waters never fail. Your people will rebuild the ancient ruins and will raise up the age-old foundations; you will be called Repairer of Broken Walls, Restorer of Streets with Dwellings.*
>
> — Isaiah 58:10-12

Considering what had happened from 1971 to 1979 while Idi Amin was president in Uganda, and how his eight-year reign of terror decimated a generation, it's no wonder the Lord gave Michael this verse. Idi Amin was known as the "Butcher of Uganda," and the estimates of those he tortured, killed, or imprisoned were estimated between one hundred thousand to a half a million people. It's interesting that the Lord has us ministering to children Cambodia, another war-torn country, where another dictator, Pol Pot, the leader of the Khmer Rouge, terrorized the people from 1975 to 1979. The Cambodian genocide was estimated at one-and-a-half to three million people dead.

When we started working with Craig, we learned that the verse the Lord gave Michael is the exact verse the He gave him before he and Loren moved to Uganda, many years before. It is on all of his church and missionary collateral.

My first trip to Uganda was in 2010. I had always wanted to go to Africa, and was so excited when the Lord opened up this ministry opportunity for us. I love the culture, the people, the food, the countryside, the exotic animals – and the precious children. They are so appreciative of any love you give or opportunity or resources you can provide. Every time I visit that country, I leave a piece of my heart there. On my way back home, I was sitting in my airline seat and had my headphones on, listening to beautiful music, when I had the inspiration to write a song about the kids in Africa and everywhere that we had PFK programs. I put down my tray in front of me and grabbed a napkin. Looking out of the window, as the sun was setting on the horizon, a lyric popped into my head. "There is hope on the horizon..." A song was birthed from my trip to Entebbe called

> So many have no one to take care of them, or relatives to show them love. For some, their spiritual state is non-existent, and they need the love and hope that only Jesus can offer.

"Songs In the Night," which we use when we present Potter's Field Kids at churches.

Songs in the Night

Lyrics by Pam Rozell
Music by Pam Rozell & Jason Ritchie

How many trials must you face
Before you learn to climb?
God will give you what you need
One child at a time
I'm gonna try to find a way
To keep you safe and warm
Use me, I'll be your hands and feet
A shelter from the storm

CHORUS
I can hear you
Your songs in the night
There is hope on the horizon
He can see you
Hear your whispered prayer
I pray to God that kids like you
Feel free from harm tonight

When I look into your eyes
So innocent and sweet
I see the shadows of the pain, your vic'tries and defeats
I see the hunger, I see the tears, as I wipe them from your face
I see the hurt, a glimpse of hope
Longing for a warm embrace

BRIDGE

Sin has scarred the human race
The canvas once was pure
Only by Your precious grace
The children will endure

How many trials will come your way?
Before you learn to fly?
We're gonna help you sprout your wings
One child at a time
We're gonna help you find a way to keep you safe and warm
God will be your hiding place
A shelter from the storm

It's mind-boggling how the Lord has grown our Kid's programs around the world. From Entebbe, we added a program in Nairobi, Kenya, and we started Potter's Field Christian Academy for kindergarten through third grade. One of the nationals who worked with us there felt led to go to the Democratic Republic of the Congo to implement a Potter's Field Kids program. We have five hundred kids in that program every weekend. We had to have a national do this work because it is too dangerous for any American to be in this region.

We are in Villarreal, Costa Rica, eight villages in Cambodia, and in Antigua, Guatemala, where our Central American Headquarters has been since 2013. We teach English to more than twelve hundred kids in the public school system there, using the Bible as our curriculum. We also have a Kids Program on the Blackfeet Reservation in Browning, Montana. In the summer of 2014, we implemented a local Potter's Field Kids Program in Whitefish, where we hold twelve to fourteen horse camps a year teaching the Bible, horsemanship, art, crafts and dance movement, and play games on horseback. We work with local "special needs" adults from Lighthouse Christian Home, and work with Foster Care (CASA) and Adoptive Families in the Flathead Valley (Child Bridge). We also host local children as well. In 2018, we will be praying about and scouting new locations in Eastern and Western Europe and the United Kingdom for potential new works.

I'm an orphan now, so I can relate a bit more than I could before with these precious children, however, I don't have, nor will I ever have, the incredible challenges that these kids face. So many have no one to take care of them, or relatives to show them love. For some, their spiritual state is non-existent, and they need the love and hope that only Jesus can offer. Their daily challenges are getting clean water and hoping they won't get parasites from the food they eat – if they have any – or the water they drink. The sanitation is inferior, and modern-day conveniences, nonexistent. My heart breaks for them, yet I see a purity of heart and an appreciation for the little things in life which we as Americans can learn from.

As Michael was at the airport, departing from his first trip to Africa, he was on the curb saying goodbye to Pastor Craig. He's never forgotten the words that were shared with him in that moment: "Mike, you can send me all the resources in the world, and I will use them. But what I really need are hands and feet to help me to implement the vision God has given me for Africa." Michael knew that God was orchestrating something wonderful, and creating a great working relationship between our ministries.

He also knew that we could definitely send some help…

Chapter 29

PASSING GOD'S GOODNESS
TO THE NEXT GENERATION

Love Lives On

Written by Pam Rozell, Claire Cloninger & Walt Harrah

I was just a toddler, but pictures they don't lie
Daddy's holding hands with me, how time flies
In the growing pains that followed through thick and through thin
My Heavenly Father all the while, was loving me through him

I had to let you go, but Daddy
I want you to know

CHORUS
Love lives on, love lives on
What we share together never will be gone
In your heart and in your faith
In the Savior that you praise
There's a circle called forever, where love lives on

Standing at the altar, you held my trembling hand

331

Smiling at me through your tears, my new life began
The love that I grew up with, now I can give away
Cause you and mama taught me well,
To love day by day

I had to let you go, but Daddy
I want you to know
(Repeat Chorus)

BRIDGE
In your final moments, if only I'd been there
To hold your hand, as you held mine
So many times with care
But this heart of mine is certain
That your life and love endure
And I can't describe, this peace I feel
Just knowing this for sure
(Repeat Chorus)

L ife is short. It's hard to believe that at the writing of this book Michael and I just celebrated our thirtieth wedding Anniversary! It truly seems like all the events you have read about within the pages of this book just happened yesterday. If I'm blessed to live as long as my parents, I can count how many summers I have left to enjoy on this earth. That is a sobering thought, and one that makes Michael and I take a look at what the Lord would still have us to do in our lives while we are here, if the Lord tarries. My dad always told me, "The first part of your life, you cruise at a pretty good clip up to age forty. Then after that, it zooms by so quickly…then you find yourself on your deathbed." I know what he means – time flies.

Lord, make me to know my end, and what is the measure of my days, that I may know how frail I am. Indeed, You have made my days as handbreadths, and my age is as nothing before You; certainly every man at his best state is but vapor.

— Psalm 39:4-5 NKJV

All men are like grass, and all their glory is like the flowers of the field; the grass withers and the flowers fall, but the word of the Lord stands forever.

— 1 Peter 1:24

Remember how fleeting is my life. For what futility you have created all men! What man can live and not see death, or save himself from the power of the grave?

— Psalm 89:47

I've experienced the death of many loved ones over the past fourteen years. My precious daddy passed away in 2003, followed by our beloved cocker spaniel, Katie, six months later. Then my favorite horse, Starbuck, passed away the next year, followed by my half-brother, Skip (James O. Souders, Jr.).

Skip never lived with us because there was a twelve-year difference in our ages. He stayed with his mom, and was living in boarding school when I came along. I first met him when I was nine years old, but I had heard of him my whole life. I was enamored with him, and we waltzed together in my aunt's living room when I first met him. He was tall, handsome, and kind; a wonderful man who we loved tremendously. He had a full-ride scholarship to the University of Michigan for football when tragedy struck. Before he had a chance to attend college, he was in a bad car accident and became a quadriplegic. His best friend was driving, and the back right seat belt had been put into in the trunk, so he couldn't put it on; he was left with a severed spinal cord, and he would never walk again. I never heard Skip complain once, and he had such a great outlook on life all his days until he passed at the age of sixty-one.

Many of my aunts, uncles, and cousins passed during this time as well. Then in 2014, our devoted and resolute mom went to be with the Lord.

> *Brothers and sisters, we do not want you to be uninformed about those who sleep in death, so that you do not grieve like the rest of mankind, who have no hope.*
>
> — 1 Thessalonians 4:13

Four other horses who were dear to my heart also died during these years, as well as two sweet goats. I love my animals with abandon. They are my four-legged kids. Even in the midst of finalizing this book, during the summer 2017, my precious Annie, our precocious dachshund who everyone called "my soul," passed away in my arms at fifteen years old.

Michael and I know that we will be held accountable for what has been entrusted to us thus far.

After I lost my daddy, Pastor Chuck told me that he still had moments of grief after losing his own father and brother in an airplane crash many years ago. I miss all those in my life who have passed. A sense of lamenting ebbs and flows over me sometimes like the rolling waves of the sea. A sound, smell, or activity will trigger pangs of sadness and anguish, and tears will flow. We weren't designed for death. We were supposed to live in Eden before the fall, and now we are longing for Heaven to be reunited with those who have gone home before us."

> "...Weeping may endure for a night, but joy comes in the morning."
>
> — Psalm 30:5 NKJV

I like to look at life as a three-act play, since that analogy resonates with me. If you give each "act" of your life thirty years, then Michael and I are coming to the end of our Act Two and are standing on the precipice of Act Three. We pray that our third act is the best one yet. Michael and I know that we will be held accountable for what has been entrusted to us thus far. We now have embarked on the "mentoring" phase of our Christian walk. We are told to pass God's goodness to the next generation.

> O my people, hear my teaching; listen to the words of my mouth. I will open my mouth in parables, I will utter hidden things, things from of old – what we have heard and known, what our fathers have told us. We will not hide them from their children; we will tell the next generation the praiseworthy deeds of the Lord, His power, and the wonders He has done.
>
> — Psalm 78:1-4

Our staff is mostly made up of Millennials, also known as Generation Y. This generation is typically described as being born during the eighties and nineties, reaching adulthood in the early twenty-first century and later. So our staff comprises ages thirty-eight down to nineteen. These are the "children" of our generation – the Baby Boomers or Generation Xers. They came of age when the Internet took off. Wikipedia states:

Although Millennial characteristics vary by region, depending on social and economic conditions, the generation is
generally marked by an increased use and familiarity with
communications, media, and digital technologies. In
most parts of the world, their upbringing was marked by
an increase in a liberal approach to politics and econom-
ics; the effects of this environment are disputed. The
'Great Recession' has had a major impact on this generation because it has caused historically high levels of unem-
ployment among young people, and has led to speculation
about possible long-term economic and social damage to
this generation.

They also give a statistic that one in four of them are unaffil-
iated with any religion. Michael and I have found that they are
definitely the "entitled" generation. We also find more people
in this age range are opting to go and live with mom and dad
again. And due to the fact that we baby boomers don't like the
thought of being "empty nesters," parents are welcoming them
back with open arms, much to the detriment of their kids. While
the exception to this, of course, is when it is a necessity for their
kids to move in due to truly falling onto hard times, and having the blessing of parents who can help them get back up on
their feet for a season, the reality is, more of these millennials
are perfectly content to live at home while pursuing hobbies and
working as baristas, rather than responsibly moving on to promising careers, starting families, or furthering their education. We
are also discovering that they are much more comfortable communicating via a device rather than through eyeball-to-eyeball
conversation, and therefore we are seeing a generation that isn't
a sociable one – "social," but not sociable. They would rather

impersonally break up a relationship with one another by texting over their cell phone.

Michael and I have always had people around us, whether touring, traveling, or living with us in a discipleship environment. Early on, during our heavy touring years, I read a biography by L.G. Parkhurst, Jr. on Francis and Edith Schaeffer's life where he and his wife started a school where anyone, especially young people, could come from all over the world in a "community" to find out more about God. They co-founded and established the L'Abri Fellowship International study and discipleship centers in Switzerland. He was an American Evangelical Christian theologian, philosopher, and Presbyterian pastor. After reading that book, I lifted up a silent prayer that one day, hopefully, Michael and I could facilitate something like this for young people in the States.

They wanted something different – an authenticity, something most of them didn't possess or weren't surrounded with. They wanted to be a part of something bigger than themselves.

When we began co-laboring alongside Pastor Don and Jean McClure over the past ten years, they too, after studying at Capernwray in England, wanted to pour into young people's lives.

During the early, formative years of our walk with the Lord, Michael and I had come out of a church that was really big on home fellowships and one-on-one discipleship. Our first home group was a "Home Builders" group that helped us in the basics of our marriage. We've always been believers in having accountability and authority over us, even today. We've already seen many who haven't finished well, and we would never want to become a statistic or casualty in this. We want to depart this earth finishing well. Therefore, we willingly place ourselves under those in authority, usually older saints who have successfully walked the Christian life of faith, examining their fruit, and hopefully avoiding the pitfalls that will continue to come our way.

When Craig asked us to send him "hands and feet" to help facilitate his work in Uganda, he didn't realize that this work would provide a beautiful solution to the trends Michael and I had already been observing in the youth of today. As we traveled from church to church in the past ten years or so, we began to see a disconnect in these eighteen- to twenty-six-year-old millennials. They were disengaged and walking out of the church. They weren't mad at their parents or the church; they were just indifferent. There was a great falling away, but not in a rebellious way. They wanted something different – an authenticity, something most of them didn't possess or weren't surrounded with. They wanted to be a part of something bigger than themselves. They wanted a "community" and experiences of their own, and we were finding that most of them needed to be taught a work ethic they didn't have.

We began to make changes. In 2004, we had started a discipleship school in Montana at which one hundred seventy-eight students had already attended. This new incarnation of our school, which launched in 2009, would be called "IGNITE." Michael asked Pastor Don if he would make a renewed commitment to give the IGNITE school at least one week per month, teaching the students and investing in our staff. He and Jean have been a part of our schools since 2007. They are invaluable in helping train up this next generation through stellar Bible teaching. They are also shining examples of working hard throughout their lives – "running with the horses" into the decade of their seventies. There is no such thing as retirement in this Christian walk. We have to work hard just to keep up with them! We want to raise up a generation of spiritually-healthy individuals who are autonomous and educated in the things of the Lord with the help of these older saints who have walked before us. It is so important to yoke yourselves with these people. How prideful to think that we, in and of ourselves, have all the answers.

Other cultures revere their elders. I wish it were so in our American culture. The Asian cultures get this so right. Americans like to refer to baby boomers and Gen Xers as "old school" – however, we must have all done something right because we are overseeing multi-million dollar ministries and businesses. The ones we want to glean from are the saints that have been in the ministry for forty to fifty years plus, people like our friends, Terry and Nancy Clark, Joe and Cathy Focht, and of course our mentors – Don and Jean McClure. We want to sit at their feet and eat their low hanging fruit that has been growing for years. And now it is our turn to become that for the millennial generation.

We stepped out in faith with this new concept for our school. The young adults we were recruiting and attracting while touring would be given a chance to sit at Jesus' feet for one year of their lives. We integrated our IGNITE interns with our Kids Programs around the world. Through the Potter's Field Kids programs, they would give of themselves to children that could never give anything back in return. They were also the answer to Pastor Craig Linquist's plea to help hold up the arms of missionary pastors by tangibly putting hands and feet onto the field.

IGNITE consists of three months of training, currently at our Headquarters in Antigua, Guatemala. The first thing we do when they arrive is take their iPhones, laptop, or iPad for two weeks so they can learn to communicate with each other and with God on a deeper level than ever before. We ask them to willingly to "turn off the noise" in their lives for this short period of time. After intensive study of characters of the Bible, inductive Bible Studies,

There is something to say for having young people walk through life with you, learning and maturing in Christ as they go.

and practical ways to survive on the field, they are then deployed to one of our locations on the field all over the world for a period of six months, or for some, part of their program is go on tour with us for a couple months, then deploy overseas. When this time is completed, they come back to Montana for one month. We found that this re-entry period is a vital time for a debriefing of their experiences on the field. It is also a time of preparation to integrate back into their home church environment where they will volunteer and serve the last two months, completing the program. They have given the Lord three hundred sixty-five days of their lives to transform them from the inside – out.

Many of these interns decide to come back to Montana and serve with PFM after they've completed their one-year program. Some decide to stay and work at their home churches, or they go back to school, or whatever the Lord has planned for them to do. In the beginning of PFM, we took on staff members at the suggestion of others, or those who "felt led" to come and serve; sometimes lead staff members would suggest hiring someone who they liked to work with in the past, and others were friends we had hired, and this yielded mixed results. Now we are primarily raising up from within our ranks, hiring our IGNITE staff for new positions, as opposed to those who just came along, as we did in the past. We find that bringing people alongside our ministry in this new way gives us better insights into the maturity level of individuals who already understand the vision of our program, which creates a better working environment. We hope we have effectively learned from our mistakes, and will continue to learn and grow as time passes.

There is something to say for having young people walk through life with you (which is what discipleship is), learning and maturing in Christ as they go. It's a beautiful thing to watch. The Lord has brought us a stellar group of young people to mentor during this season. We are making sure that everyone has been educated and is growing and maturing through IGNITE. Ninety percent of our staff today have been through our IGNITE Program, with the exception of some of us "older saints," and our pastors on staff: Steve Venable, our Executive Pastor, and Steve Miller, who heads up our Media Department. Our desire is to instill in these young people an opportunity to grow to the level they need to attain to and gain experience as they go. Our main desire is to instill a passionate walk with the Lord and an opportunity for these young people to reach their full potential in Christ Jesus. We are here to help those who want more of Jesus in their lives and want a life on mission. That we can do.

We are excited to be able to sow into our hometown, our "Jerusalem," for the first time in twenty-five years of ministry. It's awesome to watch what God is doing in our small fellowship of believers at Selah. We are using Selah as a lab of sorts, to raise up the next generation of pastors and teachers and worship leaders. My husband, who is the senior pastor, and our assistant pastors, have already ordained two young "twenty-something" men who are in training to "be passed the baton" and become future leaders in our ministry. They are given the opportunity to teach along with the veteran pastors and elders on a rotational basis on Sundays and Wednesday evenings, giving them practical experience behind the pulpit. We are also letting the younger women teach Bible studies for practical application. We are raising up worship teams as well. God is doing a new thing! He is making a way in the desert and streams in the wasteland right before our very eyes.

We are in a new, joyful season in our ministry. We are enjoying watching some of our young people marrying after meeting and spending time with each other on the field, and now they are having children of their own! I am actually getting to feel what it would've been like if I'd had my own children. The Lord has me helping some of these young brides-to-be with their weddings, and preparing them for the intimacies and intricacies of marriage. I feel it's the Lord's way of redeeming what the "locusts have eaten" in my life. He is using the broken shards of my life and the knowledge I've acquired along my journey to help transition them smoothly into married life. I'm also leading Bible studies for the girls as time allows. Michael is discipling young people on a daily basis, teaching at the school and Selah, walking out the life of faith and emulating the life of Christ to a hungry and new group of "sponges," and passing the torch to the next generation.

After having been in the ministry for so many years, we meet a lot of people who saw us do our Potter's Field presentation when they were little kids. This blesses us immensely. We are honored that the Lord is still using Potter's Field Ministries through the generations. Only God can orchestrate something like that to happen. He knew He created PFM to be a timeless audio/visual that would speak to His people throughout the years.

One such young man is Brenen Beeler, who is in his thirties and Senior Pastor of Regenerate Church in Orange County, California.

He went down to Guatemala in July of 2017 to teach our largest class of IGNITE students since its inception. Here is a look at what his Instagram posts read:

7/26/17 – "Teaching 29 missionaries and ministers-in-training who are between 18-22 that will travel all over the world for the next year of their life telling people about Jesus. They, along with their leadership team, have taught me more this week than I could ever teach them in a lifetime. Radical faith requires radical obedience."

7/25/17 – "I am flying to Guatemala right now with #donmcclure and #MikeRozell @pamrozell to teach and minister for the next 4 days. It's going to be epic. I am #blessed beyond to be partnering with some of my heroes. I first saw Mike and Pam Rozell share when I was 6 years old at Calvary Chapel Costa Mesa. I was so impacted I never forgot the "God Pot" message. And now I get to minister with them, only something that God could do."

His church is full of millennials.

We are raising up a stellar staff, mostly former IGNITE students who became 2.0s (a training program in Montana to transition into a full time staff position) who are now on staff at PFM. We also have an "IGNITE Lite" program which I will explain further in the next chapter. We have one hundred fourteen people on our Potter's Field staff worldwide. We have deployed two hundred fifty-two IGNITE students since changing over from our original concept. That makes four hundred thirty students and disciples who have come through our school since its inception in 2004!

We are watching our touring ministry expand its borders and broaden its horizons by connecting all three great passions of our lives together – Potter's Field Ministries tours, IGNITE Mission Training School, and Potter's Field Kids – that we hope will leave a legacy of winning souls, making disciples, and feeding hungry children for the next generation.

Use whatever tools the Lord gives you to pass on His goodness to the next generation, whether it's pottery, songwriting, singing, art, teaching, media, writing, horses, IGNITE, Selah, cooking – fill in the blanks. Do it with a passion and great fervor. Spend yourselves for the sake of the gospel – "Til the Whole World Hears..."

Now strap in for the ride.

The MudMan Cometh...

Chapter 30

THE MUDMAN COMETH

...But the righteous will live by his faith.

— Habakkuk 2:4 NASB

I know how it looks. But just start. Nothing is insurmountable.

— Lin-Manuel Miranda, American composer, lyricist, playwright & actor

You are never too old to set a new goal or to dream a new dream.

— C.S. Lewis, British novelist, poet, academic & Christian apologist

Writing this book has been such an augmenting and burgeoning experience. At times I never thought it would come to fruition. It seemed such an insurmountable task. This process has been so good for me. I found out how my brain works a little better. I'm not the most organized person on the planet. I tend to shrink back and not attempt to start the ominous tasks or projects that will take too long to accomplish or

345

seemingly never get done. Some good examples are: cleaning my house, cooking a meal...or writing a book. I've known for ten years that the Lord wanted me to document this account of our lives. He actually gave me the title before I started it. I would write a chapter or two, or possible chapter titles, and then leave it for a year or two. I know His timing is perfect, and as it turns out, this book is "for a time such as this." I can see that we needed twenty-five years of experience in the ministry to solidify and live out the most pertinent things that needed to be said. It has been amazing to experience – while writing down my thoughts, or things He would give me right before I would awake, or stories that would come to me on a plane between events – how the Holy Spirit would take over and lead me. It has been a wonderful journey, but also the most difficult task I have taken on in my Christian walk thus far. My prayer in writing these similitudes – which Michael and I actually walked through – is that you will etch these truths upon your heart and dare to believe in an unfathomable God who does extraordinary, seemingly impossible things. My desire is that your faith would be strengthened to believe that He answers prayers and fulfills promises, and that you would actively yield and surrender to the mighty God of the Universe.

For nothing is impossible with God.

— Luke 1:37 NLT

When Michael and I took that leap of faith to begin Potter's Field Ministries, we wouldn't have been able to comprehend the depth, breadth, or height of where and how He would be using this ministry. The Potter's Field story is truly one of the most prodigious stories that I've ever witnessed – and it happened to me. It is a story of redemption. It hasn't come without its challenges, trials, or opposition, from within and without. While in Paris, Texas, during our tour of 2012, a woman approached and gave us a prophecy. She said, "Michael will walk through a trial. Remember: 'God will close doors no man can open and open doors no man can close.' He will be okay." This was so profound, that evening I went back to the tour bus and wrote it down. Not too long thereafter, we walked through one of the most painful and distressing trials that we have walked through to date. We were in the refiner's fire, and were trusting in Him that we would come out like pure gold. A few weeks later on that same tour, we had a word from the Lord from Pastor Howard in Merritt Island, Florida: "Grace abounds. God will give us everything we need for all the work we will do. Crush Satan under your feet – he is defeated – Satan will bow to Jesus."

> We are learning as we press on in our walk that we need not fret, worry, or fear. All we have to do is keep pressing onward and upward in our call and He will take care of the rest.

Both of these incidents were so impacting – I'm actually sitting here looking at the actual, original paper that I wrote these on from five years ago so I wouldn't forget. Not only has the Lord fulfilled this in our lives, but we are blown away at how He did it, and He has blessed us a hundredfold beyond anything we could imagine. The growth that has happened in our ministry in the past five years has been unprecedented since the inception of Potter's Field.

Jesus said, *"I am the true vine, and My Father is the gardener."* (John 15:1). God is the Gardener, and He may decide it is necessary to prune the branches – that's you and me – and clear the debris that hinders growth. If we would just trust that the Gardener knows what He's doing and allow Him to do this, then the branches will produce fruit for years to come. If the branch doesn't allow the pruning, it will be stifled in its growth, and may even shrivel and die. This is when you hold onto Jesus with a death grip – like a branch, grafted into and integrated with the vine – knowing He hasn't brought you this far to leave you hanging or to see you fail or fall.

God prunes, and He moves people on, and changes are inevitable in order to grow. It's usually because certain people have become stagnant and are stunting the overall growth and direction that the Lord intends His ministry to go. Life is not constant; it is always in flux. This is what keeps us clinging to God and ascending. We are learning as we press on in our walk that we need not fret, worry, or fear. All we have to do is keep pressing onward and upward in our call and He will take care of the rest. It is so freeing. I love what our mentors say – "Just keep doing what you're doing and don't look to the right or to the left. Keep your hand on the plow. God is a just God. He will even the scales. And time will discern and take care of everything. Sit back and watch."

We have a team of people in Montana and on our staff around the world of one hundred fourteen people who "dance" together. It has been a beautiful crossing through the parted waters of the Jordan, allowing a collaboration with smart, like-minded, mature, teachable sponges as we forge ahead to "transform lives forever." Potter's Field wouldn't be who and where they are today without them. We will be forever grateful to each and every one of them and their families.

Since we serve a God of the impossible – He will take what you bring to Him, unusual things that don't make sense – like a potter and a singer – and make something beautiful of His choosing to use for His glory.

> The will of God is never exactly what you expect it to be. It may seem to be much worse, but in the end it's going to be a lot better and a lot bigger.
> — Elizabeth Elliot, Christian author & speaker

Michael and I have discussed for years that we needed to be creative and open to how the Lord would be leading us in changing the way we have done Potter's Field up to this point. We still are touring, but not as much, due to the amount of international travel that has been added as our sponsorship and programs have grown. We fly in to churches on weekends now, instead of being on the road for months at a time and living on our tour bus. A team is sent ahead of us so they can manage set up and help at the back tables. We rotate the interns and staff so everyone can travel at one time or another, either domestically or internationally. It keeps things fresh for them, and for us, and it lets them keep their finger on the pulse of what God is doing through our PFM

We were going to need the "next thing" if we were going to continue to build a legacy of taking care of children all over the world.

services and around the world with our Kids Programs. It is always a wonderful thing to see people getting saved, marriages healed, and the rededication of lives unfolding right before your eyes.

We have seen ministry trends and vehicles that God has used change drastically through the years. The era of large concert

ministries, where massive arenas are filled as they were in the eighties and nineties, are coming to a close. Most of this is due to
rapidly changing technology. The days of selling large amounts
of product are pretty much over in this Internet era. We can
order music with the click of a finger on Apple Music and iTunes
for a mere ninety-nine cents per song. As a matter of fact, that's
how you can order my music. There are even free downloads of
some of my older songs. This has record companies scrambling to
come up with new solutions in which they can still earn a profit
when investing in artists who need funds to get a project off the
ground. Even then, with opportunities like KickStarter campaigns
and YouTube, the record companies aren't required anymore for
funding and publicity. It is also easier to put out singles or an EP
(extended play) recording with half the songs of the traditional
album of the past. We still sell product at the back table at our
events, but it is nothing compared to what it used to be in the
eighties and nineties. Michael now sells his high-end, six-foot God
Pots for an "artisan-level" price, but he doesn't have the time he
used to for making pottery with all the international travel to keep
our Kids Programs running smoothly.

We will continue to tour as long as the Lord keeps opening
doors, and it has shown no evidence of slowing down, but now we
have to engage in serious time management with all of the different
avenues of ministry that the Lord has us participating in.

Michael is always finding new ways of being a better steward
of the resources God provides – both people and finances. We
were going to need the "next thing" if we were going to continue
to build a legacy of taking care of children all over the world. We
always knew that Potter's Field would look differently because we
knew we wouldn't be able to tour the rest of our lives. We wanted
to have a new vehicle which could generate financial resources for

the continuation of the work of PFM long after Michael and I are gone.

There were many IGNITE alumni – young adults we had spiritually invested in and raised up – who felt called by the Lord to come back and continue to be a part of what He was doing at PFM. To help with this transition, we began exploring "tent-making" opportunities for them – some form of small business we could manage which would provide employment for these interns while allowing us to continue their ministry training.

Michael had a conversation with our friend Joe Gregory, exploring ideas and asking advice about what our next steps should be. Joe is a very successful entrepreneur and philanthropist. He advised Michael, "Whatever it is you decide to do, Michael, stay in your wheelhouse." Michael knew what that would be. He knew food!

> **Aquila and Priscilla worked alongside Paul making tents while spreading the gospel. It was a trade they could support themselves with as they evangelized in an area.**

Michael learned of a man in a nearby town who sold tamales. He was retiring and wanted to sell his recipe, so we bought the "family recipe" for a reasonable price. Our staff, students, and interns started rolling tamales daily, and we started doing well in the Flathead Valley at local festivals, events, and farmers markets. One of our former IGNITE students, Ben Corder, came up with a name "Tamalelujah!" This was our first training ground for what was to come, but while it was a great medium for earning revenue, we couldn't do it year round, and it sparked a desire to look for a brick-and-mortar location.

Michael found a drive-thru coffee kiosk in Whitefish in a section of town called Happy Valley. It's on a major highway with lots of traffic. I had never thought about doing a business like this, but his brilliant mind is always moving forward as he seeks the Lord on the next direction for PFM. Drive-thru coffee huts are really popular in Montana because it gets really cold in the winter and you can just drive up, grab your coffee, and go. We decided that the ministry would buy the hut as a non-profit venue. It would be a place where our interns could work and make a little money. It would also be a great location to work together where discipleship and community could take place. Some of them could learn to manage a business, and it was a practical way we could teach a good work ethic to this generation.

Back in Biblical times, it was a Jewish custom to teach and provide hands-on training for sons, whether they were rich or poor, and apprenticeships for those interested in learning a trade or a craft. Aquila and Priscilla worked alongside Paul making tents while spreading the gospel. It was a trade they could support themselves with as they evangelized in an area. By listening to the Holy Spirit, Michael cracked the code of how our interns could make a living while using this business to evangelize our community. Interns are now saving their money, and some are even buying homes here. The hut was actually very affordable, and the couple who sold it had heard about us, and knew our ministry. When we went down to sign the paperwork, they didn't even ask for our driver's licenses. It was as if this acquisition was what we call "a door falling off the hinges." We didn't have to strive to make it happen – it seemed as though it should just be.

As there was a lot of competition with coffee sales in Whitefish, Michael decided to move forward by adding food to our menu. We weren't sure if we could get the hut commercially zoned for serving food due to the fact we would have to install a large exhaust fan and a grill. But when he went to the city council, they passed it. Having been a gourmet chef on that exclusive airline in his early twenties, the flame of this talent was being stoked again and was circling back around. He is a master at cooking just like he is at pottery – so much better than I am – proven in that I gained twenty pounds during our first year of marriage, exclusively from eating his food!

After about six months, Michael was itching to try something new on the menu. We talked about trying burgers, since we weren't aware of a solid "Mom-and-Pop" burger joint in the Valley. Some of the local restaurants served burgers, but Michael wanted to do a "gourmet" burger-and-fries combo that was "family affordable." He came up with a savory, scrumptious burger that was better than any I'd ever eaten. The burgers are slathered in chili, and in honor of his being a potter, he began to refer to his chili as "Mud." And that was it – we would name the burger restaurant MudMan!

All MudMan burgers come with bacon and fresh homemade fries, and are fully loaded with all the fixings: chili, cheese, bacon, lettuce, onions (or grilled onions), and tomatoes. And what would a gourmet burger be without – you got it – secret sauce!! Only Michael, the managers, and I know what's in this incredible spicy-with-a-kick sauce. (That's why it's called a "secret" sauce…so don't pry!) The burgers are so large that I can't even eat a MudMan in one sitting. We have a smaller version now, a MudBoy, and I can't even finish that one! It's a full two meals for me!

While flying back from one of our tour dates, Michael was reading a newspaper article about McDonald's. It revealed that when they added a breakfast option to their menu, their percentages skyrocketed. So when we returned that week, I got a call to drive down to the office. Michael had just come up with a breakfast sandwich option for the menu and he wanted me to be a taste tester. It was a fried egg sandwich, with or without cheese, and your choice of bacon, sausage, or chili – or choose all three for a meat lovers option – and it virtually melted in my mouth. I knew we were on to something great! I'm not a "foodie," but I crave these delicacies, the burger or breakfast sandwich, at least once a week!

Needless to say, we stopped selling the tamales soon after the burgers came along. Pastor Steve Miller, who is on our staff and is an incredible artist (he was a professor at the Art Institute of Chicago for twenty-five years), came up with our iconic logo. It is a rendering, or rather, a caricature of Michael's dashing thick hair with the signature Ray Ban sunglasses he's worn since his youth, complete with "Big Mountain," the ski runs of our Whitefish Mountain Resort, drawn in the lenses.

Word of mouth began to spread around town about how good our burgers were. We were using a local bakery to supply our buns, but they couldn't keep up with our demand, so we needed to find another solution. One of our former IGNITE interns, Michelle, had just married Joshua, one of our "national" Ugandan interns from Africa – they had fallen in love while she was on the field. He didn't want to continue to go on to university, which we help fund through PFK, but wanted to go and learn a trade so he had a way to take care of Michelle after they were married. We ended up funding his way through culinary school in Africa. We brought them both over to the States so he could learn about American culture before heading back over to Uganda to be Resident Assistants for the interns that we would be sending over for their field time during their six-month deployment. Joshua reminded Michael of his training and suggested, "Since I went to culinary school, do you think I could try to come up with a homemade bun recipe?" Working alongside Dave DeFazio, who is a chef – he and his wife, Barb, are longtime ministry friends from our Fort Lauderdale days – Joshua and he not only came up with a bun, but it was a fast-rising yeast bun that was so dense and delicious it tasted like a pastry! This is the signature bun that we are now known for in this valley, baked fresh every day.

I started putting a little bug into Michael's ear about a healthy choice for us calorie-conscious people who can't eat a lot of burgers during the month. Eventually, he added a wonderful chicken sandwich option called a MudBird, which you could order on the bun or lettuce wrapped. We also have vanilla and chocolate shakes, but since Montana is known for its huckleberries, I urged him to add a huckleberry shake option.

When I'm not writing a book or touring, I go to lunch with my dear friend, Jan Miller, Pastor Steve's wife, once a week. I've known her for almost twenty-five years. Our favorite place to go is a Chinese restaurant in an adjoining town called Columbia Falls. Every time I would drive into town en route to lunch, I would see a large "For Sale" sign in front of an old A&W drive-thru restaurant. It had been sitting there for quite some time.

The Lord was pricking my heart to ask Michael to inquire about this property, so as I was driving home one day after our lunch, I called Michael and asked, "Did you know that the old A&W is up for sale in Columbia Falls? I feel like the Lord would have us at least see what is happening with it. I think it would be a great location for another MudMan. It's in a great location on the route that everyone has to take to get to Glacier National Park, and pretty central for the locals as well." I was so sure the Lord wanted Michael to call on this property that I remained persistent in reminding him for three solid months. By the Lord's leading, I was particularly strong in my appeal for him to call one day, and he said, "We don't have any money. What am I supposed to do?" And I replied, "That's never stopped us before!"

Michael called that afternoon and met a really nice older gentleman and his wife, and they were intrigued about what we would be doing with the concept of MudMan. Michael offered something that was absurd in the "real world." He knew that if it was "of God" that this offer would be accepted. He proposed a three-year lease option to buy, with no money down, and also asked if they would come down $175,000 in the asking price. Michael explained how the all the net profits would go to feed the hungry children in our PFK programs worldwide, and it would provide a place for our interns to make money and be discipled on-site as we "did life" with them. The man said that he loved what we would be doing with the restaurant, so they agreed on the terms and sealed the deal the old-fashioned way – with a gentleman's handshake. The monthly cost was even going to be less than what Michael originally thought. The hinges fell off the door once again! God was up to something bigger than we knew...

> God is now using something as simple as a hamburger and fries, and once again we are stepping out in faith, trusting Him every step of the way!

God is now using something as simple as a hamburger and fries, and once again we are stepping out in faith, trusting Him every step of the way! A potter and a singer...and a burger-and-fry joint! Here we go! God is using something so different and off the wall to glorify Himself in this volatile, precarious, and unpredictable world that we are living in. One thing is for sure – we all have to eat to live! Of course God would use something so unlikely to proclaim His name and to engage both the believer and non-believer alike. Everyone likes the idea of sowing into something larger than themselves. Even if you aren't a Christian, the thought of humanitarian work is palatable.

Michael came up with a great concept for those who can't afford to pay to go through the IGNITE Program. He allows them to come to IGNITE Lite, where they come and work at MudMan, earning credit to put themselves through the program while we provide housing.

We have pictures of each employee lining the walls in our MudMan locations – whether IGNITE 2.0, IGNITE Lite, or full-time PFM staff member. These pictures showcase where each of them has served for six months in one of our PFK locations around the world. They also wear badges that say: "Ask me about Uganda" – or Costa Rica, Guatemala, Kenya, Cambodia, or wherever they have served. (These badges strike up some incredible conversations with our guests, and provide a great witnessing opportunity!) We also have a fifteen-minute video loop playing continually, showing each intern and the children that we take care of, for the general public to view while they eat, giving them a direct insight into the true beneficiaries of their meal.

The success that MudMan has had during its first year has been colossal. MudMan was just voted the Best Burger and Fries in the entire valley by the people in the Flathead Valley – 98,082 people as of 2016! Only a mighty God can make something like this happen.

We buy our meats from a local butcher thus supporting our local community. I've seen the simplicity and greatness of our non-profit burger business in being able to fund feeding people less fortunate in third-world countries. We feed people here to feed people all over the world! Our motto is: "Buy Local, Serve Global." Michael is so funny – he likes to joke that God sprinkles the burgers with some kind of Jesus dust. Since first opening the Hut, we have served over 130,000 burgers in just over a year. God is using a new model to reach the unchurched, the churched, and the community at large.

We were gifted a beautiful new MudMan food truck by a pastor and longtime friend from Florida that we have ministered with for years. The only contingency was that we had to park it at his church while we were in town and serve burgers. We gladly obliged. It has been a tremendous blessing. We have now moved it up to Montana, and it is booked regularly for festivals, sporting events, and farmers markets, and it is often parked in various locations serving our communities and churches. The food truck has been wildly successful – to the glory of God!

Natalia Navas, one of the girls from our IGNITE Program, lives in Guatemala. We didn't know that her dad was a developer there. He has now built a MudMan there for us. Opening in the near future, this will be our first international store, with our interns working there in the field, engaging the locals, and using it as an avenue to witness to a dying world. This will support the work in Guatemala and serve as a model for future international stores.

Michael had been talking to me about finding another location in Kalispell, the largest city within fifteen miles from us. That same week, a real estate agent and his son stopped in for a MudMan burger after hiking in Glacier National Park. He was the agent for the man we bought the Hut from. He proceeded to tell our General Manager, Jordan Cole, that his father-in-law just listed a restaurant in Kalispell that was perfect for a new MudMan location, and it seats ninety patrons. Michael and Jordan drove down to scout out the location and it was an even larger store than the one in Columbia Falls! Michael called the agent in charge of handling this acquisition immediately. When he spoke to the broker, he shared his criteria for acquiring this store: it would have to be the same deal we had at our other location. At first, the owner didn't want to lease with an option to buy, and said no to Michael's proposition. However, God had other plans, and the next morning Michael got a phone call. The owner was a Christian. He explained to Michael that the Lord wouldn't allow him to sleep. He knew that he was supposed to go through with the deal. We are slated to open the Kalispell MudMan in early 2018. As of the printing of this book, we've been asked to open another location in Cambodia as well.

> You might think you are a world changer, but it's God who changes the world. He is the Potter. You are the clay.

One of the things I love the most about my husband is his honesty. This trait is not wildly popular in the world in which we live. As a matter of fact, Jesus was eventually killed because He told the truth. Jesus was God, and He was Truth. The leaders didn't like it, and it didn't fit their preferred worldview, so they sentenced him to die on a cross. Michael has grown immensely in how he delivers the truth today. Early in our marriage he spoke truths that would cut me like a knife. Ultimately, I knew they were true, but we are told to "speak the truth in love" (Ephesians 4:15). We are also told "you shall know the truth, and the truth will set you free" (John 8:32). Michael's honesty has made me a better person, better able to see my shortcomings, and vice versa. As a friend recently said, "Honesty and sensitivity aren't good bedfellows, but when properly married they dwell in harmony!"

Faithful are the wounds of a friend, but the kisses of an enemy are deceitful.

— Proverbs 27:6 NKJV

Michael now speaks the truth in love with finesse, and that in and of itself is a miraculous transformation. He uses parables like Jesus did to drive home a point – or in modern vernacular, "word pictures." I've grown to love these, and have actually learned a bit of this skill through osmosis by living with him. Michael cares enough about people to tell them what's real without sugarcoating issues. This will garner more foes than friends, but I would rather have a friend like him in my life than someone who doesn't care enough to tell you what's real and give biblical counsel.

Michael does things and thinks in a way like no one I've ever met. His mind is abstract, ingenious, and unique, and God uses his non-linear thinking. He's always thought "outside the box." Several years ago, Apple ran a campaign which simply stated: "Think Different." Michael and I love Steve Jobs' driven spirit and innovative mind, and what he accomplished in his relatively short life was stupendous. He said:

The people who are crazy enough to think they can change the world are the ones who do.
— Steve Jobs, CEO & Co-Founder of Apple, Inc.

While Steve Jobs influenced the way we view technology and communication, he did it all for worldly gain – the iPhone doesn't bring salvation. Real change comes from God, who uses His people to touch the lives of others. You might think you are a world changer, but it's God who changes the world. He is the Potter. You are the clay. Remember to give glory where it is due!

> *Now to Him who is able to do exceedingly abundantly above all that we ask or think, according to the power that works in us, to Him be glory in the church by Christ Jesus to all generations, forever and ever. Amen.*
>
> — Ephesians 3:20-21 NKJV

I truly believe that Michael has a wonderful, God-given passion for evangelism, and by stepping out in faith and obedience, he has been used in tremendous and boundless ways, continuing to be used in the hands of the Master Potter to change, feed, disciple, and evangelize the world for His glory – "Til The Whole World Hears!"

These promises are not exclusive to us. They are for you as well. Believe He loves you. Believe He can use you. And be obedient to His call. Be the clay in the hands of the Potter, and He will make you into the vessel of His choosing. What He has for you is beyond comprehension…exceedingly, abundantly above all you can ask or think.

As we embark on this next chapter – or Act Three – I can't wait to see how God expands Potter's Field Ministries. The Lord has given me insight and a new promise into what's next for us. I will hold off on telling what that is until the next installment, but His faithfulness has never been proven wrong in our lives. He has never let me down. The Lord is now setting up Ebenezer stones of remembrance that we may never lose sight of God's goodness toward us.

Samuel then took a large stone and placed it between the towns of Mizpah and Jeshanah. He named it Ebenezer (which means "the stone of help"), for he said. "Up to this point the LORD has helped us!"

— 1 Samuel 7:12 NLT

Hopefully the stones presented in this book will be a reminder that God is mighty and ever present and active in our midst. What are the stones of remembrance in your life? I challenge you to take the time to chronicle them…to ponder and remember…to pass them on to your children and speak of the goodness of our Lord any time He opens a door for you to do so. Press on towards the goal to win the prize, keeping your eyes on Jesus!

Not that I have already obtained all this, or have already been made perfect, but I press on to take hold of that for which Christ Jesus took hold of me. Brothers, I do not consider myself yet to have taken hold of it. But one thing I do: Forgetting what is behind and straining toward what is ahead. I press on toward the goal to win the prize for which God has called me heavenward in Christ Jesus.

— Philippians 3:12-14

So until we are in the arms of Jesus, or He comes back to get us on that white horse, we will serve Him with a vengeance. Make your life count. Take risks. At the end of his life, my dad had a conversation with Michael and told him that he wished that he had taken more risks in his life. Dare to fail. Dare to succeed.

To win big, you sometimes have to take big risks.
— Bill Gates, Co-Founder of Microsoft Corp.

We didn't have a contingency plan for the success of MudMan. But we are thrilled to take on the challenge.

Only Then

Written by Pam Rozell, Claire Cloninger & Walt Harrah

Our labor in the Lord is never wasted
He always ends up blessing what we do
Now if we sow in tears
We'll reap a harvest
He's promised us in Heaven
We'll receive the crown we're due

Chorus
Only then
Will we know we made a difference
Only then
Will we understand it all
When we see the ones who love You
Who never would have known You
If we had not been faithful to Your call

We labor, for the building
Of God's Kingdom
With sleepless nights
And struggles all the way
We're pressed on every side
But not abandoned
We'll never shrink back from the task
The call is to obey

BRIDGE

Give us strength to stand
And faith to follow through
And light to lead the ones You love
To eternal life with You

As I contemplate what the Lord has done in these two "cracked pots," I am astounded and forever grateful to my Lord and my God who is our Master Potter. As I look at my towering "work of art" that is my treasured husband, and what he has become in Christ Jesus, I marvel at the handiwork of our Lord. When I see and experience how He has restored a shattered marriage, I am in awe at His power and ability to change lives. I am more in love with Michael today than I was thirty years ago. Marriage ripens and grows richer as the years pass by. It takes hard work, perseverance, daily forgiveness, loving actions, engaged conversation, quality time spent, and commitment to each other and to your God, built on the Cornerstone – The Rock – who is Jesus Christ. You can have this too. All you have to do is believe that Jesus is the Christ – the Son of the Living God.

I pray for thirty more years with this wonderful man that has been the greatest gift I've ever received from God. Stay tuned as God hopefully provides the content for thirty more chapters of "Stones of Remembrance."

Our Act Three is right around the corner.

God's Best is yet to come.

AFTERWORD
from Pastor Michael Rozell

And they overcame him by the blood of the Lamb and by the
word of their testimony…

— Revelation 12:11 KJV

As you have read through this book, you have read the testimony of my wife. You can see how she knew the Lord at a very young age, but lived out a carnal and lukewarm life for a time. Whatever you take away from this book regarding Potter's Field Ministries, while we believe and know that it started from the foundation of the earth, the moment that it all flows from for the two of us was at that altar on Wednesday night, September 30, 1987, in Costa Mesa, California, when Pam rededicated her heart to the Lord. There is no Michael and Pam Rozell, there is no Potter's Field Ministries, there is not this phenomenal and incredible staff that we get to travel, teach, and train with, there is no impact on thousands of children around the world, there is no heart in us raising up the next generation – there is absolutely none of this without the grace of God on Pam's life.

It can't be anything but clear as you read through this book that God used her to get through to me. It's hard for me to imagine how it could have happened any other way. For me, I know that not only did He bring me this woman that He had designed for me, but in His sovereignty He knew it was going to take someone who understood the depth of grace and depth of forgiveness that she had experienced herself. He was able to use the dark places she had taken Him, because of the forgiveness she absolutely knew she received. She clearly sees what He did for her and it gives her the freedom to see me the way He sees me. She doesn't look at me with temporal eyes, she looks at me with eternal purpose. She believed in God's plan for me long before I did.

And we believe that for you, for those of you who don't know that yet. There is an eternal God of the universe, who really does want to attach Himself to you.

Without His redemption, our human nature, our sinful nature, separates us from God. You see in Pam's story of her life the emptiness and pain she couldn't get away from. I'll never forget it – that night she rededicated her life to the Lord – when she came off that altar after the conversation with Pastor Chuck. She ran to me and said, "Michael, I'm born again!" and my first response was, "So, are you still Miss Georgia?" I didn't know what "born again" meant, but I can surely tell you today that from that moment on she absolutely was Spirit-filled – radioactive – and I saw "born again" lived out through her.

You are only able to pour out forgiveness and mercy and grace to the degree in which you know you have received it in your own life. Her cup was overflowing, and it has stayed that way because of the hope and the work of the cross and an empty tomb.

Therefore, I tell you, her many sins have been forgiven— for she loved much. But he who has been forgiven little loves little.

— Luke 7:47

After thirty years of being married to this woman, I can say with confidence that God never called us to be happy – He called us to be free. *"So if the Son sets you free, you will be free indeed"* (John 8:36). That's what God's plan was…for us to be free. Free from the weight of our guilt, our shame, and our fear of the future. This eternal God of the universe really does have a personal investment in you, and He wants to attach Himself to you. Giving you passion, purpose, His presence, and His power to overcome. To be used. To have impact. To make a difference.

He has made everything beautiful in its time. Also He has put eternity in their hearts, except that no one can find out the work that God does from beginning to end.

—Ecclesiastes 3:11 NKJV

Reading this book, you can honestly see that, through the testimonies of our lives, it is clear there is absolutely no life outside of God's passion for us. It is mind-blowing, a mystery, how He completes His work "from beginning to end". He has put eternity in our hearts, and no one is beyond His reach. He is relentless to place opportunities and "markers" in our lives…stones of remembrance…so we can look back and see His hand. All we have to do is yield to this God who wants to set us free.

He is here, standing at the door knocking, waiting for you to open it for the very first time, or to reopen it and give Him access once again. Don't let this moment pass. Stop and respond to Him, expressing simple words from your heart, yielding to the work the Master Potter has planned all along —

Lord Jesus, forgive me of my sins. Come into my heart and never leave. Give me a hunger to know You more, to love You more, because I believe that You loved me first. Would you baptize me in the power of Your Spirit, giving me a hunger for Your Word? From this day forward, I'm Yours. And I mean it. In Jesus' name, Amen.

That was the prayer that I prayed under the piano twenty-six years ago. He set me free from a life of rage and addiction, and He continues to mold me and shape me. I'm not the man that I want to be, but I'm not the man that I was last year. And Lord willing, next year others will be able to look at me and say I'm not the man I was this year. The work that He began, He will and does see to completion as we yield to His absolute, complete authority over our lives (Philippians 1:6).

And as if this book is not testimony enough, He will do *"exceedingly abundantly above all that we ask or think..."* (Ephesians 3:20 NKJV).

ACKNOWLEDGEMENTS

How do you describe a miracle? *Michael and me* – it's an example when two people decide to surrender their lives and hearts completely to an Almighty God (and to each other), submitting one to another in order for God to heal and restore. This is a story of redemption – the redemption of two lost souls and the redemption of a shattered marriage that God put together again, and and how He decided to use these vessels to shine His light through the cracks of their lives. When the Lord gave me the title for this book over a decade ago, I didn't know what writing it would entail. It would involve hours of solitude and, thankfully, many completed journals that I've kept through the years which helped guide me through the process, with details long forgotten, along with the leading of the Holy Spirit. Of course, it takes an army of dedicated soldiers of the Lord to keep Potter's Field Ministries going on a daily basis who we will forever be thankful for during the writing process. We can't do anything apart from all of you! God has gathered a stellar team of people to forge ahead to further His Kingdom, "for such a time as this."

I finished this book twenty-five years to the day that we started "officially" touring as Potter's Field Ministries, on October 3, 1992, at Satsuma Baptist Church. I finished the body of the book (excluding finishing touches) on October 3, 2017. It is also the date that my pastor, Chuck Smith, slipped from this life to the next into His Heavenly home – October 3, 2013. He has passed God's goodness to the next generation. God is good!

> *Therefore, my beloved brethren, be steadfast, immovable, abounding in the work of the Lord, knowing that your labor is not in vain in the Lord.*
>
> — 1 Corinthians 15:58

I want to thank my husband, Michael, for allowing me to pour my heart into "our story" these past few months, and not caring that I "let the house go." Also for allowing me to be in front of a computer screen for countless hours as I wrote *"in my own little corner, in my own little chair…"* as the Rodgers and Hammerstein song literally replayed in my mind every day while I beheld my favorite view in Whitefish, from my window overlooking the valley.

Thanks to Joanna Chung, Lorie Welch, Christa Stoltzfus, Megan Cole, Rheanna Taylor, Sydnie Fowler, Kendra Scharite, Roberta Rozell, Jan Miller, Caitie Dawson, Monica Guitierrez, Anna Scott, Autumn Robison, and Brooke McClain so much for praying for this book daily, endless hours of scanning pictures, reading, making copies, editing revisions, always being there, and being "my precious girls" that I love so much! I am honored to work alongside you.

To Don and Jean McClure, our spiritual mentors and dear friends for years; for offering encouragement, insight, and helpful critiques on this book and in our lives. Roger and Traci Gales and Tony and Donna Croteau for faithful service and loyal friendship through the years. Steve and Michelle Venable, Steve and

Jan Miller, Craig and Loren Linquist, our Board of Directors, our Field Overseers around the world, Bruce and Marilyn Riley, the entire PFM staff, and our MudMan team – without you keeping the wheels turning, this book wouldn't be possible; our dear sweet 101-year-old friend, Fern Scrivner, who still is a faithful prayer warrior – thanks for praying for this book and PFM. Thanks to Cindy Watt Clough who encouraged me and helped start me out on this journey to write more than fifteen years ago.

Thank you Austin and Shannon Hiatt; Assistant Director – IGNITE, Jordan Cole; General Manager – MudMan, Derek Scharite; Assistant Manager – MudMan, Ryan Fowler, Dave and Barb DeFazio, Kevin and Renee Hanks, Neal and Jade McCormick, Matt McClaine, Dainon Taylor, and Theo Opdenaker.

Thanks so much Brett Burner at Lamp Post Publishers for exhorting me for two years when we would present PFM at your church to write this book. I knew when we met you that you were the one to publish it. Thanks for your heart and passion for the Lord and for your desire for truth to translate onto the written page. I grew so much and loved the process. I'm so glad to know and love your family: Karla, your lovely wife, Gideon, Paloma, and Silas.

Also thanks to Marianne Wiest, for the cover and portrait photos – you truly are an artist with your camera. You know how to capture the essence of the soul that God placed in each of us through your lens.

Thanks most of all to King Jesus for saving us (from ourselves) and remolding us into vessels of honor of Your choosing, to use at Your discretion. I couldn't have done this arduous task without the leading and inspiration of Your Holy Spirit, leading and guiding sometimes into the wee hours of the morning; also on flights, between tour dates, horse camps, listening to sermons, or upon awakening from sleep. It was harder than I expected, but my prayer is that this book will touch the hearts of those who read it and they will be drawn unto You – the author and finisher of our faith – the God of miracles who wants to and is waiting to do impossible things in our lives.

About the Author

Pam Rozell is the Co-Founder, along with her husband, Pastor Michael Rozell, of Potter's Field Ministries, an international touring parachurch ministry, preaching for twenty-five years in churches, crusades, and conferences with a potter's wheel and original songs. Based in Montana, together they founded Potter's Field Kids programs around the world, the IGNITE Mission Training School, IGNITE Lite and IGNITE 2.0, and MUDMAN Burgers, where they are discipling millennials and raising up the next generation to pass on the Good News of the Gospel. Pam has a Bachelor of Arts degree in Journalism, and is also a conference and retreat speaker. She and Michael have been married thirty years and reside in Whitefish, Montana, with their PFM family, dogs, horses, and goats.